Women & Men Communicating

CHALLENGES AND CHANGES

WOMEN & MEN COMMUNICATING

CHALLENGES AND CHANGES

LAURIE P. ARLISS
Ithaca College

DEBORAH J. BORISOFF
New York University

HARCOURT BRACE JOVANOVICH COLLEGE PUBLISHERS

Fort Worth   Philadelphia   San Diego   New York   Orlando   Austin   San Antonio
Toronto   Montreal   London   Sydney   Tokyo

EDITOR IN CHIEF   Ted Buchholz

ACQUISITIONS EDITOR   Janet Wilhite

DEVELOPMENTAL EDITOR   Terri House

PROJECT EDITOR   Laura Hanna

PRODUCTION MANAGER   Kathleen Ferguson

BOOK DESIGNER   Peggy Young

COVER ILLUSTRATION   Rebecca Ruegger

Address Editorial Correspondence to: Harcourt Brace Jovanovich College Publishers
301 Commerce Street, Suite 3700
Fort Worth, TX 76102

Address Order to: Harcourt Brace Jovanovich College Publishers
6277 Sea Harbor Drive
Orlando, FL 32887
1-800-782-4479, or 1-800-433-0001 (in Florida)

Printed in the United States of America

Library of Congress Catalogue Number: 92-71051

ISBN: 0-03-074656-6

2 3 4 5 0 3 9 9 8 7 6 5 4 3 2 1

PREFACE

It is a different experience growing up male or female in our culture. Boys and girls, and women and men, learn distinct communication styles. Their attitudes toward relationships, toward the world of work, and toward participating in the family, are distinct. Even the stereotypes and behavioral expectations we have for women and men differ.

Especially after the Industrial Revolution, the roles for women and men became clearly defined. Men belonged in the world of work; they were expected to provide for the family. Women belonged in the home; they were supposed to act as caretakers for the family's emotional needs. Times, however, have changed. Educational opportunities have opened to women as well as to men. Economic realities mean that for the majority of women, working outside of the home is no longer a frill or "just a second income." Their incomes are essential for the family's survival. Socially, women and men both have been encouraged to expand their behavior. Men are encouraged to develop their emotional sides, to learn to become more nurturing and vulnerable in their relationships. Women, in contrast, are urged to develop assertiveness skills, to become more independent in their interactions with others.

It is often easier to prescribe changes in behavior than it is to actually realize these changes. How we reconceptualize and develop ourselves, our relationships with others, and our roles as professionals reflect some of the challenges facing women and men today. These challenges provide the rationale for writing this book. Because we move from the self to the world outside of the self, we have organized the chapters in this book to reflect this movement.

Part One looks at why women and men communicate differently and how these differences are manifested. Judy Pearson and Roberta Davilla in Chapter 1 look at what we mean by gender and what it means to be a man or a woman in our culture. The effect of gender on our capacity to develop intimate relationships is addressed by Deborah Borisoff in Chapter 2. But gender differences are not limited to U.S. culture. How these differences exist cross-culturally is discussed in Chapter 3 by David Victor. In Chapter 4, Linda Costigan Lederman examines gender differences in intrapersonal communication and intrapersonal relationships.

Part Two of the book considers gender and communication in the context of personal relationships. Developing cross-sex friendships is considered in Chapter 5 by William Rawlins. Laurie Arliss traces communication in romantic relationships in Chapter 6. And Kathleen Galvin and Joyce Hauser look at gender and communication within the frameworks of first-marriage families (Chapter 7) and stepfamilies (Chapter 8).

In Part Three, we move from the realm of personal relationships to the world of education and of work. Girls and boys receive different educations and are not reflected equally in educational materials, according to Pamela

Cooper (Chapter 9). Nor are men and women welcomed equally in the corporate sector, as Lea Stewart and Dianne Clarke-Kudless reveal in Chapter 10. The final four chapters of the book scrutinize gender differences in distinct fields—fields selected because they reflect large numbers of both women and men. Cindy Victor examines the difficulties women, especially, face in their efforts to enter the legal field (Chapter 11). Elaine Jenks explores gendered communication in health care settings (Chapter 12). In Chapter 13, Judi Brownell presents the impact of women's and men's communication in the hospitality industry. And in the final chapter, Marcia Rock reveals the difficulties that women, primarily, confront in the broadcasting industry (Chapter 14).

The contributing authors represent some of the leading scholars in the area of gender studies and related fields. We are fortunate to enable you to read what they have to say on topics that are assuredly of interest to students around the nation. We invite you to listen to their voices.

Laurie Arliss
Deborah Borisoff
E D I T O R S

$\mathcal{T}$ABLE OF CONTENTS

LAURIE ARLISS (Ph.D., State University of New York at Buffalo) is an Associate Professor of Speech Communication at Ithaca College in Ithaca, New York. Gender issues are central in all of her teaching and research interests. She has taught courses in the subject, presented seminars to professional and educational audiences, and published books, book chapters, and journal articles on male-female interaction. Her recent text, *Gender Communication* (Prentice-Hall, 1991), surveys reported sex differences in verbal and nonverbal aspects of communication and discusses them in relation to sex stereotypes, sexist language practices, and competing explanatory theories. This volume extends the discussion by addressing important questions about the nature and impact of recent changes in personal and professional environments. Arliss has also authored a text entitled *Contemporary Family Communication: Messages and Meanings*, in which gender issues are prominent in the examination of challenges and changes in the American family.

DEBORAH BORISOFF (Ph.D., New York University) is Associate Professor of Speech Communication, Director of Speech and Interpersonal Communication, and Deputy Chair of the Department of Communication Arts at New York University. She has co-authored or co-edited five books on communication, has published fifteen book chapters and journal articles, and has presented over fifty convention papers and keynote addresses at state, regional, national, and international conferences. She is co-author of *The Power to Communicate: Gender Differences as Barriers*, 2nd edition (Waveland Press Publishers, 1992). In addition, she has served as a communication consultant to Fortune 500 companies, government agencies, and individual executives. Her research and writing address gender differences and communication, conflict management, listening, crosscultural communication, and organizational communication. She is the current editor of *The Speech Communication Annual*.

JUDI BROWNELL (Ph.D., Syracuse University) is Associate Professor of Managerial Communication at the School of Hotel Administration, Cornell University. She teaches graduate and undergraduate courses in organizational and managerial communication and participates regularly in the school's executive education programs. She has designed and conducted training programs for a wide range of education and work organizations. Brownell is author of *Building Active Listening Skills* (Prentice-Hall, 1986) and co-author of *Organizational Communication and Behavior: Communicating for Improved Performance (2+2=5)* (Holt, Rinehart, and Winston, 1989). She has published articles in such journals as *Communication Education, The Journal of Business Communication, Communication Quarterly, The Journal of Business Education,* and the *Western Communication Journal.*

PAMELA COOPER (Ph.D., Purdue University) is Professor of Communication Studies at Northwestern University. Her teaching and research interests center around gender and communication, classroom communication, and children's literature. She has written and published extensively in all three areas. Her publications include *Speech Communication for the Classroom Teacher,* and two co-authored texts, *Communication Between the Sexes* and *Look What Happened to Frog: Storytelling in Education.*

DIANNE CLARKE-KUDLESS (M.B.A., Fairleigh Dickinson University) is Managing Director for Enterprise Services, a company specializing in organizational behavior and performance, and a part-time lecturer at Rutgers University. Her specialty is designing programs to improve organizational performance and influence customer behavior. She is currently the National Director for the Women's Network, American Society for Training & Development (ASTD). Her work has been published by IBM, AGS/nynex, Technical Publishing Inc., and Data Training, and she is a career planning columnist for National Federation for Business and Professional Women (NJ). Clarke-Kudless has worked with many companies, including Dun & Bradstreet, General Foods, Sea-Land, Chubb & Son Inc., Research-Cottrell Companies, AGS/nynex, and On-Line Software, where she has implemented corporate performance programs.

ROBERTA ANNE DAVILLA is a doctoral candidate at Ohio University. Davilla's primary research areas are family communication and gender communication, with particular focus on studying children. Her publications include the instructors' manual for *Gender and Communication* by Pearson, Turner, and Todd-Mancillas; "Let's Go Krogering: A Naturalistic Study," to be published in *Speech Communication Annual*; and other pedagogical articles and manuals pertaining to teaching and directing the basic communication course. She is the recipient of the 1991 ICA Outstanding Graduate Student Teacher Award at Ohio University.

KATHLEEN M. GALVIN (Ph.D., Northwestern University) is Professor at Northwestern University. In 1988, she was awarded the prestigious "Excellence in Teaching Award" at Northwestern. She presently serves the University in the capacity of Associate Dean of the School of Speech. Galvin is also a well-known scholar who has published widely in the areas of classroom communication and family communication. She is co-author of *Person to Person: An Introduction to Speech Communication* (National Textbook Company, 3d ed., 1989) and *Family Communication: Cohesion and Change* (Scott Foresman, 3d ed., 1991). Galvin has presented more than 200 workshops in family communication for professional and community groups.

JOYCE HAUSER (Ph.D., Union Institute) is Assistant Professor in the Department of Speech Communication at New York University. Some twenty years ago she became Chief Operating Officer of Marketing Concepts and Communications, Inc., whose client roster included many of the most illustrious privately and publicly held medical and corporate companies. Also, she worked as a broadcaster with NBC radio for thirteen years. In 1985 she served as a mediator and arbitrator for the Victim Services Agency and the Institute for Mediation and Conflict Resolution. Dr. Hauser has authored many articles on mediation as a possible alternative to legal action and communication as a family issue. Hauser is included in Marquis' "Who's Who In the World," "In the East," "In Industry and Finance," "Advertising," and "American Women," and was honored by the National Cancer Society as one of the "Top Fifteen Women in America."

ELAINE B. JENKS (Ph.D., Pennsylvania State University) is Assistant Professor of Communication Studies at West Chester University. Her major teaching and research interests are health communication and gender communication. Her doctoral dissertation and many of her scholarly presentations are concerned with interpersonal communication in health care settings. Of particular interest in her recent work are the implications of gender integration in health care settings and the resultant challenges for men and women.

LINDA COSTIGAN LEDERMAN (Ph.D., Rutgers University) is Chair of the Department of Communication at Rutgers University. She specializes in instructional and interpersonal communication, with an emphasis on experiential learning. Her research focuses on the use of qualitative methods, especially simulations, games, and focus group interviews, to generate qualitative data about affective and behavioral dynamics associated with verbal communication. She has written four books and twenty book chapters and/or journal articles; presented more than one hundred conference papers and professional seminars; and designed and published a variety of communication simulations and games, including L & L Associates' *The Carrot and the Stick,* and Lindlee Enterprises' *The Marble Company Game* (with Lea P. Stewart, Simcorp), and *Pass It On.* Lederman is immediate past editor of *Communication Quarterly,* one of the nation's oldest scholarly journals of communication. She has served as President of the Eastern Communication Association, President of the Tri-State Communication Association, and Chair of the Commission on Experiential Learning, Speech Communication Association.

JUDY C. PEARSON (Ph.D., Indiana University) is Professor of Interpersonal Communication and Director of Graduate Studies in Interpersonal Communication at Ohio University. She has taught elementary through graduate school in the Midwest, West, and South. Among her fifteen textbooks are *Understanding and Sharing: An Introduction to Speech Communication,* now in its fifth edition, and *Gender and Communication.* She has published over fifty articles in the major journals in communication and psychology and has presented nearly 200 papers at professional meetings. Her most recent book, *Lasting Love: What Keeps Couples Together,* has been discussed in over 250 newspapers, ten magazines, on radio programs, and on television shows, including CNN *Prime Time, CBS This Morning,* and ABC's *Jenny Jones Show.*

WILLIAM K. RAWLINS (Ph.D., Temple University) is Associate Professor of Communication at Purdue University. He has published numerous articles and book chapters on the subject of cross-sex friendship, with special focus on the rhetorical challenges inherent in such friendships due to cultural definitions of masculinity and femininity. Rawlins also has published a text on the subject, *Friendship Matters* (Aldine de Gruyter, 1992).

MARCIA ROCK is co-author (with Marlene Sanders) of *Waiting for Prime Time: The Women of Television News.* Rock is a journalism professor at New York University and an independent producer whose work has aired frequently on public television. She has won two local Emmy Awards in the category of Arts/Cultural/Historical Programming: one for "On the Road Again: The Singing Angels in China," a documentary about a Cleveland youth choir's trip through China in 1983; the other, from the New York Chapter of NATAS, for "McSorley's New York," a documentary essay that chronicles the history of New York's Irish immigrant community and explores the role McSorley's has played in the cultural and political life of the city. Her profile of the North Carolina writer Reynolds Price aired on WNET in 1992. Her most recent documentary, "Village Writers: The Bohemian Legacy," aired twice on the PBS station WNYC in 1991. She is currently working on a documentary on Northern Ireland.

In 1988 Rock traveled to Israel and produced a documentary on the media coverage of the Intifada in Israel, "Israel Through the News," which takes a close look at the problems inherent in the television medium when covering violence. Rock is creator and executive producer of "New York Windows," a series of short news features produced by her students. Her students have won numerous awards, including first prize in 1989 and second prize in 1990 and 1991 from the Academy of Television Arts and Sciences Student Awards in News and Public Affairs, and the Robert F. Kennedy Journalism Award.

LEA P. STEWART (Ph.D., Purdue University) is Associate Professor at Rutgers University and specializes in organizational communication and gender. She has written or edited four books, published twenty-one book chapters and journal articles, and designed a variety of communication simulations and games for instructional use. She is the co-author of *Communication Between the Sexes*, 2nd edition (Gorsuch Scarisbrick Publishers, 1990). Her publications have appeared in journals such as the *Journal of Communication, Communication Monographs, Academy of Management Journal*, and *Communication Quarterly*. Stewart has served as a consultant to numerous organizations, including TRW, AT&T, and the Federal Aviation Administration.

CINDY RHODES VICTOR (J.D., University of Michigan Law School) is a partner practicing law in the firm of Howard and Howard in Bloomfield Hills, Michigan. She has authored numerous articles on legal issues, including AIDS in the workplace and sexual harassment.

DAVID VICTOR (Ph.D., University of Michigan) is Associate Professor of Management at the Eastern Michigan University College of Business, where he teaches international business communication, managerial communication, and international management at both the graduate and undergraduate levels. Dr. Victor is the author of *International Business Communication* (Harper Collins, 1992) and co-author (with Deborah Borisoff) of *Conflict Management: A Communication Skills Approach* (Prentice-Hall, 1989), as well as several scholarly articles in international management and business communication. He is a frequent consultant to business in the United States and abroad. He has also received two U.S. Department of Education federal grants in the area of international business, and in 1991 was the first professor in the Distinguished Visiting Foreign Professor program at the *Instituto Technologico y de Superiores de Monterrey* in Mexico.

WOMEN & MEN
COMMUNICATING

CHALLENGES AND CHANGES

CHAPTER 1

THE GENDER CONSTRUCT: UNDERSTANDING WHY MEN AND WOMEN COMMUNICATE DIFFERENTLY

AUTHORS   Judy Pearson, Ohio University
Roberta Davilla, Ohio University

POINTS TO BE ADDRESSED

- The difference between sex and gender
- The process of gender identification
- Differences between male and female development
- Differences between male and female ways of knowing
- Differences between male and female ways of being

Now, more than ever before, men and women are recognizing the need to understand the differences that separate them. We have always relied on male-female relationships in the private world of the family, but legal and social changes now demand that we feel comfortable in a wide range of public male-female associations. The difficulty of relating to another individual is logically complicated when that individual is perceived as "different," but understanding the sources of difference can provide both enlightenment and comfort. In this book, the urgency of understanding male-female communication is addressed by communication scholars. Each chapter focuses on an important aspect of gender communication or examines gender issues in an important setting. The authors attempt to characterize the unique challenges inherent in male-female interaction at a time of great change.

Prior to examining specific aspects of interaction between men and women, it is useful to consider the important process by which we come to know ourselves as gendered individuals in a world where gender matters. While researchers in the physical sciences continue to seek answers to biological questions, researchers in the social sciences work to clarify the social, moral, and linguistic dimensions of gender differences. In this introduction, we explain the difference between biological sex and its socially constructed correlate, gender. We discuss the development of gender identity, and explain how men and women emerge with unique ways of knowing and ways of being. We argue that male-female interaction is affected by the unique experiences of being male and being female in our society.

Although biological sex has probably always been of interest to researchers and educators, the focus on gender is relatively new. Before the mid-1970s, the term "sex" was used to refer to biological differences that existed between people. Research on "sex differences" simply categorized people on the basis of their biological differences. A variety of forces came together in the mid-1970s to encourage a reconceptualization of gender. One influence was the work of psychologists such as Sandra Bem (1974, 1975a, 1975b), Janet Taylor Spence, Robert L. Helmreich, and J. Stapp (Spence, Helmreich & Stapp, 1974a, 1974b; Spence & Helmreich, 1978). Carol Gilligan (1982) contributed to the debate with her landmark book, *In a Different Voice*, a few years later.

Bem's work is an exemplar of the new research and theory on gender. Before this time, people were categorized on masculinity and femininity measures as being more or less of each of these measures. In other words, masculinity was placed on one end of the continuum and femininity was placed on the other end, as illustrated in the figure below.

MASCULINITY   FEMININITY

An individual, through a series of questions, would be categorized as either masculine or feminine or somewhere between the two extremes. We should observe, however, that the more masculine one indicated that he or she was, the less feminine he or she would be. An individual could not be rated high in both masculinity and femininity nor low in both categories.

In private conversations, Bem has explained that she felt limited by this conceptualization of masculinity and femininity. She perceived herself as possessing a number of both masculine and feminine traits. In other words, she felt that she should score high on both masculinity and femininity. Instead, when she was categorized, her score indicated that she was somewhere between masculinity and femininity and was thus viewed as neither feminine nor masculine.

Bem (1974) created a new way to measure and to conceive of sex roles in the Bem Sex Role Inventory. She suggested that masculinity and femininity are separate dimensions and that one might be high in masculinity and low in femininity (masculine), low in masculinity and high in femininity (feminine), high in masculinity and high in femininity (androgynous), or low in masculinity and low in femininity (undifferentiated). This view is depicted below.

HIGH IN
FEMININITY

ANDROGYNOUS   FEMININE

HIGH IN MASCULINITY   LOW IN MASCULINITY

MASCULINE   UNDIFFERENTIATED

LOW IN
FEMININITY

Although the differences in Bem's conceptualization may appear to be fairly simplistic, her perspective radically altered the way women and men were categorized. In the past, women and men were viewed as different because of biological traits and they were categorized on masculinity-femininity scales in a unidimensional way. Bem suggests that people should be categorized based on the extent to which they have internalized societal standards for masculine and feminine behaviors. In addition, both biological males and biological females could be feminine, masculine, androgynous or undifferentiated.

Sex and gender are thus not identical constructs. As Maya Angelou (1986) so aptly wrote in *All God's Children Need Traveling Shoes*,

> I had long known that there were worlds of difference between males and men as there were between females and women. Genitalia indicated sex, but work, discipline, courage and love were needed for the creation of men and women.

Sociologists, psychologists, and communication researchers generally agree that sex refers to one's biological or physical self while gender refers to one's psychological, social, and interactive characteristics (see, for example, Bernard, 1971; Lipman-Blumen and Tickamyer, 1975; Pearson, 1975; Stroller, 1968).

Researchers in the physical sciences continue to be interested in biological sex. Social scientists are more likely to focus on gender or gender roles because they have traditionally examined our social lives. Nonetheless, a relationship exists between sex and gender. Indeed, women are more likely than men to behave in a feminine way, while men are more likely than women to behave in a masculine manner.

To what extent does one's biological sex influence that individual's social and psychological gender? Patricia MacCorquodale (1989) explains,

> . . . the relative weight given by a belief system to social versus biological factors results in an ideology that maximizes or minimizes sex differences. Within both feminist and traditional systems of belief, there is a division between those who believe the influences of biology are indirect and mediated by society (social constructionists) and those who believe that direct effects of biology endow each gender with certain essential characteristics (biological essentialism) (Sayers, 1982: 95).

Although the nature vs. nurture argument continues to be debated in some quarters, an even more complicated discussion now ensues. The newer argument concerns the tolerance and fluidity with which an individual can comfortably move among gender identifications. Stable gender identity is not a universally accepted experience. Researchers (Imperato-McGuinley, 1979; Money, 1972) vary in their views about how gender identity becomes fixed. John Money asserts that gender identity is formed during a child's first three years. Julianne Imperato-McGuinley, on the other side, believes that gender remains flexible during childhood. Once the hormones during puberty "take hold," gender identity becomes established.

Imperato-McGuinley (1979) studied sexually incongruous children from rural Santo Domingo villages. The people exhibited an inherited deficiency known as DHT-deficiency and had ambiguous genitalia. Eighteen of the people had been raised as females. At puberty, these "females" experienced lowering of their voices and the growth of a penis and scrotum. The phenomenon was common enough to warrant the word that translated literally means "penis at twelve." Of the eighteen children raised as girls, only two experienced sex role confusion. The other sixteen were successful in assuming the male gender role and married and fathered children.

The researcher drew two conclusions from her study. The first was that gender identification is not unalterably fixed, but evolves throughout childhood. The second conclusion was that when the sex of rearing conflicts with the biologically based sex, the biological sex prevails. On the one hand, the study provides evidence for a more fluid understanding of gender identification. On the other, it supports biological determinism.

The new conceptualization of gender allows us to assert that, to some extent, our social interaction influences gender. Our communicative exchanges tell us what our roles are and encourage or discourage us from internalizing predispositions that relate to masculinity or femininity. Symbolic interactionists suggest that people develop through three stages (see, for example, Mead, 1977). The prepatory phase includes the stage in which infants imitate others by mirroring. In the play stage, the child responds simultaneously in a generalized way to several others. The child generalizes a composite role by considering all others' definitions of self. The person thus develops a unified role from which he or she sees the self. This perception is the overall way that other people see the individual. People unify their self-concepts by internalizing this composite view. This self-picture emerges from years of symbolically interacting or communicating with others.

The integrated self tends toward the behaviors others encourage and away from behaviors that others discourage. From birth, people are treated differently because of genitalia. Male and female babies are dressed in different kinds and colors of clothing. Parents respond differently to male and female infants (see, for example, Nancy Bell & William Carver, 1980). Male and female babies are described with different adjectives: boys are strong, solid, and independent, while girls are loving, cute and sweet. People describe identical behavior on the part of infants differently if they are told the infant is a "boy" or a "girl" (see, for example, Condry & Condry, 1976). Preschool children observe commercials and cartoons on television, are read books, and play with toys in which "appropriate" sex roles are depicted. In many ways, people are treated differently because of their biological sex.

Because of such differences in treatment, it is not surprising that women and men develop differently. Carol Gilligan (1982) helped to explain differences in the moral development of women and men through a psychological approach. Lawrence Kohlberg's (1958; 1969; 1973; 1976; 1981) previous work in moral development relied on studying only male subjects. "Standard" stages of moral development were created, and females did not fit into the "norm." Kohlberg presumed that females were deviants and no research was done at that time to see if females morally developed through a differing process.

Gilligan (1982) attempted to correct this problem by studying women. She suggests that relationships and issues of dependence are experienced very differently by males and females. Through socialization and subsequent moral development, males rely on separation and individuation to establish their gender identity. Feminine identity does not depend on the achievement of separation from the mother or on the development of individuation. Because masculinity is defined by separation while femininity is defined through attachment, male gender identity is threatened by intimacy and female gender identity is threatened by separation.

To amplify this point, Gilligan (1982) cites Lever, who studied role-taking during conflict resolution. Lever observed children at play, and reported that when a dispute erupted, girls ended the game, while boys elaborated the rules for resolving disputes. Lever concluded that boys learn independence and the organizational skills necessary for coordinating activities groups of people through play. By learning the socially approved rules of the game, boys are better able to deal directly with competition from both their friends and their enemies. However, girls learn cooperation, not competition. They play in smaller, more intimate pairs, usually in private places. When disagreements erupted while playing a game, girls were quick to end the game. The significance of maintaining the primary relationships was tantamount for girls. Their identities were fostered in cooperative relationships with others, rather than individual goal-achievement and rule-following.

The message that Gilligan underscores is that, presumably from socialization differences, women and men have different voices of experience. Neither is superior, but the male voice has been traditionally the voice heard. Standards based on male behaviors are created and females are therefore left out. When female experiences are questioned in the pursuit of knowledge, a problem of what to do with those experiences results.

M. Belenky, B. Clinchy, N. Goldberger, and J. Tarule (1986) similarly showed that women's ways of knowing and being are distinctive from men's. They conducted extensive interviews with women who were in a variety of education settings. The institutions from which the female students were selected ranged from a traditional Ivy League college to an "invisible college," a human service agency that assisted women in caring for their children. A goal of the study was to utilize William Perry's epistemological framework and expand it. Perry (1970) had studied the intellectual and ethical development of undergraduate students at Harvard University. However, most of his subjects were males and the result was a useful design charting their epistemological development. Due to the proliferation of research on males' experiences, Mary Field Belenky and her colleagues chose to study only women's experiences in terms of their relationships to various institutions.

These researchers grouped women's knowing perspectives into five categories: silence, a voiceless position that is subject to external approval; received knowledge, in which women gain externally generated knowledge but do not create knowledge of their own; subjective knowledge, which is knowledge created intuitively, personally, and privately; procedural knowledge, in which women are included in the learning and application of objective procedures for communicating knowledge; and constructed knowledge, in which women create their own knowledge, and the value of both subjective and objective knowledge is recognized (Belenky et al., 1986: 15).

In order to explain differences in ways of knowing, Belenky and her associates cite two stories related by two middle-aged women. The first woman recollected how, on the first day of a science class, the professor brought in a jar filled with beans and asked the class to tell him how many beans were in the jar. The class members shouted out many different guesses. The professor responded to their attempts by stating that they should never trust their own senses, and invited the class to go on a mysterious journey into the realms of scientific inquiry, with the professor as their guide. The young female first-year college student dropped the course later that day and never went near a science classroom again.

The second woman remembered, on her first day in a philosophy class, how a philosophy professor entered the room and placed a large cardboard cube on the desk. The professor asked the students what the object was. The students responded that the object was a cube. The professor pressed her students by asking what a cube was. The students stated that a cube contained six sides. The professor asked, "But how do you know?" She pointed out that it was impossible for anyone to see all six sides simultaneously. The cube existed because of intelligence, and the brain invented the sides that were not physically seen. Each student was able to invent the truth about cubes.

These examples illustrate the differences in ways of knowing. The first illustration envelops the silent and received knowledge perspectives; knowing can only be realized through an external source. The external source generates superior knowledge and the student/learner of this knowledge must seek approval of what is learned and what is "right." The science professor was the authority; he could teach his students the "truth." Students were to rely on his authority rather than recognizing and relying on their own knowledge. The second story illustrates subjective, procedural, and constructed knowledge. The students/learners in this situation were confirmed in their assessment of what they already knew in terms of their own experiences. The philosophy professor confirmed the students' individual, intuitive knowledge. They were all authorities and their "truths" were confirmed.

Women and men are treated differently, they develop differently, and their ways of knowing are discrete. These differences are apparent in our language. The importance of language was explained by Cheris Kramarae (1981): "Language is used in social contexts; used to construct and maintain social relationships between and among women and men" (vii). With her colleagues, Muriel Schulz and William M. O'Barr (1984), Kramarae adds,

> . . . it is only within the latter part of the twentieth century that the study of language implies for most scholars simultaneous concern with society. Language is, after all, spoken by people in social contexts as they communicate about human concerns." (9)

An increasing amount of research demonstrates that the symbols we use to communicate are man-made. The language that we use was created primarily by men, for men. The words we have available reflect male experience and they encourage male domination.

What are some obvious examples of man-made words? Let us consider the language of business. Although the business world may be viewed as an area that is open to both women and men, when one listens carefully, it appears to be primarily a "male club." Many business cliches, for example, come straight from sports—a decidedly male activity. If you want to be successful, you may have to "keep you eye on the ball," be a "boy wonder," "keep your head down," be a "team player," be a "pinch hitter," and "tackle the job." What do you avoid? You don't want to be in the "penalty box," "under fire," "under the gun," be in the "cellar," be a "disqualified player," have a "jock mentality," or be "caught with your pants down."

We can also build the argument that language is male-dominated when we deal with the so-called generic pronouns. When we talk about generic people using the singular, which pronoun do we choose? In general, people use the male form to refer to both men and women: "he," "his," and "him" can refer to a male in some cases and to either a male or female in other cases. We never use "she" and "her" to refer to men, or to both women and men. We may question why these forms are not equally appropriate.

Kramarae (1981) observes that language does not serve all of its users equally well. Women are left out far more often than men, but both men and women may find that language limits the expression of their experience. Kramarae offers four theoretical frameworks from which to understand the relationship between gender, language, and social structure. Among these are the muted group framework, the reconstructed psychoanalysis framework, the speech styles framework, and the strategy framework.

The muted group theory is based on the notion that people who are dominant in a particular social hierarchy determine the communication system of that social group; people who are subordinate are "muted." The subordinate group is further rendered inarticulate because the dominant group creates language based on their own world view. The subordinate group has different perceptions and the need for different language; however, no allowance has been made either for that differing perception or the language that would correspond to it. Kramarae offers the basic assumptions of this theory, applying it to women and men.

1. Women perceive the world differently from men because of women's and men's different experiences and activities, rooted in the division of labor.

2. Because of their political dominance, the men's system of perception is dominant, impeding the free expression of the women's alternative models of the world.

3. In order to participate in society women must transform their own models in terms of the received male system of expression (3).

The reconstructed psychoanalysis approach is derived by Kramarae from the original theorizing of Sigmund Freud and his reinterpreter Jacques Lacan. She explains that Lacan argues repeatedly that the unconscious is a language and thus psychoanalysis is linguistic analysis. Through the acquisition of language we are located (as female or as male) into a social structure. In learning our language we

> learn dichotomous opposition: speech/silence, science/poetry, logic/intuition, author/reader — masculine/feminine. (66)

Kramarae notes that this approach "stresses symbolism over cognitive development" (66).

Lacan does not subscribe to a fixed reality in which words have a one-to-one correspondence with some concept within that reality. Instead, words have only a relationship to each other. Further, according to Kramarae, a "language code represents and authorizes social hierarchies, and the ideological superstructure (the system of ideas of the culture)" (67). The child's acquisition of a language thus renders him or her a social being within a particular ideological superstructure. Kramarae concludes:

> What I stress here is that language has, for Lacan, the central, all-informing role; the human is formed by language. The language code gives individuals their construction of reality, and their location in that reality, including their gender identity. (67–68)

The speech styles approach may be viewed as a more fluid or dynamic approach than is either the muted group theory or the reconstructed psychoanalysis theory to understanding gender. This theory suggests that women's and men's speech behavior is based on their perception of their social group. In other words, women and men communicate in ways that are distinctive because they are placed in different, and apparently relevant, social groups. Kramarae explains that this somewhat static approach to language and gender is made more dynamic by the addition of three emphases:

> (1) the ways that distinctive speech can be used by members of a group to create solidarity and to exclude members of out-groups from some interactions;
> (2) the ways that dominant group members use the distinctive features, actual or perceived, of the speech of subordinate groups as a focus for ridicule; and
> (3) the ways that speakers manipulate their speaking styles to emphasize or de-emphasize particular social identities (91).

The speech styles approach allows us to examine women and men as two linguistic groups, just as blacks, and whites, and other subcultures have been placed into separate social groups. We can also consider both the convergence and divergence of members of the two social groups as they mirror the behavior of the other social group in cross-sexed interactions, or as they refuse to accommodate a speaker of the other social group. We can examine how women, as a subordinate group, can alter their linguistic usage to be viewed more positively by others. Finally, we can learn about women's challenges to male predominance in the linguistic arena (Kramarae, 1981: 91).

Anthony Mulac, John Wiemann, Sally Widenmann, and Toni Gibson (1988) tested the convergence theory recently and found "greater differences in gender-linked language behavior in same-sex than in mixed-sex dyads" (315). Both women and men appeared to converge in their language when speaking to members of the opposite sex. These researchers claim that the behavioral convergence may be based on the sex-role stereotypes that exist in opposite sex interactions.

The strategy model is based on the idea that all communication is "strategic," a term broadly understood, based on Brown and Levinson's (1978) definition, as

> (a) innovative plans of action, which may still be (but need not be) unconscious, and (b) routines—that is, previously constructed plans whose original rational origin is still preserved in their construction, despite their present automatic application as ready-made programs. (90)

Kramarae explains the reasoning that leads to the strategic model:

1. Industrialized capitalism has sharpened a division between the labors of women and men, and a separation in the location of their activities. . . .

2. Authority (legitimate power, authorized power to command) is associated with the public sphere and men have clear monopoly of this. . . .

3. As a consequence of the division of labor, the separation of spheres, and the use of differential allocation of resources and legitimate power, women and men will use different strategies to influence others and shape events. (119)

In order to fully understand why men and women communicate differently, it is important to remember the distinction between sex and gender and, accordingly, to realize that gender is socially constructed. Because the lessons we learn about ourselves and our world are often gender-specific lessons, women and men develop differently. As children and later as adults, females and males are treated differently, so it is hardly surprising that our ways of knowing and ways of being are distinct. Language perpetuates current societal constructions of women and men and encourages both differences and dominance. Students of communication need to be keenly aware of the influence of gender in male-female interaction. However, we must also realize that, because it is socially created, the gender construct can and does change. In a time of tremendous legal and social change, we must all be ready for the interpersonal challenges that lie ahead.

REFERENCES

Adler, E. S. 1984. *A Proposal for a Course on the Sociology of Work and Family* (Working paper No. 133). Wellesley, MA: Wellesley College Center for Research on Women.

Angelou, M. 1986. *All God's Children Need Traveling Shoes*. New York: Random House.

Argyle, M. 1975. *Bodily Communication*. New York: International Universities Press.

Argyle, M., and M. Williams. 1969. Observer or observed? A reversible perspective in person perception. *Sociometry* 32: 396–412.

Banks, T. L. 1988. Gender bias in the classroom. *Journal of Legal Education* 38: 137–146.

Belenky, M. F., B. M. Clinchy, N. R. Goldberger, and J. M. Tarule. 1986. *Women's Ways of Knowing: The Development of Self, Voice, and Mind*. New York: Basic Books.

Bernard, J. 1971. *Women and the Public Interest: An Essay on Policy and Protest*. Chicago: Aldine-Atherton.

Bell, N. J., and W. Carver. 1980. A reevaluation of gender label effects: Expectant mothers' responses to infants. *Child Development* 51: 925–927.

Bem, S. 1974. The measurement of psychological androgyny. *Journal of Consulting and Clinical Psychology* 42: 155–162.

_____. 1975a. Androgyny vs. the tight little lives of fluffy women and chesty men. *Psychology Today* 9: 58–59.

_____. 1975b. Sex-role adaptability: One consequence of psychological androgyny. *Journal of Personality and Social Psychology* 31: 634–643.

Brown, P., and S. Levinson. 1978. Universals in language usage: Politeness phenomenon. In E. N. Goody, ed., *Questions and Politeness: Strategies in Social Interaction*. Cambridge, England: Cambridge University Press.

Campbell, K. K. 1985. The communication classroom: A chilly climate for women? *Association for Communication Administration Bulletin* 51: 68–72.

Condry, J., and S. Condry. 1976. Sex differences: A study of the eye of the beholder, *Child Development* 47: 812–819.

Cooper, P. J. 1987, November. *In or Out of the Pumpkin Shell? Sex Role Differentiation in Classroom Interaction*. Paper presented at the annual meeting of the Speech Communication Association, Boston, MA.

DeFrancisco, V. L. 1989, November. *What Gets Said When We're Not Listening? A Critique of Conversation Analysis Methods in the Study of Communication Between Women and Men*. Paper presented at the Women's Caucus, Speech Communication Association Convention, San Francisco, CA.

Education department sees enrollment fluctuating in the decade. 1990, January 3. *The Chronicle of Higher Education*, 2.

Fausto-Sterling, A. 1985. *Myths of Gender: Biological Theories about Women and Men*. New York: Basic Books, Inc.

Gilligan, C. 1982. *In a Different Voice: Psychological Theory and Women's Development*. Cambridge, MA: Harvard University Press.

Goldberg, P. 1968. Are women prejudiced against women? *Transaction* 6: 28.

Halberstadt, A .G., C. W. Hayes, and K. M. Pike. 1988. Gender and gender role differences in smiling and communication consistency. *Sex Roles* 19: 589–604.

Hall, R. M. 1985. Classroom climate for women: The tip of the iceberg. *Association for Communication Administration Bulletin* 51: 64–67.

Hall, M., and B. Sandler. 1982. *The Classroom Climate: A Chilly One for Women?* Washington, DC: Association of American Colleges, Project on the Status and Education of Women.

Hill, C. L. 1988. Sexual bias in the law school classroom: One student's perspective. *Journal of Legal Education* 38: 603–609.

Hughey, J. D., and B. Harper. 1983, November. *What's in a Grade?* Paper presented at the annual meeting of the Speech Communication Association, Washington, DC.

Imperato-McGuinley, J., R. Peterson, T. Gautier, and E. Sturla. 1979. Androgens and the evolution of male-gender identity among male pseudohermaphrodites with a 5-alpha-reductase deficiency. *New England Journal of Medicine*, 300: 1236–1237.

Jenkins, M. M., J. M. Gappa, and J. Pearce. 1983. Removing bias: Guidelines for student-faculty communication. In *Sex and Gender in the Social Sciences: Reassessing the Introductory Course*. Annandale, VA: Speech Communication Association.

Kohlberg, L. 1958. *The Development of Modes of Thinking and Choices in Years 10 to 16*. Unpublished doctoral dissertation, University of Chicago, Chicago, IL.

_____. 1969. Stage and sequence: The cognitive-development approach to socialization. In D. A. Goslin, ed., *Handbook of Socialization Theory and Research*. Chicago: Rand McNally.

_____. 1973. Continuities and discontinuities in childhood and adult moral development revisited. In Collected Papers on Moral Development and Moral Education. Moral Education Research Foundation, Harvard University, Cambridge, MA.

_____. 1976. Moral stages and moralization: The cognitive-developmental approach. In T. Lickona, ed., *Moral Development and Behavior: Theory, Research and Social Issues*. New York: Holt, Rinehart & Winston.

_____. 1981. *The Philosophy of Moral Development*. San Francisco, CA: Harper & Row.

Kramarae, C. 1981. *Women and Men Speaking: Frameworks for Analysis*. Rowley, MA: Newbury House Publishers, Inc.

Kramarae C., M. Schulz, and W. M. O'Barr, eds. 1984. *Language and Power*. Beverly Hills, CA: Sage Publications, Inc.

LaFrance, M. 1985. The school of hard knocks: Nonverbal sexism in the classroom. *Theory into Practice* 24: 40–44.

Lipman-Blumen, J., and A. R. Tickamyer. 1975. Sex roles in transition: A ten-year perspective. *Annual Review of Sociology* 1: 297–338.

Long, J. E., D. Sadker, and M. Sadker. 1986, April. *The Effects of Teacher Sex Equity and Effectiveness Training on Classroom Interaction at the University Level*. Paper presented at the annual meeting of the American Education Research Association, San Francisco, CA.

Maher, F., and K. Dunn. 1984. *The Practice of Feminist Teaching: A Case Study of Interactions among Curriculum, Pedagogy, and Female Cognitive Development* (Working paper No. 144). Wellesley, MA: Wellesley College Center for Research on Women.

Malovich, N. J. 1984, August. *Curriculum Analysis Project for the Social Sciences: Integrating Scholarship about Sex and Gender into College Coursework*. Paper presented at the annual convention of the American Psychological Association, Toronto, Ontario, Canada.

Markel, N., L. Prebor, and J. Brandt. 1972. Biosocial factors in dyadic communication: Sex and speaking intensity. *Journal of Personality* 23: 11–13.

Martin, J. R. 1985. *Transforming the Liberal Curriculum: Rewriting the Story of Sophie and Emile* (Working paper No. 156). Wellesley, MA: Wellesley College Center for Research on Women.

MacCorquodale, P. 1989. Gender and sexual behavior. In K. McKinney and S. Sprecher, eds., *Human Sexuality: The Societal and Interpersonal Context*. Norwood, NJ: Ablex, 91–112.

MacIntosh, P. 1983, February. *Interactive Phases of Curricular Revision: A Feminist Perspective*. Paper presented at the Claremont College Conference, "Traditions and Transitions: Women's studies and a balanced curriculum," Claremont, CA.

McDermott, M. 1983, April. *The Impact of Classroom Interaction Patterns on Students' Achievement-Related Beliefs and Behaviors*. Paper presented at the biennial meeting of the Society for Research in Child Development, Detroit, MI.

Mead, G. H. 1977. Quoted in *Sociology: Human Society* by Melvin De Fleur et al. Glenview, IL: Scott, Foresman, 138.

Money, J., and A. Ehrhardt. 1972. *Man Woman/Boy Girl*. Baltimore, MD: Johns Hopkins University.

Moreau, N. B. 1984. Education, ideology, and class/sex identity. In C. Kramarae, M. Schulz, and W. M. O'Barr, eds., *Language and Power*. Beverly Hills, CA: Sage Publications, 43–61.

Mulac, A., J. M. Wiemann, S. J. Widenmann, and T. W. Gibson. 1988. Male/female language differences and effects in same-sex and mixed-sex dyads: The gender-linked language effect. *Communication Monographs* 55: 315–335.

Nadler, M. K., and L. B. Nadler. 1989, November. *An Empirical Investigation of Perceived and Actual Sex Differences in Classroom Communication*. Paper presented at the Speech Communication Association convention, San Francisco, CA.

National Center for Education Statistics. 1989. *Digest of Education Statistics, 1989.* (Publication No. NCES 89-643). Washington, DC: U.S. Government Printing Office.

Pearson, J. C. 1975. *The Effects of Sex and Sexism on the Criticism of Classroom Speeches.* Unpublished doctoral dissertation, Indiana University, Bloomington, IN.

_____. 1985. *Gender and Communication.* Dubuque, IA: William C. Brown Company.

Perry, W. G. 1970. *Forms of Intellectual and Ethical Development in the College Years.* New York: Holt, Rinehart & Winston.

Rieke, R. D. 1985. The classroom climate: A chilly one for women? A response. *Association for Communication Administration Bulletin* 51: 73–74.

Rosenfeld, L. B. and M. W. Jarrard. 1985. The effects of perceived sexism in female and male college professors on students' descriptions of classroom climate. *Communication Education* 34: 205–213.

Rosenfeld, L. B. and M. W. Jarrard. 1986. Student coping mechanisms in sexist and nonsexist professors' classes. *Communication Education* 35: 157–162.

Sadker, M., and D. Sadker. 1985. Sexism in the classroom. *Vocational Education Journal* 60: 30–32.

Sadker, M., and D. Sadker. 1986. Sexism in the classroom: From grade school to graduate school. *Phi Delta Kappan* 67: 512–515.

Sayers, J. 1982. *Biological Politics.* London: Tavistock.

Schuster, M. R., and S. R. Van Dyne. 1983. *Feminist Transformation of the Curriculum: The Changing Classroom, Changing the Institution* (Working paper No. 125). Wellesley, MA: Wellesley College Center for Research on Women.

Schwister, M., N. S. Rich, and C. Hossman. 1984. Opening career options for males and females — A workshop for K–12 teachers, *Education* 105: 125–131.

Spence, J. T., R. Helmreich, and J. Stapp. 1974a. The personal attributes questionnaire: A measure of sex-role stereotypes and masculinity-femininity. *JSAS Catalog of Selected Documents in Psychology* 4: 127.

_____. 1974b. Ratings of self and peers on sex-role attributes and their relation to self-esteem and conceptions of masculinity and femininity. *Journal of Personality and Social Psychology,* 32: 29–39.

Spence, J. T., and R. Helmreich. 1978. *Masculinity and Femininity: Their Psychological Dimensions, Correlates, and Antecedents.* Austin, TX: University of Texas Press.

Stoller, R. J. 1968. *Sex and Gender, on the Development of Masculinity and Femininity.* New York: Science House.

Zimmerman, D. H., and C. West. 1975. Sex roles, interruptions and silences in conversation. In B. Thorne and N. Henley, eds., *Language and Sex: Difference and Dominance.* Roxley, MA: Newbury House Publishers, 105–129.

CHAPTER 2

THE EFFECT OF GENDER ON ESTABLISHING AND MAINTAINING INTIMATE RELATIONSHIPS

AUTHOR   Deborah Borisoff, New York University

POINTS TO BE ADDRESSED

- Intimacy as a dance metaphor
- The background and need for the study of intimacy
- Definitions and traits of intimate relationships
- Barriers to intimate relationships
- How gender differences sustain barriers to intimacy
- Moving towards intimate relationships: breaking down barriers

In the introduction to their edited text on intimate relationships, Perlman and Duck (1987) note that psychologists, sociologists, family scientists, and communication experts "are all making important contributions" to the study of personal relationships, thereby reflecting the recent multi-disciplinary aspect of this field (9). However, in many important works on intimacy and intimate relationships, the gender differences that often create barriers to intimacy and how these differences are reflected in the communication process are notably absent. This chapter, therefore, attempts to fill this void by integrating into the literature on intimacy the important aspects of interpersonal communication that reflect how men and women acquire and express different styles of communication. Such understanding will contribute to our knowledge of the concept of intimacy in our culture and will facilitate breaking down the barriers to intimate relationships that are a product of cultural expectations.[1]

INTIMACY: A METAPHOR IN MOTION

U. Weisstein (1968), in his work in literary theory, points out that the durability of legendary themes and heroes is related directly to the fact that these heroes and themes reflect our own lives and situations. "In every mind devoted to justice," he observes, "there is an Antigone. . . . These heroes are in us, and we in them; they partake of our lives, and we see ourselves reflected in their shapes. . . . Our myths and our legendary themes are polyvalence: they are the indices of humanity, the ideal forms of the tragic destiny, the human condition" (131).

If these heroes reflect our lives; our relationships, an interesting image emerges when we consider the relationship between Paul Valéry's heroes, Faust and Luste, as they strive toward an intimate relationship. Faust, the protagonist, embodies the intellect. Luste, the play's heroine, represents the heart. Although the two characters struggle for closeness, they remain uncertain about their own feelings and about their relationship. Critic K. Weinberg (1976) observes, "They need one another as interpreters, and as refracting mirrors that reflect one upon another with a certain degree of distortion" (27). These characters are never able to realize their love. They are never able to achieve the intimacy they desire because they are so staunchly grounded in their male/female identities. When Luste is away from Faust and is filled with the physical stirrings he arouses in her, she tries to intellectualize her feelings. This intellectual process, imposed on a woman who represents pure feelings, fails to illuminate and prevents her from fully understanding herself. In the case of Faust, every time he is with Luste, he is unable to maintain the intellectual process because of the physical stirrings she arouses in him. This emotional process, imposed on a man who represents pure intellect, thwarts his mental exercise and prevents him from completing the work that would enable him to understand himself.

Luste tries to display Faust's intellect and fails. Faust attempts to express the emotions so much a parte of Luste. He, too, fails. The image of the two protagonists as they interact throughout the play is that of a dance—one, however, that is out-of-step. Yet the message conveyed by the heroes' circumstance is one that can be heeded today: to remain in the purely mental plane of the intellect is frustrating. It does not illuminate. To remain in the purely emotional plane of feeling is weakening, and, equally, cannot illuminate without the seeds of understanding. While Faust brings Luste to the point of wanting to understand herself through his intellectual example, Luste, through her physical presence, brings Faust to the point of wanting to live. The image of a dance not quite in sync pervades the image of intimate relationships. Harriet Goldhor Lerner (1989) entitles her book *The Dance of Intimacy*, yet the dance she describes is not at all in step. L. Rubin (1983), in her work *Intimate Strangers*, the title of which itself reflects a contradictory image, calls intimacy among married couples an "approach-avoidance dance" (65). Intimate relationships between couples are fraught with difficulties. Many of these difficulties are rooted in the differences that lead to gender identity and gender roles in our society.

This chapter will address some of these differences in the context of recent research on intimacy, explore how many of these barriers stem from the ways in which women and men are encouraged to express intimacy in their communication strategies, and conclude by presenting ways in which some of these barriers can be diminished. While Faust and Luste as literary figures may represent the epitomes of intellect and emotion, as our culture has begun to change, along with it we see changes emerging in our expectations for women's and men's communication. As the boundaries for acceptable communication for women and men expand, these changes will help blur the lines that separate man and woman, Faust and Luste.

THE STUDY OF INTIMACY: BACKGROUND AND IMPORT

Although the study of intimacy began around the turn of the century with the writings of George Simmel (see Perlman and Fehr, 1987), research in the area has been limited, primarily for two reasons. First, scholars have found it difficult to locate enough suitable subjects willing to participate in longitudinal studies. Second, until the late 1960s and early 70s, according to D. Perlman and B. Fehr, self-disclosure was not considered appropriate behavior—especially for men.

A major factor contributing to an increased interest in intimate relationships, however, was the finding that positive close relationships are beneficial for both psychological and physical well-being in the young as well as the elderly. The work of E. Klinger (1977) with 138 college students, for example, revealed that for 89 percent of the subjects, personal relationships made their lives meaningful. Reis' (1984) work with the elderly reflected positive psychological and health benefits when subjects maintained intimate connections. Conversely, and not surprisingly, the absence of intimate bonds can have negative effects. Perlman and Fehr (1984) refer to a series of studies conducted in 1976 and 1977 that demonstrated the potentially dire consequences that can occur when individuals lack intimate relationships: higher rate of suicide among men was related to the absence of close male bonds (H. Goldberg, 1976); depression for women was ten times more likely when they lacked someone to confide in (Brown and Harris, 1978).

Interest in intimacy as an area of study has increased considerably. Perlman and Fehr (1987) maintain that there is now greater acceptability as self-disclosure as a behavioral style in U.S. culture. The increased receptivity to the study of intimacy and heightened interest in self-disclosure can most likely be related as well to the aforementioned studies connecting health to intimate relationships.

Evidence of this increased interest in the area is apparent in the writings of scholars and practitioners from a variety of disciplines. Basic to understanding how men and women function in intimate relationships is understanding first what we mean by intimate relationships.

INTIMATE RELATIONSHIPS: DEFINITIONS AND TRAITS

The term intimacy, E. Hatfield (1982) tells us, stems from the Latin word *intimus*, which means "inner" or "innermost" (208). Researchers in the field offer a wealth of definitions.

For Chelune and his colleagues (1984), intimacy is a *quality* of relationships that they define as "a subjective appraisal, based upon interactive behaviors, that leads to certain relational expectations" (13). For them, intimacy is based on self-disclosure, transactional exchange, mutuality, and shared experiences. Thus their definition of an intimate relationship is "a relational process in which we come to know the innermost, subjective aspects of another, and are known in a like manner" (14).

Hatfield (1984) defines intimacy as a *process* rather than a behavior: "a process in which we attempt to get close to one another: to explore similarities (and differences) in the ways we both think, feel, and behave" (208).

In their work, L. Acitelli and S. Duck (1987) regard intimacy as a potent cultural norm affected by the individual engaged in an intimate relationship, by the social and cultural expectations that govern the way we can express feelings of intimacy, and by the behavioral constraints that define the form of the relationship (297). Thus intimacy in a friendship, in a familial context, in a courtship, and in a marriage will vary.

For one of Rubin's (1983) male interviewees, the mask symbolizes the distinction between ordinary and intimate relationships. For him, intimacy is "putting aside the masks we wear in the rest of our lives" (68).

Regardless of the definitions they offer, scholars who study intimacy concur that to achieve the closeness inherent in intimate relationships, the following relational characteristics are required:

1. *Knowledge* of the innermost being of one another, which is achieved through self-disclosure and validation of the partner

2. *Mutuality* in the relationship, where shared values, ideas, and attitudes contribute toward understanding

3. *Interdependence* of one another for the emotional and physical well-being of the relationship

4. *Trust* in the relationship and in one another

5. Reciprocal *Commitment* to a relationship

6. Open and supportive *Communication*

7. *Time*, for it is normally over time that we are able to develop the trust required in intimate relationships

Understanding the components of intimate relationships is easy. Achieving intimacy, however, may be difficult. As the following section reveals, there are several fears that can impose potent barriers on the development of intimate relationships. (See box on page 19 for a comparison of the traits and barriers to intimate relationships.)

BARRIERS TO INTIMATE RELATIONSHIPS

Despite the benefits of intimacy, powerful barriers to establishing intimate connections exist. Too often, these barriers prevent individuals from taking the risks required to form intimate bonds. Many writers have articulated the fears that impede intimacy. Several of these fears stem from the cultural norms for men's and women's behavior. Below is presented a partial list of some of the frequently cited concerns.

1. FEAR OF EXPOSURE:

No one enjoys being regarded negatively. Yet many individuals equate disclosing fears and concerns with weakness, or with what S. Jourard (1971) terms being "psychologically naked" (39). Many individuals, consequently, keep secret those feelings that may be interpreted as signs of weakness.

2. FEAR OF ABANDONMENT:

Many individuals, according to Hatfield (1984), believe that if they are not perfect, they will not be loved. They fear being abandoned and isolated. This fear is another compelling force that impedes developing intimate connections. If one does not risk being loved, one does not risk being abandoned.

3. FEAR OF REPRISAL/ATTACK:

Knowledge is power. Individuals fear disclosing intimate information about themselves that can be potentially damaging if revealed to others. We become vulnerable when we reveal ourselves, especially if we cannot trust this information will be guarded.

4. FEAR OF LOSS OF CONTROL:

Several writers point to the fear of loss of control as particularly problematic for men. Hatfield (1984), for example, explains that men are expected to maintain control of their thoughts and feelings. As a result of this expectation, many men cannot express easily their feelings because they regard this expression as a loss of control. V. Derlega (1984) explains the negative consequences that can result when men mask their inner thoughts and feelings in order to not risk losing control or power in a relationship: "If . . . loving, including self-love, entails knowledge of the unique needs and characteristics of the loved person, men as well as women must be willing to incur the potential of being hurt" (7).

5. FEAR OF LOSS OF INDIVIDUALITY:

L. Rubin (1983) refers to the fear of loss of individuality as the loss of the "me" in a relationship. For psychologist H. Lerner (1989), we risk being engulfed by others when we have not sufficiently developed the self we bring to intimate relationships (53). And, in an earlier work by E. Hatfield (1982), a potent risk of intimacy is the fear "that one would literally disappear as he or she lost himself [sic] in another" (212).

6. FEAR OF CREATING A POWER IMBALANCE:

For some individuals, if their partner is more vested in the relationship than they are, the potential exists for relinquishing power to the partner. This "power" can be reflected through control of monetary resources, sexual behavior, emotional control, and the like. Regardless of its source, such imbalances may reflect inequality in relationships.

The six fears presented above coincide, according to D. Morris (1971), with a tendency in our culture to equate tenderness with weakness and vulnerability. The fear of being hurt or controlled—through abandonment, rejection, exposure, resources, and so on—may become so compelling that we may never achieve the closeness for which we so ardently strive.

7. PERCEPTION AS A BARRIER TO INTIMACY:

The connotative aspect of words is, according to Aaron T. Beck (1988) a potential threat to intimacy (22). Because individuals come to a communication exchange with their own view of the world, the way one *perceives* or *interprets* the meaning of messages in a relationship has an enormous influence on how he or she will respond. Beck provides a cogent example: If one partner in a relationship equates a loud voice with rejection, then that individual may feel angered or hurt, or misunderstood when the other partner raises his or her voice, regardless of how the partner intended the message. For Beck, the perceptions of the receiver are of at least equal importance to the sender's message. His contention reflects the notion that there are multiple realities to which individuals respond.

COMPARATIVE SUMMARY OF THE TRAITS AND BARRIERS TO INTIMATE RELATIONSHIPS

Traits	Barriers
1. Knowledge of each other through self-disclosure	1. Fear of exposure of being less than perfect
2. Interdependence for emotional and physical well-being	2. Fear of loss of individuality; the drive to be independent
3. Trust in each other and in the relationship	3. Fear of betrayal; one is vulnerable to being attacked
4. Commitment to a reciprocal relationship	4. Fear of a power imbalance, especially if one partner is more vested in the relationship
5. Open and supportive communication	5. Communication that is misunderstood, misinterpreted, or defensive

Several barriers presented in this section are general in nature and are not necessarily linked to gender differences in the development of women and men in our culture. However, many differences in the communication styles of women and men serve to sustain or increase difficulties in establishing, conveying, and maintaining intimate relationships. As the following section demonstrates, these differences can have an enormous impact on the quality of intimate relationships.

GENDER DIFFERENCES IN COMMUNICATION:
SUSTAINING BARRIERS TO INTIMACY

Over thirty-five years ago, Theodore Reik (1954) suggested that gender has a significant effect on the connotative interpretation of language:

> Men and women speak different languages even when they use the same words. The misunderstandings between men and women are thus much less a result of linguistic and semantic differences, but of emotional divergences when the two sexes use identical expressions (15).

Reik's observation has not been contradicted. In fact, C. Gilligan's (1982) longitudinal studies on women's moral voices reflect the problems that can emerge when women and men use similar words to encode experiences of the self; of social relationships: "Because these languages share an overlapping moral vocabulary, they contain a propensity for systematic mistranslation, creating misunderstandings which impede communication and limit the potential for cooperation and care in relationships" (173).

Reik's and Gilligan's words are striking because they eloquently attest to several reasons why men and women so often experience difficulty developing and maintaining intimate relationships.

The reasons women and men learn different ways of speaking and the way these differences are articulated inform our understanding of the way couples communicate and affect our perception of intimacy within relationships. As we examine the many differences in the identity formation and communication styles of women and men, we can see how these differences may create or sustain barriers to intimacy.

1. THE MEANING OF THE SELF

Independence, activity, strength, intelligence, and competitiveness are terms normally regarded as masculine in U.S. culture. Connection, passivity, weakness, emotion, and compromise, in contrast, are typically assigned to women. These gender traits are so pervasive that they cross international boundaries. In a comprehensive 30-nation study, Williams and Best (1982) report that these characteristics are consistently gender-linked. The self-concept influences, in turn, the way we interact with others. If men are encouraged to achieve independent identities, if women are supposed to seek "connections" with others, the desires and expectations each gender will have in defining, establishing, and maintaining intimacy with a member of the opposite sex will be affected. Rubin (1983) describes how women's desire to seek closeness and men's wish to remain independent often result in a push-pull situation. That is, as women strive to get close to the men they love, the men, for whom too much closeness signals suffocation, begin to retreat. This retreat creates the desire in women to "clasp" further, which results in greater distancing. This kind of behavior illustrates a basic contradiction: One of the positive characteristics of intimate relationships is interdependence and open communication; one of the major barriers to intimacy is the fear of losing one's individuality. If men have learned to place a high value on independence and authenticity, they will be reluctant to move towards the interdependence essential for positive intimate bonds. Women, too, may suffer from the motivation to connect. H. Lerner (1989) points out that women receive conflicting messages: they are supposed to develop the self, yet, they are expected to subordinate the self to the needs of others. "We all," she adds, "by virtue of being female, have learned to please and protect relationships by silencing, sacrificing, and betraying the self" (126). As long as the masculine and feminine selves are perceived as diametrically opposed, the dance of intimacy that Lerner describes will remain problematic.

2. THE ABILITY TO SELF-DISCLOSE: STRENGTH OR WEAKNESS

Self-disclosure—the ability to open up, to make oneself vulnerable, to validate the ideas and feelings of others—is an important quality of intimate relationships. Not surprisingly, the ability to self-disclose and *what* is disclosed are gender-related. "Men and women differ little, if at all, in how much they are willing to reveal to one another," Rubin (1983) tells us (215). What it *is* that they reveal, however, may be another matter. Men more readily disclose views and attitudes. Women are more likely to reveal fears and feelings. Additionally, women *receive* more disclosure from others—this is a matter of reciprocity. Men may learn from the role models in their lives that emotional vulnerability is unacceptable male behavior. Such knowledge follows them into their relationships with others as well. V. Derlega and A. Chaikin (1976) found that women and men are regarded differently when they disclose personal problems. They report that in male-male and/or male-female dyads, when a male stimulus person disclosed a personal problem, he was viewed more negatively than when he remained silent. (The image of the strong, silent type is evoked here.) The opposite results were obtained when female stimulus persons were evaluated. It appears that even if men *want* to become open about their feelings and their emotions, the negative assessment of such behavior would discourage them from doing so.

3. THE MEANING OF PERSONAL RELATIONSHIPS: A MATTER OF INTERPRETATION

The way each gender may approach, participate in, and evaluate intimate relationships is influenced by the way men and women interpret these relationships. What may be a desirable, safe situation for one individual may be perceived of as a threat to another. Gilligan (1982) reports that significant differences exist in the way women and men interpret personal and impersonal situations (39–42). In a series of studies, Gilligan and her colleagues found that when asked to interpret a picture of a couple, men projected more violence into scenes of personal affiliation than did women. In contrast, when more impersonal pictures were shown to groups of male and female students, women projected more violence into the interpretation of these scenes than did the men.

If aggression is viewed as a response to the *perception* of danger, then these findings are especially salient when we acknowledge that women and men may *perceive* danger in different social situations: "men [see] danger more often in close personal affiliation than in achievement and [construe] danger to arise from intimacy, women perceive danger in impersonal achievement situations and construing danger to result from competitive success" (Gilligan, 1982: 42). The men in Gilligan's studies used such terms as "betrayal," "deception," "humiliation," and "smothering" when describing the interaction and relationship between the couples shown in the pictures. If men interpret closeness as threatening or stifling, we can begin to understand more fully the reluctance they may feel when the women in their lives ask for closeness.

4. THE EXPRESSION OF INTIMACY: A MATTER OF COMMUNICATION STYLE

S H E: "I just don't understand. Why can't he tell me he loves me!"
H E: "Of course I love her. I show her that I do. Why do I have to tell her?"

S H E: "My job was making me miserable. When I came home I wanted to talk about it."
H E: "I don't understand her. She told me she was unhappy at work. I told her what steps she should take to change jobs."
S H E: "He just doesn't get it."

These two examples are stereotypical, illustrating the kinds of communication that distance couples and erect barriers to close relationships. Anthropologists D. Maltz and R. Borker (1982) found several differences in the communication styles of men and women: Boys learn conversation around competitiveness and dominance while girls learn conversation around affiliation and equality; men may use aggressiveness as a form of conversation with no ulterior motive while women regard their partner's aggressive behavior as disruptive to the relationship; men use questions to seek information while women also use questions as a form of conversation maintenance; men may be more uncomfortable with silence and thus tend to speak at greater intervals; and, when women discuss problems and share experiences, they tend to be reassuring while men, in contrast, are more likely to want to seek solutions to problems rather than to listen empathetically.

In the second example, the man may interpret his behavior as being helpful: he wants to offer a concrete solution to his partner's situation. The woman, however, may erroneously interpret his suggestions as an attempt to control. He is, consequently, mystified when she rejects his efforts to help out. She desires what D. Tannen (1990) calls "the gift of understanding," but her male partner has instead offered "the gift of advice" (50).

Tannen suggests that such differences in the communication styles of men and women need to be scrutinized differently than they have been in the past. Rather than approach gender differences and communication as solely culturally related, we may need to regard the languages of women and men as cross-cultural communication: "If women speak and hear a language of connection and intimacy, while men speak and hear a language of status and independence, then communication between women and men can be like cross-cultural communication, prey to a clash of conversational styles" (1990: 42).

According to psychologist P. Noller (1987), women and men not only send different verbal messages, but husbands and wives send different nonverbal messages. In her work with married couples, Noller found that wives used more smiles with positive messages, employed more types of behavior regarded as positive communication, and used generally more communication overall. Husbands, in contrast, "used similar behavior for each message type, relying generally on eyebrows, particularly eyebrow raises and flashes, whether they were sending positive or negative messages" (158). Noller further found that males tend to send a greater number of neutral messages than females (163).

Women and men have integrated all too well those lessons of their childhood that taught them to give or deny their feelings and ideas a voice. So ingrained are the behavioral expectations for women and men that many are only dimly aware of how they communicate and how this communication may be interpreted by others. If women continue to reside in the emotional plane, and if men inhabit primarily the realm of ideas rather than feelings, it will be difficult to break down the communication barriers in intimate relationships.

BREAKING DOWN BARRIERS:
TOWARD INTIMATE RELATIONSHIPS

In 1928, Carl Jung observed that "there is no coming to consciousness without pain" (cited in Rubin, 1983: 72). These words are appropriate for considering intimate relationships. No matter how strongly individuals desire intimacy, achieving intimacy is difficult. To work towards productive intimate relationships, men and women should consider the following steps that can decrease barriers to intimacy.

1. INTIMACY REQUIRES INDEPENDENCE

Independence and intimacy are interrelated. One cannot achieve intimacy without the capacity for independence, and vice versa. Hatfield (1984) notes that "People who lack the ability to be independent *and* intimate can never really be either" (213). Women, who are expected to be nurturing and other-centered, need to develop the independent self. Men, who are encouraged to develop their independent side need to develop the emotional self.

2. ACCEPTANCE OF THE SELF

One of the barriers to intimacy is the fear that when others learn that we are less than perfect, they will reject us. Yet real closeness cannot occur unless we do, in fact, accept who we are—good traits and bad. According to Lerner (1989), such closeness occurs "most reliably not when it is pursued or demanded in a relationship, but when both individuals work consistently on their own selves" (68). Women and men need to scrutinize societal expectations for being the "perfect" man or woman and acknowledge that it is impossible to achieve an ideal. When we work on those traits that define who we are rather than on those that we think others might *expect* us to have, we can begin to define the authentic self.

3. ACCEPTANCE OF OTHERS

A major element in L. Buscaglia's (1984) criteria for maintaining loving relationships is to validate others. Accepting other individuals and encouraging their self-expression reflect a gift of love that can be given only when women and men are truly able to enter the frame of reference of their partners.

4. ENCOURAGE OPEN, CLEAR COMMUNICATION

As basic as the concept of communication is, we are often so intent on expressing our own ideas, concerns, and feelings that we ignore our partner's feelings. Also, we are likely to interpret the communication of others from our own point of view. This tendency leads to miscommunication. In the preceding section, several gender-related communication strategies were described as contributing to barriers to intimate relationships. For women and men to understand each other, they must first be sensitive to the ways their own communication styles can create communication breakdown.[2] Second, they must willingly suspend judging their partner as they take steps to bring these communication styles closer together. Third, women and men need to include in their own communication the appropriate communication strategies of both genders. Fern Johnson (1983) called this technique "code-switching," a technique she advocated for women. In a later work, E. Aires (1987) advocated this strategy for women and men.

5. MAINTAIN A BALANCE OF POWER

Perlman and Fehr (1984) report that greater relationship satisfaction is possible when a balance of power exists (27).

Studies on communication processes, conflict management, and relationship development support the importance of the role of equality in transactional communication. Individuals who are insensitive to the words of others while staunchly defending their right to assert their concerns, D. Barnlund observes (1979), deny others any meaningful role in the communication exchange. In his work on group conflict, J. Gibb (1961) distinguishes between defensive and supportive communication environments. He demonstrates that equality, an important component of a supportive environment, is necessary for productive communication. Works by noted linguists, psychologists, and communication specialists directly link communication satisfaction between men and women to the perceived amount of access both genders have to communication (Aires, 1987; D. Borisoff and L. Merrill, 1992; B. Eakins and R. Eakins, 1978; C. Gilligan, 1982; J. Hall, 1984; C. Kramarae, 1981; R. Lakoff, 1975; D. Maltz and R. Borker, 1982; J. Pearson, 1985; D. Tannen, 1990).

Borisoff and D. Victor (1989), in their work on productive conflict management, propose the following four communication strategies to maintain equality in the communication exchange: encourage each other's participation in the communication process; listen fully to and respect one another's ideas, beliefs, attitudes and experiences; confirm each other's assertions through appropriate feedback; and, communicate fairly by avoiding blaming, attacking and making sarcastic remarks. When couples believe that they have equal access to communication, they report greater satisfaction in the relationship (Beck, 1988; Hatfield, 1982, 1984: Lerner, 1989; Rubin, 1983; Tannen, 1990).

Achieving both independence and interdependence in successful intimate relationships reflects the ability, in Rubin's (1983) terms, for couples to "move comfortably between separation and unity" (95). Interdependence, especially, is not easily achieved because we become most vulnerable when we love. By demonstrating the barriers to intimate relationships and gender differences in how intimacy is defined and expressed, this chapter shows that men and women regard differently the risks that are a part of intimate relationships. By abandoning part of the rational self, Buscaglia (1984) suggests, we are able to achieve the kind of intimate relationship that he relates to happiness:

> We are far too rational in our relationships, far too ordered, organized and predictable. We need to find a place, just this side of madness and irrationality, where we can, from time to time, leave the mundane and move into spontaneity and serendipity, a level that includes a greater sense of freedom and risk (116).

In the case of Faust and Luste, the protagonists introduced at the beginning of this chapter, the heroes are destined never to find such happiness. Faust, in despair, eventually dies by his own hand. Guided solely by intellect and reason, the hero finds the temptation of the emotional side insufficiently compelling to alter either his character or his destiny. But Faust is, after all, a literary figure fixed in a moment in time, and for both women and men in their relationships, time has progressed significantly in the last half-century.

NOTES

1. Although the authors who write on intimate relationships acknowledge that there are many different kinds of intimate relationships (for example married couples, parent-child, friendship ties, gay and lesbian couples), the majority of the research on intimacy has, to this point, been conducted on heterosexual couples who are married. Because part of the purpose of this paper is to integrate the research on gender differences and human communication into the work on intimate relationships, it was considered most productive to utilize the predominant research. Therefore, this chapter focuses on intimacy and communication within heterosexual couples.

2. Several comprehensive works report on verbal and nonverbal gender differences in human communication. Some of the recent works include those by Deborah Borisoff and Lisa Merrill (1992), Barbara Eakins and Gene Eakins (1978), Judith Hall (1984), Cheris Kramarae (1981), Robin Lakoff (1975), and Judy Pearson (1985).

REFERENCES

Acitelli, L. K. and S. Duck. 1987. Intimacy as the proverbial elephant. In D. Perlman and S. Duck, eds., *Intimate Relationships: Development, Dynamics, and Deterioration*. Beverly Hills, CA: Sage Publications, 297–308.

Aires, E. 1987. Gender and communication. In P. Shaver and C. Hendrick, eds., *Sex and Gender*. Beverly Hills, CA: Sage Publications, 149–176.

Barnlund, D. C. 1979. Communication: The context of change. In C. David Mortensen, ed., *Basic Readings in Communication Theory*, 2d ed. New York: Harper & Row, 6–26.

Beck, A. T. 1988. *Love is Never Enough*. New York: Harper & Row.

Borisoff, D., and L. Merrill. 1992. *The Power to Communicate: Gender Differences as Barriers*, 2d ed. Prospect Hts., IL: Waveland Press.

_____. 1991. Gender issues and listening. In D. Borisoff and M. Purdy, eds., *Listening in Everday Life: A Personal and Professional Approach*. Lanham, MD: University Press of America, 59–86.

Borisoff, D., and D. A. Victor. 1989. *Conflict Management: A Communication Skills Approach*. Englewood Cliffs, NJ: Prentice-Hall.

Brown, G. W., and T. Harris. 1978. *Social Origins of Depression: A Study of Psychiatric Disorders in Women*. New York: Free Press.

Buscaglia, L. F. 1984. *Loving Each Other: The Challenge of Human Relationships*. New York: Fawcett Columbine.

Chelune, G. J., J. T. Robison, and M. J. Kommor. 1984. A cognitive model of intimate relationships. In V. J. Derlega, ed., *Communication, Intimacy, and Close Relationships*. Orlando, FL: Academic Press, 11–40.

Derlega, V. J. 1984. Self–disclosure and intimate relationships. In V. J. Derlega, ed., *Communication, Intimacy, and Close Relationships*. Orlando, FL: Academic Press, 1–9.

Derlega, V. J., and A. L. Chaikin. 1976. Norms affecting self–disclosure in men and women. *Journal of Consulting and Clinical Psychology*, 44: 376–380.

Derlega, V. J., and J. Grzelak. 1979. Appropriateness of self–disclosure. In C. J. Chelune, ed., *Self–disclosure*. San Francisco: Jossey-Bass.

Eakins, B. W., and R. G. Eakins. 1978. *Sex Differences and Human Communication*. Boston: Houghton Mifflin.

Gibb, J. 1961. Defensive communication. *Journal of Communication*, 11: 141–148.

Gilligan, C. 1982. *In a Different Voice*. Cambridge, MA: Harvard University Press.

Goldberg, H. 1976. *The Hazards of Being Male: Surviving the Myth of Masculine Privilege*. New York: Nash.

Hall, J. 1984. *Nonverbal Sex Differences: Communication Accuracy and Expressive Style*. Baltimore, MD: Johns Hopkins University Press.

Hatfield, E. 1982. What do women and men want from love and sex? In E.R. Allgeier and N.B. McCormick, eds., *Gender Roles and Sexual Behavior*. Palo Alto, CA: Mayfield.

————. 1984. The dangers of intimacy. In V.J. Derlega, ed., *Communication, Intimacy, and Close Relationships*. Orlando, FL: Academic Press, 207–220.

Johnson, F. L. 1983. Political and pedagogical implications of attitudes towards women's language. *Communication Quarterly*, 31: 133–138.

Jourard, S. M. 1971. *The Transparent Self*. New York: Van Nostrand–Reinhold.

Jung, C. G. 1928. *Contributions to Analytic Psychology*. New York: Harcourt, Brace & Co.

Klinger, E. 1977. *Meaning and Voice: Inner Experiences and the Incentives in Peoples' Lives*. Minneapolis: University of Minnesota Press.

Kramarae, C. 1981. *Women and Men Speaking*. Rowley, MA: Newbury House.

Lakoff, R. 1975. *Language and Woman's Place*. New York: Harper & Row.

Lerner, H. G. 1989. *The Dance of Intimacy*. New York: Harper & Row.

Maltz, D., and R. Borker. 1982. A cultural approach to male–female miscommunications. In J. J. Gumperz, ed., *Language and Social Identity*. Cambridge, England: Cambridge University Press.

Morris, D. 1971. *Intimate Behaviors*. New York: Random House.

Noller, P. 1987. Nonverbal communication in marriage. In D. Perlman and S. Duck, eds., *Intimate Relationships: Development, Dynamics and Deterioration*. Beverly Hills, CA: Sage Publications, 149–175.

Pearson, J. C. 1985. *Gender and Communication*. Dubuque, IA: William C. Brown.

Perlman, D., and S. Duck, eds. 1987. *Intimate Relationships: Development, Dynamics, and Deterioration*. Beverly Hills, CA: Sage Publications.

Perlman, D., and S. Fehr, eds. 1987. Development of Intimate Relationships. *Intimate Relationships: Development, Dynamics, and Deterioration*. Newbury Park, CA: 13–24.

Reik, T. 1954. Men and women speak different languages. *Psychoanalysis*, 2: 3–15.

Rogers, C. 1961. *On Becoming a Person*. New York: Houghton Mifflin.

Rubin, L. B. 1983. *Intimate Strangers: Men and Women Together.* New York: Harper & Row.

Stockard, J., and M. M. Johnson. 1980. *Sex Roles: Sex Inequality and Sex Role Development.* Englewood Cliffs, NJ: Prentice–Hall.

Tannen, D. 1990. *You Just Don't Understand: Women and Men in Conversation.* New York: William Morrow & Co.

Valéry, P. 1941. Luste, or the crystal girl. Trans. David Paul. In J. Mathews, ed., *Paul Valéry Plays*, Vol. 3. New York: Pantheon Books, 1960, 5–140.

Weinberg, K. 1976. *The Figure of Faust in Valéry and Goethe.* Princeton, NJ: Princeton University Press.

Weisstein, U. 1968, *Comparative Literature and Literary Theory.* Trans. W. Riggan. Bloomington, IN: Indiana University Press.

Williams, J. E., and D. L. Best. 1982. *Measuring Sex Stereotypes: A Thirty Nation Study.* Beverly Hills, CA: Sage Publications.

A CROSSCULTURAL PERSPECTIVE ON GENDER

AUTHOR   David A. Victor, Ph.D.
Department of Management
Eastern Michigan University

POINTS TO BE ADDRESSED

- Defining culture
- Understanding the connection between gender and culture
- Arguments explaining male domination
- Cultural approaches toward gender differences
- Interaction attempting to ignore gender differences
- Interaction attempting to reinforce gender differences
- Managing cultural differences

CULTURE AND COMMUNICATION

This chapter discusses cross-cultural differences in gender and communication. Behavioral and communication differences exist between the sexes in every society. The way in which these differences are manifested, however, changes radically from one culture to another. To the extent that culture affects virtually every aspect of life, culture shapes the nature of gender differences in any given society. Moreover, the way in which people communicate is inextricably intertwined with the culture in which they were raised. Indeed, as John Condon and Fathi Yousef (1985) have indicated, "we cannot separate culture from communication." (34–35). Consequently, the premise of this chapter is that the culture in which one is raised directly influences both the way one communicates and the way in which one perceives gender roles.

CULTURE DEFINED

Before proceeding, it is necessary at this point to briefly define the rather protean term culture. Alfred Kroeber and Clyde Kluckhohn discovered more than 300 definitions of the term in use. The number of definitions has since increased and these definitions have themselves grown even more unclear because of the fact that living—to use the words of ethnologist James Clifford (1988)—in an "ambiguous, multivocal world makes it increasingly hard to conceive of human diversity as inscribed in bounded independent cultures" (23).

Still, for our purposes we can define culture as what Glen Fisher (1988) calls the programming of a mindset. Culture, in Fisher's definition, begins at birth: "the infant mind is somewhat like a blank tape, waiting to be filled, and culture plays a large part in the recording process" (45). Culture is the part of behavior that is at once learned and collective. In other words, culture is taught rather than instinctive or innate. No particular culture is therefore natural while others are unnatural. And culture is collectively reinforced and handed down, so that culturally determined behavior can function only within the larger context of a group (the members of the culture itself).

CULTURE'S INFLUENCES ON COMMUNICATION

Culture affects virtually every aspect of life, from economics to religion, from language to kinship structures. Culture shapes social organization, of which formal and informal views of proper and improper sex roles form an important subset. In almost every culture, people learn to communicate differently with those of the same sex than they do with those of the opposite sex. Indeed, in many languages, the actual formation of the words one uses changes according to whether the speaker is a man or a woman. Additionally, the vast majority of the world's languages strengthen gender distinctions by using gender-linked word construction. In English, gender distinctions exist in the third person singular (that is, whether one uses "he" or "she") and the use of the word "man" to stand for "humankind"—as in the opening lines of the U.S. Declaration of Independence, in which "all men are created equal" (which at least partially formed the defense against woman's suffrage in the United States for well over a century). Culture, however, affects gender roles in many ways beyond linguistic distinctions. Culture, by shaping the way in which its members think and view the world around them, lays the underlying foundation on which are built all gender relations within that particular society—including communication.

In all cultures, men and women are raised differently. Cultural values regarding the roles of men and women are taught, modeled, and learned at an early age. For example, in the United States, girls may be encouraged to play with dolls as pretend babies (a nurturing activity) while boys are likely to be discouraged from such play. This difference in play activity, in turn, begins to reinforce certain cultural expectations of girls and boys. No innate nurturing predisposition necessarily moves girls to play with dolls; the activity is culturally learned. In turn, one can argue that gender role differences in large measure result from the combined activities of such culturally reinforced learned behavior.

Lillian Breslow Rubin (1976) has written that men and women "are products of a process that trains them to relate to only one side of themselves—she, to the passive, tender, intuitive, verbal, emotional side; he, to the active, tough, logical, nonverbal, unemotional one" (116). Rubin's remark is itself admittedly culturally biased; she erroneously describes gender roles in her own country (the United States) as if they were universal. Still, the position she holds remains valid: men and women are taught at an early age to communicate differently.

OTHER VIEWS

It would be incorrect to claim universal agreement, that gender role differences derive from cultural factors. While this view is suggested here, it is important to discuss at this point the century-long debate that has raged over the causes of the inequality of the sexes.

The chief argument against culture as the sole determinant of gender differences rests in the high degree of similarity of several factors in gender inequality, regardless of culture. With only a few exceptions among cultures in some parts Melanesia and among some early Native American societies, male dominance is traditional in virtually all cultures. Additionally, studies of the perception of certain male and female traits have shown considerable universality, regardless of cultural differences. For example, J. E. Williams and D. L. Best (1982) found in a study of gender traits in 29 nations that people associated men with such traits as "dominant," "forceful," and "strong-willed," and associated women with such traits as "emotional" and "submissive" (16).

The preponderance of male dominance has been attributed largely to two causes outside of culture: sociobiology and psychology. The one undebatable conclusion among proponents of all three sources, however, is that with few exceptions most societies traditionally have placed men in a dominant position relative to women. The near universality of traditional male dominance in most societies, regardless of culture, tends to support the view that either sociobiology or psychology is the source of gender inequality.

THE SOCIOBIOLOGICAL ARGUMENT

Briefly, sociobiology extremists such as Edward O. Wilson (1975) assert that all behavior is rooted in biology. While such so-called biological determinists represent a minority position among sociobiologists, considerable attention has been given to supposedly innate biological causes of male dominance. These include arguments rooted in the concepts of male bonding genetically reinforced through natural selection to favor male group hunting needs over millenia (Tiger, 1969); in male biologically caused aggressive behavior leading to male dominance over aggressive females (Goldberg, 1974; Wilson, 1975); in male biological superiority in physical strength and consequently in primitive warfare (Harris, 1974); and in the biological female impedients of childbearing, either through direct removal from the nondomestic area at the time of childbirth (Scheinfeld, 1947) or through greater female vulnerability during pregnancy and the early stages of childrearing (Collins, 1972). It also should be pointed out that while most of the proponents of sociobiological causes of female inequality are themselves men, this is not entirely the case. Notably, such prominent female feminist theorists as Ann Oakley (1972), Alice Rossi (1977) and Janet Sayers (1982) are critical of those who overlook entirely the role of biology in creating gender disparity.

THE PSYCHOLOGY ARGUMENT

Whether innate and universal psychological differences in male and female behavior lead to male dominance is among the most widely argued of all questions in research on gender differences. In *The Psychology of Sex Differences* (1974), Eleanor Emmons Maccoby and Carol Nagy Jacklin cite over 1,200 articles and books published by the mid-1970's on this subject. The number has since continued to grow. The argument supporting psychological causes of gender inequality has its source in the theories of female castration complex tentatively set forth by Sigmund Freud in an essay entitled "Some Psychical Consequences of the Anatomical Distinction Between the Sexes" (1925). Although Freud himself questioned the completeness of his observations, his theories on the subject led to arguments among his followers and opponents regarding psychological causes of sex inequality. These debates have manifested themselves in a host of subjects ranging from differences in perception, cognitive styles, learning ability, and achievement motivation to self-concept and self-respect, power relationships, approach-avoidance conflicts, memorization ability, and general temperament. Most feminist theorists have outrightly rejected Freud's theories as inadequately developed, perverted by the pervasive Victorian sexual repressiveness of his own era or (in the case of Jeffrey Masson's scathing 1984 criticism) on the grounds that Freud falsified his observations for personal reasons. Still, several major feminist theorists (Mitchell, 1974; Chodorow, 1978) have suggested that innate psychological differences may exist and that psychological theories—if not necessarily Freud's works—remain applicable to an understanding of the sources of gender differences.

CULTURAL APPROACHES TOWARD THE ROLE OF GENDER DIFFERENCES

The role of culture in socializing male and female behavioral traits, including communication, was pioneered by Margaret Mead (1963, 1973), who was among the first theorists to recognize that those traits we think of as masculine or feminine are actually culturally taught and learned, not inherent qualities. While in the 1980s, Derek Freeman (1983) and others have attempted to raise some doubts regarding Mead's methodology, her central views regarding the way in which cultural factors shape views of gender remain intact and continue to be seen as valid. Still, it would be somewhat too facile to discount all other influences. To some extent, biological or psychological factors may—along with cultural influences—affect gender differences.

What should concern us most here, however, is not the theories behind these differences but the reality of their existence. The fact that sex roles differ is universal but the ways in which those differences manifest themselves are culturally specific. A German sees behavioral differences between the sexes as readily as a Saudi, but the nature of those differences vary markedly precisely because those differences manifest themselves differently in German culture and in Saudi culture. Because of this, communication between and among the sexes in Germany differs, for cultural reasons, from that in Saudi Arabia. Essentially, cultural approaches to gender differences manifest themselves in three broad categories: 1) interaction attempting to ignore gender differences; 2) interaction attempting to reinforce gender differences; and 3) segregation between the sexes with limited interaction.

At this point it is important to note that within-culture differences can occur in the actual way these tendencies are manifested. That is, individual differences or resistance to such categories may represent important exceptions or subcultures varying markedly from the culture as a whole.

INTERACTION ATTEMPTING TO IGNORE
GENDER DIFFERENCES

In the cultures of several nations, including the United States, people have attempted to consciously redefine sex-trait stereotyping. Efforts have been made to ignore gender differences in communication (and actions). Particularly in the realm of politics and the workplace, steps have been taken to eradicate gender stereotyping through legal or face-losing penalties.

For the most part, these attitudes represent a revamping of society— a change from a tradition of male dominance toward an egalitarian ideal. Thus in the United States, a societal ideal—the equality of men and women—has been encouraged and reinforced by antidiscrimination legislation. This has led many contemporary Americans to consider non-sexist language, and the ignore perceived gender differences in communication practices (particularly in the workplace or in political forum). Moreover, the attempt to eradicate sex-trait stereotyping has led to efforts to disprove assumptions about sex characteristics. Thus, the Russell Reynolds Associates' study entitled "Men, Women, and Leadership in the American Corporation" (1990) was undertaken specifically to empirically determine the validity of commonly held U.S. stereotypes about nurturing (managing style) versus aggressive (leadership style) approaches to work in executive positions. The test, in short, was designed "to test several hypotheses related to the 'glass ceiling' that prevents women from reaching the top-most executive positions in corporations" (3). It is significant that the survey designers expected to find clear sex differences in management approaches, but that "contrary to expectations, the study found that a majority of women in both line and staff positions were leader-style executives. In contrast, male executives tested as expected: leaderstyle in line positions, managerstyle in staff positions" (ii). Moreover, "80 percent of executives in every category (97 percent of male leader-style executives) reported that the gender of people working under them 'didn't matter'" (ii). In short, the Russell Reynolds study indicates a movement toward perceived sexual equality among business leaders.

Perceptions of sexual equality are important because they affect the direction that the business community is likely to follow. Perhaps more importantly, the move toward sexual equality in the United States signifies a cultural manifestation of U.S. values. The ideal of gender nondifferentiation is no more natural or unnatural that any other culturally derived ideal. Instead, the tendency to strive toward a gender equality in which sex-trait differences are ignored has its roots in culture. U.S. culture (in part, as an outgrowth of its political system) attempts to teach and reinforce an ideal of innate equality among people that is often counteracted by the status and the value of work. The status and the value of work in the United States, in turn, is usually linked directly to the price paid for the labor. Gender equality as an ideal has roots in the U.S. political system of equality for all; the means of its attainment is culturally tied to the economic equality of the sexes.

To some extent, change along these lines is already evident in the United States. The increasing number of women working in a paid occupation and the entry of women into traditionally male occupations has been pervasive in the United States over the last thirty years. As of 1990, two-thirds of all U.S. married mothers with a husband present worked outside the home (Green, 1991). This is significant because women working in traditionally unpaid jobs (for example, childrearing, housework) have no direct economic self-definition. While such work remains work, it nonetheless is judged as unpaid or fee labor and therefore denigrated by U.S. cultural norms. Moreover, the percentage of U.S. women in such traditionally male occupations as engineer, physician, and lawyer have grown from 1.2 percent, 4.1 percent and 6.5 percent, respectively, in 1950 (Bates, et al., 1983) to 6 percent, 17 percent and 18 percent, respectively, in 1990 (Green, 1991). The result is an increasing trend toward gender integration in business communication, and, increasingly, society as a whole.

Still, despite the positive messages culturally conveyed regarding work for wages and increase of jobs for women in traditionally male occupations, U.S. women remain far from being the economic equals of U.S. men. Women who do work for wages still predominate in the lower paid, so-called "pink collar" jobs. As a result, women make up the vast majority of clerical positions (secretaries, typists, bank tellers), which pay less money for the associated labor than the managerial, technical, or professional occupations in which women, despite increasing numbers, still represent a marked minority.

INTERACTION ATTEMPTING TO REINFORCE GENDER DIFFERENCES

A second culturally determined view of women is particularly common in the countries of northern Europe and many other highly industrialized nations.

This is an economic equality in which sex-trait stereotypes are reinforced or even exaggerated. These cultures reinforce sex-trait stereotypes as a way to bring different human qualities into daily life and, especially, into the workplace. Consequently, more women than men may be called on to use those interpersonal skills that they are perceived through culturally learned sex stereotyping as feminine. Conversely, in these cultures, men are seen as naturally better able to carry out tasks requiring those analytic skills that are culturally perceived as being more masculine. The key point here, however, is that both sets of sex-trait stereotypes are viewed as positive by the culture as a whole and in the workplace in particular. As a result, women are not encouraged to behave more like men to succeed, but are encouraged by workplace advancement to cultivate the sex-traits stereotypes attributed to them by the society as a whole.

The most comprehensive analysis of this view toward economic equality retaining sex-trait reinforcement is the Dutch management researcher Geert Hofstede's (1984) study on cultural differences in the perception of gender-linked traits in workplace. Hofstede did not assign given behaviors to either gender, but merely examined—using what he termed a masculinity-femininity index—how often such behavior occurred in the workplace in 40 countries.

Hofstede correlated as feminine those answers that showed people orientation, interdependence, fluid views of sex roles, leveling (rather than excelling), quality of life, sympathy for the unfortunate, intuition, emphasis on serve (rather than achievement), a "work to live" philosophy, and a belief that differences in sex roles should not mean differences in power. He correlated as masculine those responses that indicated a materialistic orientation, emphasis on performance and growth (over quality of life), clearly differentiated sex roles, excelling (versus leveling), decisiveness, sympathy for the achiever, a "live to work" philosophy, and a belief that men should dominate in all settings.

His categories themselves reflect common Dutch stereotypes, a function of Hofstede's own culturally acquired stereotyping of the sexes. None of these traits are themselves biologically feminine or masculine. Still, Hofstede did not link either gender to either category. Men in some cultures could predominantly have feminine behavior; women in some cultures could predominantly have masculine behavior. He found whole societies masculine or feminine. Nevertheless, Hofstede did establish precise correlations between the amount of masculinity or femininity in a culture to the degree of differences between men and women in specific areas. Thus, he found that "in more feminine countries more working women are in the qualified jobs, and in higher education the same courses tend to be taken by women and men" (203–04). He also indicated that he found "some evidence that in more masculine countries fewer men are positive toward the idea of seeing women in leading positions" (204)

It is interesting to note that Hofstede's most feminine countries—notably the four Nordic states—are among those countries most strongly emphasizing economic parity through sex-stereotype reinforcement and are also those having the most parity between the sexes in professional and administrative occupations. Thus, for example in Sweden, 15 percent of the men and 15 percent of the women hold such jobs; and in Norway, 13 percent of the men and 10 percent of the women hold these positions (Taylor, 1985: 361)

SEGREGATION BETWEEN THE SEXES
WITH LIMITED INTERACTION

The last category of cross-cultural differences in the perception of gender is one in which gender differences are reinforced and in which men and women are limited or excluded from full interaction. Men are encouraged to interact only with other men and those women who are members of the immediate family. Even then, the subjects and degree of interaction may be limited. Women, in turn, are either expected primarily to interact only with other women and male family members or even to interact with no other person, male or female, outside the family. Thus, women are expected to act within the private sphere while men are expected to act within the public sphere. Women acting in the public sphere are rare and are given a pseudo-male status for the purpose of their actions.

Various arguments exist to explain gender segregation, ranging from the role of religion to theories of labor distribution in agricultural or hunter-gatherer societies. Women are culturally taught to be submissive to men in the public sphere (although they may dominate in the private sphere of the home). The women in these societies may view themselves as oppressed or view themselves as self-fulfilled, depending on the cultural value placed on their role in society.

MANAGING CULTURAL DIFFERENCES IN THE
PERCEPTION OF APPROPRIATE COMMUNICATION
AMONG AND BETWEEN THE GENDERS

A tendency exists within every individual to view his or her own culture as intrinsically better than other cultures. This is called ethnocentrism. To some extent, ethnocentrism is impossible to overcome entirely, because culture is modeled and learned at so early in life that cultural norms appear to be universal norms against which differences are judged. To the extent that an individual will never leave the confines of his or her own culture, ethnocentrism hold poses no problem. The world, however, is growing increasingly multicultural. International information systems, mass media reports, international trade, and other factors make ethnocentrism a weakness.

To the extent that one's own view of gender roles is culturally determined, ethnocentrism plays a part in how one will view gender differences. Because of ethnocentric influences, a tendency exists to see one's own cultural attitudes toward gender roles as right and others' views as wrong. This is even true when a culture is attempting to redefine gender roles and gender roles are therefore in a state of flux. For example, a tendency exists in the United States to denigrate societies in which the sexes are segregated. Discussion of the marked differentiation of the sexes into private-female and public-male life is likely to provoke a negative reaction among North Americans, who are likely to see such divisions as somehow wrong rather than merely different. It is important to note that the sources of such condemnation are themselves culturally rooted and may in themselves have a sexist source. This is precisely because, as mentioned above, the private sphere has no direct economic measurability and is thus devalued according to U.S. cultural norms. The reasons for the U.S. cultural attribute of devaluing the private sphere, however, may have been culturally derived by devaluing the traditional role of women's work.

The key to effective cross-cultural communication is in the suspension of ethnocentric biases as much as possible. Ethnocentrism, in turn, is diminished through increased crosscultural awareness. As a result, the more one recognizes cross-cultural differences in gender perception as not intrinsically wrong but simply different, the more likely gender-linked differences in culture will no longer impede communication.

Cultural relativity and communicative flexibility are at the heart of cross-cultural communication. Concepts of right and wrong are themselves derived from such culturally linked factors as religion and political organization. In a broader sense, one can believe that one's religion or political system is superior to that of all others, but in an immediate sense it is unlikely that one will convert an individual to one's religion or political persuasion as a prerequisite to communication. Cross-cultural communication, therefore, presupposes, to some extent, the suspension of values of right and wrong.

Differences in what are perceived as proper gender roles across cultures, however, are often so mutually offensive to both parties that communication can not proceed. To illustrate with a simple nonverbal communication example, dress attributions across cultures may prove so marked that communication stops. Thus, Saudis may be so offended by a bare-armed woman that they can not continue to talk. Conversely, North Americans may be so outraged to see a woman in a chador that they feel compelled to effectively end all channels of communication.

The intercultural communicator, then, is faced with an issue that communicators in a single culture do not face. To overcome cultural differences in gender role perception it is necessary to be flexible about what is and is not acceptable behavior for each gender. This chapter has attempted to describe the three broad categories of gender-role perception into which most of the world's cultures fall. No attempt has been made to discuss the individual cultures; such a discussion in a broad overview would be impractical here. It would, however, be highly advisable for the intercultural communicator to prepare in advance for communication with someone from another culture by studying in detail the specifics of gender-role attributions in that culture.

While the intercultural communicator need not in every instance accommodate other cultures' differences in the perception of the proper relationship of the sexes, it is nonetheless a prerequisite to effective communication. If the communicator cannot accommodate such differences, he or she can choose to cut off communication altogether. But once the commitment is made to carry on a dialogue outside of one's own culture, it is necessary to remain as flexible to differences as possible. To the extent that this chapter has provided some direction toward that end, it will have served its function.

REFERENCES

Bates, U., et al. 1983. *Women's Realities, Women's Choices: An Introduction to Women's Studies*. Oxford: Oxford University Press.

Chodorow, N. 1978. *The Reproduction of Mothering: Psychoanalysis and the Sociology of Gender*. Berkeley: University of California Press.

Clifford, J. 1988. *The Predicament of Culture*. Cambridge, MA: Harvard University Press.

Collins, R. 1972. *Conflict Theory of Sexual Stratification. In Family, Marriage and the Struggle of the Sexes*. H. Dreitzel, Ed., New York: Macmillan.

Condon, J., and F. Yousef. 1985. *An Introduction to Intercultural Communication*. New York: Macmillan.

Fisher, Glen. 1988. *Mindsets: The Role of Culture and Perception in International Relations*. Yarmouth, ME: Intercultural Press.

Freeman, D. 1983. *Margaret Mead and Samoa: The Making and Unmaking of an Anthropological Myth*. Cambridge, MA: Harvard University Press.

Freud, S. 1925. Some Psychical Consequences of the Anatomical Distinction Between the Sexes. In J. Strouse, ed., *Women and Analysis*, pp. 108–141. New York: Grossman.

Goldberg, S. 1974. *The Inevitability of Patriarchy*. New York: William Morrow.

Green, S. D. 1991. American Women and Change, *The World and I* vol. 6; No. 4: 469–81.

Harris, M. 1974. *Cows, Pigs, Wars and Witches*. New York: Vintage.

Hofstede, G. 1984. *Culture's Consequences: International Differences in Work-Related Values*. Beverly Hills, CA: Sage Publications.

Kroeber, A. L., and C. Kluckhohn, 1954. *Culture: A Critical Review of Concepts and Definitions*. New York: Random House.

Maccoby, E. E., and C. N. Jacklin. 1974. *The Psychology of Sex Differences*. Stanford, CA: Stanford University Press.

Masson, J. 1984. *The Assault on Truth: Freud's Suppression of the Seduction Theory*. New York: Farrar, Straus and Giroux.

_____. 1973. *Coming of Age in Samoa*. New York: William Morrow.

Mead, M. 1963. *Sex and Temperament*. New York: Dell.

Men, Women, and Leadership in the American Corporation. 1990, November. New York: Russell Reynolds Associates, Inc.

Mitchell, J. 1974. *Psychoanalysis and Feminism.* New York: Random House.

Oakley, A. 1972. *Sex, Gender and Society.* New York: Harper Colophon Books.

Rossi, A. 1977. A Biosocial Perspective on Parenting. *Daedalus* 106: No. 2. 1–22.

Rubin, L. B. 1976. *Worlds of Pain: Life in the Working-Class Family.* New York: Basic Books.

Sayers, J. 1982. *Biological Politics: Feminist and Anti-Feminist Perspectives.* New York: Methuen.

Scheinfeld, A. 1947. *Women and Men.* London: Chatto & Windus.

Taylor, D., et al. 1985. *Women: A World Report.* Oxford: Oxford University Press.

Tiger, L. 1969. *Men in Groups.* New York: Random House.

Williams, J. E., and D. L. Best. 1982. *Measuring Sex Stereotypes: A Thirty Nation Study.* Beverly Hills, CA: Sage Publications.

Wilson, E. O. 1975. *Sociobiology: The New Synthesis.* Cambridge, MA: Harvard University Press.

GENDER AND THE SELF

AUTHOR   Linda Costigan Lederman, Rutgers University

POINTS TO BE ADDRESSED:

- The development of the self-concept and gender
- The self as a composite of multiple selves
- Communication within the self: intrapersonal communication
- Relationships within the self: intrapersonal relationships
- Gender differences in intrapersonal and interpersonal communication
- A transactional model of intrapersonal and interpersonal communication

Differences in the ways men and women talk, behave nonverbally, and develop and/or maintain relationships are the subject of much written discussion and analysis. We know, for example, that men and women in our culture are socialized into different ways of handling interactions. In this regard, women learn to emphasize relational dimensions while men generally learn to be more message-attentive. A good deal has been said about the implications of such contrasts for personal and professional interaction. Many related gender issues are raised and discussed in later chapters of this book. This chapter, however, is devoted to an area that is less often written about: gender and the self.

One's sense of self is a critical component of any communication interaction (D. Cushman, B. Valentinsen, and D. Dietrich, 1982; N. Kuipner and C. Rogers, 1979; H. Markus, 1983). This chapter describes the communication that takes place within the self, also known as *intrapersonal communication*. It is argued here that an awareness of intrapersonal communication is critical to individual well being, particularly because it results in intrapersonal relationships (L. Lederman, 1988), which, in turn, affect *interpersonal communication*.

In keeping with the theme of this volume, special attention is paid to gender differences in intrapersonal communication. An important question arises as we examine gender issues in relation to the self: If women and men form distinct self images, what are the implications for male-female communication? Because so many of the significant interpersonal relationships in our culture are cross-sex, this question deserves serious consideration.

Many of the concepts presented in this chapter are illustrated by excerpts from interviews the author has conducted with college students. Although the examples here are quite specific to the lives of the interviewees, they help to demonstrate how a sense of self emerges, how various facets of the self become distinct and subsequently communicate with one another, and how the resultant intrapersonal communication affects relationships with others.

DEFINING THE SELF

Each of us has a sense of self, or self-concept. From the moment of birth, we are in the process of what Carl Rogers (1961) refers to as "becoming." We are in the process of gathering information about ourselves and developing a concept about that self. Our daily experiences continuously shape our understanding of who we are, including a sense of ourselves as male or female. But we do not develop a self-concept in isolation. In fact, most theorists emphasize the profound influence of social interaction on the formation of the self concept (K. Gergen, 1982; E. Goffman, 1972). It is in social interaction that the self is born and developed. We come to think of ourselves as humorous by the laughter of others, as socially attractive by the attention others pay to us, and so on. We also evaluate the quality of our interpersonal relationships by the ways in which others treat us. We come to regard ourselves as good brothers/sisters, wives/husbands, friends, or co-workers based on interaction with others.

Thus, the self is a product of interpersonal communication. At the same time, however, we know quite well that an individual's self image has a profound effect on his or her communication with others. We make communicative choices based on our current understanding of who we are, assuming that others see us as we see ourselves. An individual who believes he or she is amusing to others will risk offering witticism. An individual who sees him- or herself as a leader will risk offering direction. In truth, the relationship between intrapersonal communication and interpersonal communication is highly complex. The two levels of communication are mutually influential, nearly inseparable. It is very difficult to segment the process of self-concept formation, but, for the purposes of understanding the importance of gender on the emerging sense of self, it may be useful to begin at the beginning—at birth.

When a new baby is born, one of the first questions asked is about the child's biological sex. Once others know "what the baby is," they can talk about the baby as "he" or "she" and address it appropriately (L. Stewart, A. Stewart, S. Friedly, and P. Cooper, 1990). Of course, they know which pronouns to use and whether to suggest a masculine or feminine nickname. But research indicates that adults even use different adjectives to describe male and female infants, focusing on the size, strength, and bodily activity of baby boys and the beauty, sweetness, and facial responsiveness of baby girls. In truth, males and females begin to develop gendered self-images very early in life, first in interaction with parental figures, later with other adults, all of whom are well-schooled in gender-appropriateness and provide distinct messages to boys and girls about "who they are."

As a child grows, the self-concept continues to be influenced by what others say. Through face-to-face interaction, parents, teachers, and peers all provide children with vital information necessary for self-concept formation (H. Blumer,

1975; C. Cooley, 1967). For instance, teachers tell children how smart they are through grades and verbal comments. Even young children become remarkably adept at interpreting the meaning of the various symbols used to evaluate their ability. Although teachers are the primary source of information about academic ability, parents and friends often offer verbal comparisons ("You're the smartest girl in your class" or "Your brother is the smart one in the family"). In similar exchanges, we teach children how athletic, attractive, humorous, considerate, and generally desirable they are, which assists them in forming self-images.

Thought of in this way, it is clear that the self arises from social experience. This is why gender-related differences in our culture are part and parcel of how we come to see ourselves. In one of the interviews conducted by the author, a young woman told of a vivid memory from kindergarten. When asked to list the things she had learned about how to treat others, she responded "Be nice, be kind, and hold hands when we cross the street." She went on to explain the source of these lessons: "I think that the voice that I am always criticizing myself with is like an internalized parent figure. Sometimes that voice sounds almost like a mother—like my mother." This explanation demonstrates the close relationship between intrapersonal messages and interpersonal messages. Also, because the "rules" named by the kindergartner were characteristically female, it suggests that her sense of gender-appropriateness was learned in communication with an adult, in this case her mother.

The same interview demonstrates that the messages learned early in life can be quite powerful. Even as an adult, the subject was influenced by her mother's messages: "Like when I will have an argument with her, I will be totally against what she is saying. But then I will start telling myself things that I know are clearly her speaking. Yet I am talking for her and I'm talking to me." Later in the chapter, specific characteristics of "self talk" and other examples of intrapersonal conflict will be examined in more detail. For now, let's return to the nursery to consider another source of information about the self, a source that is arguably even more powerful than direct messages about gender-appropriateness.

Research has revealed that adults actually behave differently toward boys and girls, just as they behave differently toward mature men and women (Stewart, Stewart, Friedly, and Cooper, 1990). Often behavioral choices contain implicit messages about the significance of being male or female in the culture. Because much of what we know of ourselves is learned in social interaction, examining gender-specific communication is critical to understanding the process of self-concept formation. Through observation and interaction, children learn that females and males behave differently and have different speaking "rights" (P. Treichler and C. Kramarae, 1983). Of course, both sexes of parents have a wider range of rights than children, but, in all likelihood, children will notice that fathers typically interrupt more than mothers and engage in more simultaneous speech with their daughters than with their sons.

Such observations are significant, because the sense of self begins in interactions characterized by these and other gender-related inequities in conversational patterns. It is in these interactions that our images of who we are and the behaviors we can expect from others are born and nurtured. No one may have ever explicitly taught us as children that little boys would be interrupted less than their sisters, but such lessons are all too often the outcome of early patterns of interaction between children and adults.

When an adult listens to or interrupts a child, the youngster observes the adult's actions and attributes meaning to them. The meanings attached to communicative behaviors become incorporated into the child's sense of self. It is not that anyone necessarily tells girls that they are inherently less worth listening to than boys are. It is that little girls are listened to less than the boys with whom they talk. And boys and girls learn from their experience in these interactions that there is something inherently more worth listening to when boys speak (Treichler and Kramarae, 1983). This may explain why so many studies, conducted in diverse settings, indicate that men take far more turns at talk, and considerably longer turns, than their female counterparts.

Of course, adult males and females can challenge such gender-related inequities and work for change in their private and public lives, but it is important to keep in mind that the roots of gender bias are firmly embedded in the self-concepts of many adults.

RECOGNIZING MULTIPLE SELVES

Based on the discussion thus far, it may seem that the self is a single entity. In actuality, the self is comprised of multiple parts that evolve and function separately. The notion of multiple selves is critical to understanding intrapersonal communication. The concept was first articulated at the end of the nineteenth century by William James. James (1890) identified three distinct selves: the material self, the social self, and the spiritual self. These categories still apply today. The material self is defined in relation to the physical aspects of the individual and his or her world. It concerns itself with material objects: the individual's body and the various artifacts amassed and used by the individual, such as clothing, jewelry, cars, houses. The social self is concerned with the self in relation to others, with the self as brother/sister, friend, co-worker, and so on. The spiritual self cares for the individual's essence, his or her very spirit.

The complex nature of the self was further developed by George Herbert Mead (1934), who differentiated between the "I" and the "me." The "I" is the impulsive, unorganized, unpredictable self. Mead used the term "me" to identify the generalized other, who monitors the "I" and provides direction and guidance. One college student demonstrates how the distinction helped generate the structure for a writing project: "I remember my sophomore year of college, I was taking a short story class and I was going through a real traumatic time in my life. I wrote a short story about it and what it ended up being was the conversation that was going on in my head. I put it in the form of two different characters."

Our understanding of multiple selves was added to by the transactional psychologists, who identified three ego states: the child, the parent, and the adult (C. Jung, 1956; E. Berne, 1962; D. Barnlund, 1970). The child is the spontaneous self, the parent the ethical self and the adult the rational self. Each of us has all three ego states firmly in place by the time we reach maturity. One ego state may be more powerful in controlling behavior, but, according to the transactional psychologists, intrapersonal conversations between the three ego states are normal and desirable.

The existence of multiple selves creates the capacity for "self-reflection" (L. Thayer, 1968). That is, because the separate selves exist within one person, they can view one another as "objects" and evaluate one another, variously commending and criticizing. For example, the spiritual and social selves may find fault with the material self, which wants to have all the worldly trappings indicative of success. The spiritual self may disdain the goal, while the social self may object to valuing work over relationships.

In terms of gender differences it is interesting to speculate about whether the various selves develop differently in men and women. In terms of James' triumvirate, for example, it may be that men invest more in their material selves, because of their historical domination of public sphere. Traditionally, men have assumed the burden as "breadwinner," so they may attend more to this aspect of self. Women, conversely, have traditionally been the "kin keepers" in our culture, responsible for nurturing family and friendship relationships. Consequently, they may invest more in the social self. Though the lines that divide male and female experiences are becoming less rigid in contemporary times, the majority of early childcare is still performed by women, which, in turn, limits their participation in the material world. Their male partners are seldom afforded "leaves" to nurture family relationships full time. It remains to be seen if this contrast is related to decision making among the various selves or is simply the outcome of a sociopolitical environment that does not offer equal freedom for men and women.

Similarly, stereotypes indicate that women are perceived as more emotional than men and men as more rational than women. If so, this distinction may indicate the prominence of the child ego state in females and the adult in males. Women also appear to be more concerned with politeness and etiquette than men, indicating that they may have a more dominant parent ego state. Again, it is unclear whether the various selves gain strength because the social world requires gender-appropriateness or vice versa. One fact remains clear, however. In many cases, life's important decisions are made in tandem with a member of the "opposite sex." As a result, men and women often find themselves engaged in interpersonal, as well as intrapersonal dialogue, as the multiple selves attempt to reconcile competing alternatives and make acceptable choices.

In the next section, the interdependence of intrapersonal relationships and interpersonal relationships is further developed.

CHARACTERISTICS OF
INTRAPERSONAL RELATIONSHIPS

As a multifaceted system, the self inevitably develops relationships between its parts. These are called intrapersonal relationships (Lederman, 1988). Intrapersonal relationships provide important connections among the multiple selves. The resultant relationships affect and are affected by our relationships with others. Attitudes, feelings, and thoughts about the self influence communication just as strongly as attitudes, feelings, and thoughts about the other. Prior to examining the complex interplay between intrapersonal and interpersonal relationships, it is necessary to discuss in more detail the vehicle that makes intrapersonal relationships possible: self-talk.

Just as we learn how to talk to one another, we also learn how to talk to ourselves, offering commentary, reactions, suggestions, and advice. Such utterances may be listened to or ignored, but typically, patterns of self-talk emerge and intrapersonal relationships are formed. Unlike interpersonal exchanges, self-talk is often ongoing and continuous. One woman describes her intrapersonal communication: "It's like an internal Muzak. It just goes on and on and I don't even know it's there until I stop and listen to what it is that I am saying to myself about me." In comparing her self-talk to the background music played in elevators and restaurants, this interviewee attests to its continuous nature. In addition, her description indicates that she does not always listen. Just as it is possible to sit in a lecture hall and drift away mentally, so too is it possible to drift away while engaging in self-talk.

Indeed, the inner world of self-talk may compete with the external world for the individual's attention. As one college man reports, "I remember I was sitting there watching TV, but my mind was going off on a tangent. It was telling me, 'I should not have done that; I should not have gotten that nasty.' I would have to tell myself to come back and watch TV and not worry about it. 'You did the right thing.' But then I would find myself drifting back off again and I would have to come back again and say 'Watch TV. Don't feel bad. You did the right thing.'" This description, like the one above, indicates that individuals variously attend to or dismiss messages offered by the self. Self-talk is continuous, but it can be tuned in and out.

All of the interview excerpts provided here demonstrate that individuals can describe self-talk in remarkably vivid and specific terms. In fact, most people can recreate the content and the emotion of the internal dialogues contained in self-talk. Often, such dialogues reveal the quality of an individual's intrapersonal relationships. It should hardly surprise us that intrapersonal relationships can be good or bad, happy or troubled, close or distant (Lederman, 1988). In this regard, they are like any relationships with another person.

Intrapersonal relationships are highly significant because they can enhance or impair self-esteem. Self-talk can potentially provide a constant and rich source of esteem, but this is not always the case. It we continually put ourselves down, we feel differently about ourselves than if we continually praise ourselves. Just as one person who holds another in low esteem can provide disconfirming, destructive messages, so can the self communicate contempt and disapproval. In most instances, self-esteem is not a single, fixed commodity, but a dynamic set of entities that is highly variable. Self-esteem can be compartmentalized, or distributed unequally among the various selves. One individual may admire the adult part of himself or herself, but disapprove of the child. Another may enjoy the child and disapprove of the parent for trying to squelch his or her spontaneity. Similarly, the material, spiritual, and social selves need be held in equal esteem. Because there are multiple selves, and multiple relationships among the selves, there are multiple levels of self-esteem.

Like all long-term, continuous relationships, intrapersonal relationships are subject to change and modification over time as one party (the self) gets to know the other (itself) more fully. Thus, an intrapersonal relationship, like an interpersonal relationship, has a history. The nature and valence of the relationships develops and stabilizes over a wide range of experiences. We may not even be aware of how we think about and behave toward ourselves because the process becomes so familiar that it is no longer noticeable. Still, most individuals learn to value their intrapersonal voices. As one college man stated, "It is a conscious process when I am trying to work through a problem or I am trying to decide something. I try to talk to myself as a way to get two different opinions even if they are both my opinion."

An important facet of any intrapersonal relationship is the amount of self-knowledge. We may, for example, know more about ourselves as students than we do about ourselves as employees. Similarly, most young adults know more about themselves as children than as parents. According to some researchers, men and women differ greatly in terms of self-knowledge. Women have been reported to pay more attention to themselves as relationship partners. They monitor their own relational behavior and assess their supportiveness, understanding, and so on, in interpersonal terms. Men, in contrast, reportedly possess more self-knowledge about task-related abilities, such as career and athletic talents. They monitor their individual behavior, too, but tend to see it in isolation from or in direct competition to the behaviors of others.

As you might expect, problems sometimes arise in intrapersonal relationships. Often, problems are associated with stressful situations. If we are experiencing difficulties in our personal relationships, we may find ourselves riddled with self-doubt and inner conflict, which, in turn, may further complicate our communication with others. Similarly, when we feel that we have done a poor job on some task and are not happy with ourselves about it, interpersonal problems often emerge. The close relationship between interpersonal conflict and intrapersonal conflict suggested by these two examples is of great significance in male-female communication. Keep in mind that men and women may be troubled by different kinds of stress, but typically call on one another to understand and even empathize.

In sum, many dimensions exist in intrapersonal communication. This means that intrapersonal communication can be affected by gender-related issues, just as interpersonal and mediated communication can. In the next section, a model of interpersonal communication is expanded to include intrapersonal relationships. By taking a more comprehensive view of an interpersonal exchange, we can better clarify the impact of gender.

MODELING INTRAPERSONAL COMMUNICATION

Because of its complexity and importance, communication within the self must be viewed as an integral part of any dyadic exchange. To illustrate, let's create a simple model of communication between two individuals (A and B). The object of their exchange is labeled X.

If we view this communication as transactional, we assume that it consists of two parts, the relationships between A and B and the exchange of messages about X. That is, though the talk itself may seem to be about the subject X, the participants also share valuable information about their relationship. In this way, they are attempting to achieve "co-orientation," not only toward X, but also toward one another (T. Newcomb, 1953; E. Baudhuin, 1974).

Obviously, the relationships between A and B affects their communication. If, for example, A and B view themselves as friends, and the subject of conversation is A's brother (X), B will be more apt to speak well of X. If A and B are adversaries, the communication about X might be quite different. Indeed, one of the most significant reasons for using a transactional model to discuss communication is that it points out the impact of relationships on communication. The transactional model makes explicit that messages exchanged between two people do not exist apart from their relationship with one another. As W. Wilmot (1980) explains, communication between people begins with them taking another into account, a relational dimension.

Of course, it is very difficult to "take another into account" without attending to his or her biological sex. As mentioned, even infants are viewed as distinct based on this information. The gender composition of a dyad, then, can have a profound influence in terms of who says what to whom and in what ways. Two women would logically talk quite differently than two men, even if they were discussing the same event. Presumably, though, the similarity between the partners would facilitate the exchange. Cross-sex exchanges, in contrast, would be more problematic. Studies verify that men and women tend to use different language, different vocal patterns, different turn-taking behaviors, and even different nonverbal behaviors (Stewart, Stewart, Friedly, and Cooper, 1990).

But a simple transactional model does not go far enough in depicting the full impact of gender differences on male-female communication. An expansion is needed that includes potential gender differences in intrapersonal communication. An expanded transactional model is presented in Figure 4.2 below.

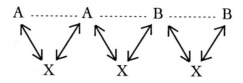

By adding two sets of intrapersonal relationships (A-A and B-B) to the model, we can more fully realize the complexity of the exchange. All of the arrows in the model signify the potential for reciprocal effects. Just as the relationship between A and B affects and is affected by the discussion of X, so too are the intrapersonal relationships of both A and B, which, in turn, act back upon the A-B relationship and the discussion of X. Though it may be disconcerting in its complexity, the expanded model accurately reflects the reality of communication. Most importantly, it indicates that intrapersonal and interpersonal communication go on simultaneously and are mutually influential.

THE IMPACT OF GENDER ON COMMUNICATION

The expanded transaction model provides a useful framework for understanding the profound effect that gender has on communication. As discussed earlier, the self is developed in early communicative exchanges, which tend to be gender-specific. Girls and boys learn who they are through direct messages about themselves and indirect messages contained in gendered communicative choices. By the time they can challenge such inequities, they have already developed a solid self-image, which makes change stressful.

Meanwhile, male-female relationships take on added significance as a child passes through adolescence and into adulthood. Comfortable same-sex friendships among age mates gradually yield to more heterogeneous relationships developed in educational, professional, and social settings. Many important pairings will be cross-sex, so understanding sex differences in intrapersonal communication is critical to effective interpersonal communication.

Many studies indicate that women are more supportive interpersonally than men. Others suggest that men are more honest and critical than women (Treichler and Kramarae, 1983). Similarly, studies verify that women are more accommodating than men (Wheeless and Berryman-Fink, 1985). These and other findings are easier to understand if we attend to the intrapersonal process that accompanies communicative choices. It is not that women do not know how to be more direct and critical. It is not that men do not know how to be more accommodating. Rather, individuals of both sexes have learned to view and evaluate their own behavior in light of the prevailing images or maleness and femaleness in the culture. Indeed, there is no reason to believe that individuals are more critical in self-evaluation than in other types of evaluation, so their intrapersonal messages may be especially harsh in this regard. It is essential that we realize the origin and function of self-talk if we hope to achieve mutually acceptable cross-sex relationships, whether at work or at home.

Communication is a complex and lifelong process. Much of what we become and how we think about ourselves is formed while we talk with one another. Our sense of ourselves and our sense of value to others—indeed our relationships with others—are formed as we talk with others. Men and women in this culture form much of their sense of manliness or womanliness in the same communication process in which we develop our other facets of self-concept. This chapter provides a review of some of the most important dynamics at work in the process in which that sense of self is formed. Because we are continually shaping and reshaping, defining and redefining that sense of self, knowing about these processes is important. The more we know about how we have come to see ourselves and think of ourselves, the more we know about the power we have to re-examine our self-concepts and to develop the people we are in the process of becoming.

REFERENCES

Barnlund, D. C. 1970. A transactional model of communication. In K. K. Sereno and C.D. Mortensen, eds., *Foundations of Communication Theory*. New York: Harper & Row, 83–102.

Baudhuin, E. S. 1974. A general semantics systems model of communication. *Etc.: A Review of General Semantics* 31: 415–424.

Berger, C. R., and J. J. Braddac. 1982. *Language and Social Knowledge*. London: Edward Arnold Ltd.

Berne, E. 1962. *Transactional Analysis in Psychotherapy: A Systematic Individual and Social Psychiatry*. New York: Grove Press.

Blumer, H. 1975. Symbolic interactionism. In R. W. Budd and B. D. Ruben, eds., *Approaches to Human Communication*. Rochelle Park, NJ: Hayden.

Cooley, C. H. 1967. *Human Nature and the Social Order*. New York: Schocken Books.

Cushman, D. P., B. V. Valentinsen, and D. Dietrich. 1982. A rules theory of interpersonal relationships. In F.E.X. Dance, ed., *Human Communication Theory: Comparative Essays*. New York: Harper & Row, 90–119.

Gergen, K. J. 1982. From self to science: What is there to know? In J. Suls, ed., *Psychological Perspectives on the Self, Vol. 1*. Hillsdale, NJ: Erlbaum, 129–149.

Goffman, E. 1972. The presentation of self to others. In J. G. Manis and B. N. Meltzer, eds., *Symbolic Interaction: A Reader in Social Psychology*. 2d ed. Boston: Allyn and Bacon, 234–244.

Hitkins, J. W. 1977. The epistemological relevance of intrapersonal rhetoric. *Southern Speech Communication Journal* 42: 220–227.

————. 1988. Intrapersonal discourse and its relationship to human communication: Rhetorical dimensions of self-talk. In C. V. Roberts, K. W. Watson, and L. L. Barker, eds., *Intrapersonal Communication Processes: Original Essays*. New Orleans, LA: Spectra Incorporated, 36–68.

James, W. 1890. *The Principles of Psychology*. New York: Holt.

Jung, C. G. 1956. *Psyche and Symbol: A Selection from the Writings of C. G. Jung*. New York: Doubleday and Company.

Kelley, H. H., et al. 1983. *Close Relationships*. New York: W. H. Freeman.

Kuipner, N. A., and T. B. Rogers. 1979. Encoding of personal information: Self-other differences. *Journal of Personality and Social Psychology* 35: 633–678.

Lederman, L. C. 1988, April. Intrapersonal relationships: A new construct. Paper presented to the Eastern Communication Association, Baltimore, MD.

Markus, H. 1977. Self-schemata and processing information about the self. *Journal of Personality and Social Psychology* 35: 63–78.

_____. 1980. The self in thought and memory. In D. M. Wegner and R. R. Vallacher, eds., *The Self in Social Psychology*. London: Oxford University Press.

_____. 1983. Self-knowledge: An expanded view. *Journal of Personality* 51: 543–565.

Mead, G. H. 1934. *Mind, Self and Society from the Standpoint of a Social Behaviorist*. Chicago: University of Chicago Press.

Newcomb, T. 1953. An approach to the study of communication acts. *Psychological Review* 60: 367–386.

Rogers, C. 1961. *On Becoming a Person*. Boston: Houghton-Mifflin.

Stewart, L. P., A. Stewart, S. Friedly, and P. Cooper. 1990. *Communication Between the Sexes*. 2d ed. Scottsdale, AZ: Gorsuch Scarisbrick Publishers.

Swann, W. B. 1983. Self-verification: Bringing social reality into harmony with the self. In J. Suls and A. G. Greenwald, eds., *Psychological Perspectives on the Self*. Vol. 2. Hillsdale, NJ: Erlbaum, 33–66.

Swann, W. B., and S. J. Read. 1981. Self-verification processes: How we sustain our self-conceptions. *Journal of Experimental Social Psychology* 17: 351–372.

Thayer, L. 1968. *Communication and Communication Systems*. Homewood, IL: Richard D. Irwin.

Treichler, P. A., and C. Kramarae. 1983. Women's talk in the ivory tower. *Communication Quarterly* 31:2: 118–132.

Wheeless, Virginia Eman, and Cynthia Berryman-Fink. 1985. Perceptions of Women Managers and Their Communicator Competencies. *Communication Quarterly* 33: 137–147.

Wilmot, W. W. 1980. *Dyadic Communication*. 2d ed. Reading, MA: Addison-Wesley.

FOOTNOTES

1. Seven college women were interviewed about the ways in which they talk to themselves about themselves for a major research project on which the author is working. In addition, three college men were interviewed. These interviews will be referred to throughout the chapter and direct quotes will be taken from them and used as illustrations of some of the concepts discussed in the chapter.

COMMUNICATION IN CROSS-SEX FRIENDSHIPS

AUTHOR   William K. Rawlins, Purdue University

POINTS TO BE ADDRESSED

- Comparison of friendship and romantic love
- Gender differences in same-sex friendship
- Cross-sex friendship as borderwork
- Cross-sex friendship as a rhetorical challenge
- Advantages of cross-sex friendships

Friendship between a woman and a man? For many people the idea is charming, but improbable. Either it leads to "something else"—that is, romantic involvement—or comments by significant others in their immediate social network or by third parties in the work setting make the friends feel too uncomfortable to continue their close affiliation. *Whether* and *how* you think such relationships can endure as mutually fulfilling ends-in-themselves indicates your thoughts about several key social issues, including how women and men should behave and feel in personal relationships, and what boundaries exist between friendship and love.

This chapter examines research concerning this surprisingly uncommon and often vexing interpersonal relationship in order to identify the communication challenges facing such friends. I begin by comparing friendship and romantic love to display their similarities and differences. Next, I outline gender patterns in same-sex female and male friendships and the related issue of women's versus men's perceptions of cross-sex bonds. I argue that how women and men view their relationships in general has implications for the possibilities that exist in female-male relationships. I then critically examine the gender disparities in expectations of friendships and suggest certain ideal-typical scenarios of conducting cross-sex friendships. The chapter closes with a consideration of central concerns in the rhetorical management of cross-sex friendships and a description of their advantages.

COMPARING FRIENDSHIP AND ROMANTIC LOVE

Friendship and romantic love are similar and different in important ways. First, both are personal relationships privately negotiated between particular individuals. People choose friends and romantic partners based on their distinctive qualities as persons. Nobody can compel someone to love or befriend another. However, two individuals can develop a mutual attachment of friendship or romance in unlikely arrangements (like the friendship portrayed in the movie *Driving Miss Daisy*) and even forbidden circumstances (as when prison guards and their prisoners fall in love). Potentially then, because of private negotiation, both friendships and romances can transcend social dictates and sanctions.

Next, friendships and romantic bonds require a considerable investment of emotional energy (Rawlins, 1982). Close friends as well as lovers feel substantial affection for one another and care deeply about what happens to their partners. Finally, friendship and love both demand loyalty and fidelity. In developing a private relationship characterized by mutual trust, affection and commitment, lovers as well as close friends depend on the other to be there when needed and to be loyal in times of trouble.

But there are also significant contrasts between friendship and romance. While romantic love usually involves a strong sexual component, friendship manifests a strong spiritual attraction. Consequently, love relationships are potentially more volatile and characterized by perceived urgency (W. Rawlins, 1982). Further, love does not imply equality while friendship emphasizes it (L. Rangell, 1963; M. Horton, 1973; R. Brain, 1976). Sometimes in the struggle for "the upper hand" in love relationships, persons withhold commitment from each other, playing games of "brinkmanship" to keep the other off balance or trying to make the other jealous even at the risk of losing the relationship (J. Sprey, 1969). In contrast, the more "serene" caring of friendship (I. Lepp, 1966), coupled with its emphasis on equality and mutual benefit, usually results in comparatively fewer passionate struggles (except, of course, for competitions fueled by similarities between friends).

Moreover, Lepp (1966) maintains that romantic love is exclusive because it "can only exist as reciprocity between two people" (53). M. Roberts (1982) also cites "exclusivity" as a definitive attribute of romantic love in contrast to friendship. The exclusive claims of romantic partners make them possessive about each other. For this reason many societies institutionalize love relationships, thereby socially sanctioning the restricted attachment of two persons (Lepp, 1966; Brain, 1976). By contrast, friendship is typically not as jealous and can be shared; friends are enriched by experiencing the friendship of other people. Rangell remarks, "Friendship stands in fact between genital love, with its exclusivity to one or a few chosen objects, and the 'all-embracing love of others' seen in religious ascetics . . ." (49). Lepp (1966) argues that those who maintain that a person can only have one true friend conceive of friendship as similar to love. However, the fact that some friends do become possessive and jealous suggests that any distinctions between the exclusivity of friendship and romantic love are a matter of degree (Rawlins, 1982).

Lastly, romantic involvement between a man and a woman is much more celebrated than cross-sex friendship in American culture. Brain (1976) argues that romantic love receives "insane intensification" in our culture, both in its own right and as a prelude to marriage. But we need not look any farther than common parlance to hear people regretfully or defensively describing a cross-sex affiliation as "just friends." Meanwhile, other persons report aspiring to "more than friendship" in their cross-sex attachments. In contrast to the countless love stories we hear told in songs and see enacted on screen, cross-sex friendship is rarely acclaimed or depicted as an ongoing, freestanding bond. This relational category lacks its own master narrative in our culture. How many stories can you think of that richly portray or endorse the lasting, devoted friendship of a man and a woman as an end in itself? Even the film *When Harry Met Sally*, which attracted so much attention to the question of enduring cross-sex friendship, ultimately proves to be another tale of romantic love. The characters' cross-sex friendship is only a stage in the development of the latter, more celebrated attachment.

GENDER PATTERNS IN SAME-SEX FRIENDSHIPS

Traditional sex roles continue to influence significantly the character of friendships in America. Scholars repeatedly observe differences between males' and females' same-sex friendships across the life course (Rawlins, 1992). J. Gottman (1986) concludes that "Gender is the most potent psychological determinant of friendship choice in middle childhood" (140). In trying to explain the prevalence of same-sex friendships among children, C. Rubenstein and C. Rubin (1984) allude to the well-known preference for similar others in children's friendships, adult encouragement of these choices, and sex-role stereotypes within the peer group that reinforces them.

In comparing the friendships of girls with those of boys, fairly consistent tendencies have been described. Beginning around age seven, boys tend to play in groups, and girls prefer to play with one other girl (J. Lever, 1976; H. Foot, A. Chapman, and J. Smith, 1977; T. Berndt, 1982). While fifth and sixth grade boys' friendships are expansive, allowing other boys to join in, D. Eder and M. Hallinan (1978) found those of girls to be more exclusive, making it rather difficult for other girls to become friends.

Girls' friendships are also more intimate than those of boys. For example, fourth grade females shared more secrets than males in K. Rotenberg's (1986) research. And in their study of fifth and sixth graders, W. Furman and D. Buhrmester (1985) report that the girls indicated significantly more intimacy, affection, and enhancement of worth than the boys did. Though there were no initial gender differences in the ratings of same-sex friendships across a sample of second, fifth, and eighth graders, the girls exhibited a steady increase in intimate disclosure and a "striking increase during preadolescence in the significance of same-sex friends as intimacy providers" (1111). In contrast, the boys' levels remained fairly constant. By and large, girls are more apt to have a same-sex "chum" and share greater intimacy as opposed to mere sociability (Seiden and Bart, 1975).

Continuing these trends, adolescent female friendships are characterized as "involved" (J. Fischer, 1981), more exclusive and intimate than males'

F. Hunter and J. Youniss, 1982), closer emotionally (E. Douvan and J. Adelson, 1966; J. Youniss and J. Smollar, 1985), and more inclined to disclose and discuss personally involving topics (F. Johnson and E. Aries, 1983; Youniss and Smollar, 1985). Adolescent girls prize their close friends for evaluating experiences and aiding in their personal development (M. Richey and H. Richey, 1980). However, the characteristic emphasis placed on loyalty, confidence, and commitment in these bonds often fosters intense jealousy between friends and rejection of others desiring to join their conversations (N. Karweit and S. Hansell, 1983; E. Douvan and J. Adelson, 1966; J. La Gaipa, 1979; B. Bigelow and La Gaipa, 1980; N. Feshback and G. Sones, 1971).

In contrast, adolescent male friendships are described as "uninvolved" (J. Fischer, 1981), more inclusive and group-related than females' (I. Kon and V. Losenkov, 1978), less disclosive, and concerned mostly with activity-oriented issues (F. Johnson and E. Aries, 1983; Youniss and Smollar, 1985). Although they do begin to air mutual concerns by mid to late adolescence, males tend mostly to value their friends' companionship and the enjoyment of doing activities together (Richey and Richey, 1980; Smollar and Youniss, 1982). However, since males' friendships typically emphasize activity, achievement, and leadership, closeness can be inhibited or problems can arise due to feelings of competition between friends (N. Karweit and S. Hansell, 1983; E. Douvan and J. Adelson, 1966; Richey and Richey, 1980).

Throughout their adult lives, men's modal pattern of friendship emphasizes each individual's rights and personal autonomy (Gilligan, 1982). While assuming this basic stance toward relationships, they do things together, share activities and fun, and provide instrumental help on a reciprocal basis. But men also typically limit their vulnerability by revealing little about themselves to their friends, largely avoiding the discussion of feelings or personal issues and focusing more on activities and objective issues, such as sports or politics (Rawlins, 1992). Overall, their relationships exhibit restrained emotional involvement (Fox, Gibbs, and Auerbach, 1985).

In contrast, female friends typically enact a moral vision of mutual obligations and responsibilities, wherein relationships are primary and individuals are viewed as essentially connected with one another (Gilligan, 1982). For women, the satisfactions of friendship are usually associated with extensive interdependence. Their pattern of activities interconnects their lives, encourages emotional sharing and intimacy, and incites ongoing tensions between caring versus utility and judgment versus acceptance (Rawlins, 1992). Sharing both mundane and fundamental concerns, disclosing personal feelings and values, and supporting each other by talking things through cultivates close involvement between women friends.

Females' greater intimacy competence in friendships across the life course partially derives from the fact that more females embrace the challenge and consequently learn how to communicate with close friends sooner. Such interaction remains an important part of their everyday lives (Rawlins, 1992). In contrast, a considerable number of males practice the "hail-fellow-well-met" and activity-oriented carriage appropriate for routine male role requirements and ultimately useful for the world of work but not for facilitating intimacy.

GENDER DIFFERENCES IN PERCEPTIONS OF CROSS-SEX FRIENDSHIPS

The contrasts evident in male and female same-sex friendships extend to their orientations to cross-sex relationships. Consequently, males and females tend to derive unmatched benefits from their cross-sex friendships. Researchers have found that males confide more in their best female friend than their best male friend (M. Komarovsky, 1974; K. Olstad, 1975; H. Hacker, 1981). And though undergraduate males mentioned more male "best friends" than female ones in Olstad's (1975) study, they reported spending more time with their female friends and consulting them more about significant decisions. Finally, young men describe giving less, knowing the other person and being known better, feeling closer (R. Buhrke and D. Fuqua, 1987), and obtaining greater acceptance and intimacy in their cross-sex versus same-sex supportive relationships and friendships (S. Rose, 1985).

In contrast, women receive more acceptance and intimacy from their female friends than from their male friends; only companionship, an activity-oriented pursuit, increases with males (Rose, 1985). Females declare knowing the other and being known better by same-sex others (Buhrke and Fuqua, 1987). They indicate feeling happy more frequently in close same-sex bonds, as opposed to males' prevailing happiness in cross-sex intimacy (V. Helgeson, P. Shaver, and M. Dyer, 1987). And both men and women are more apt to search for females than males in times of stress (Buhrke and Fuqua, 1987). Finally, though men reported feeling that their same- and cross-sex friendships served similar functions, Rose (1985) observes, "Women's expectations for friendship do not seem to be fulfilled to the same extent by men friends as by women friends" (72). Taken together, the research findings comparing males' and females' same- and cross-sex friendships support Komarovsky's (1976) contention that men have greater emotional dependence than women on their cross-sex relationships. N. Chodorow (1976), in turn, argues that exclusive relationships with men are insufficient for women, who also need bonds with women.

Males' undifferentiated view of women may overly constrict their behaviors options and undermine their emotionally rewarding cross-sex friendships. The stereotypical male outlook includes several tendencies that potentially subvert cross-sex friendship (Rawlins, in press). First, males are more apt than females to view both men's and women's behaviors in a more sexualized manner (A. Abbey, 1982). Abbey (1982) remarks, "Males do seem to perceive friendliness from females as seduction, but this appears to be merely one manifestation of a broader male sexual orientation" (830). Second, many males acknowledge their sexual motivations for forming cross-sex friendships, which women recognize, rendering them suspicious and reluctant to form friendships with males (Rose, 1985). On their part, most females describe platonic motives (Rose, 1985). Third, males often perceive a responsibility to take initiative and assert masculine sexuality (J. Pleck, 1975).

However, it should be noted that attracting a romantic partner is a crucial pursuit during young adulthood for both genders. One study reports that both genders view males more positively than females as "first-initiators" of hetero-sexual relationships, and that both sexes prefer indirect initiations; in addition, males indicate more willingness to take the lead (S. Green and P. Sandos, 1983). Further, being friends prior to romantic involvement: (1) avoids much of the "brinkmanship" of sexual game-playing and strategically withheld com-mitments; (2) presents less risk to either party's self-esteem; and (3) better facilitates a more positively toned and gradual break-up, as well as a return to friendship in the event that the love relationship does not work out (Rawlins, 1982; S. Metts, W. Cupach and R. Bejlovec, 1989). Viewed in this way, cross-sex friendship makes considerable sense as a precursor to romance.

It is primarily men who find it difficult to develop cross-sex relationships free of romantic involvement. Rubin, L. Peplau, and C. Hill (1980) assert that men believe more in a "romantic ideology" and therefore "may be more ready to fall in love quickly with a wider range of partners while women tend to be more deliberate and discriminating about entering into a romantic relation-ship" (824). Research indicates that males feel they are supposed to take the initiative in cross-sex bonds and try to transform "just friendships" into romantic or sexual relationships (R. Bell, 1981). Women seem better able to manage their feelings cognitively and are "less likely to be swept off their feet into a deep love relationship" (Rubin, Peplau and Hill, 1980: 832). Yet, when women do develop romantic attachments to men, they are more liable to with-draw from their same-sex friendships to facilitate exclusive commitment than men are (S. Rose and F. Serafica, 1986). Distinctive relational aptitudes and inclinations persist.

CRITICALLY EXAMINING GENDER DISPARITIES IN FRIENDSHIPS

It should be noted, however, that the incongruities typically associated with men's and women's friendships are much less evidence in their closer and more enduring bonds (P. Wright, 1982). While women frequently disclose more to their friends than men do, D. McAdams (1985) found no significant differences when intimacy motivation was examined. In other words, males who were highly motivated to be close with their friends revealed as much to them as similarly inclined females. Likewise, D. Ginsberg and J. Gottman (1986) did not observe gaps in disclosure between comparably close male and female pairs of friends. Finally, in a study of same-sex best friendships, N. Ashton (1980) reported no difference in the males' and females' self-disclo-sure, emphasis on communicative ability, or intimacy.

Thus, some quandaries emerge in attempting to appraise and compare the closeness and overall worth of the typically reported same-sex friendships of men and women. For example, M. Caldwell and Peplau (1982) noted a provocative "discrepancy between subjective reports of intimacy in friendship and objective measures of intimate interactions" (731). Though both men and women were describing best friends, defined abstractly by them in terms of heightened communication, disclosure, and confidence, in actuality, the women emphasized "emotional sharing and talking" privately with a single best friend, while the men stressed "activities and doing things together" with a group of friends (Caldwell and Peplau, 1982). Consequently, the authors suggest that males and females may employ separate standards for evaluating the intimacy of their friendships, and what constitutes closeness for men may not suffice for women (Caldwell and Peplau, 1982).

Apparently, males and females characteristically use different evaluative standards to appraise the disclosure, shared activities, and affection occurring in their friendships (Rawlins, 1992). Women rate communicative exchanges with men lower than their interactions with female friends because they are accustomed to more intimate and personal discussions than men typically pursue, and therefore experience unmet expectations. On their part, men may actually perceive themselves as spontaneous and trusting conversants though they seldom share issues that offer emotional insight or render them vulnerable (L. Davidson and L. Duberman, 1982). Further, many men think their feelings are best revealed through their actions and that too much revelation is "unmanly" (D. Williams, 1985). For these reasons men often must learn from women what it means to talk about their feelings in a manner that women perceive as "opening up" and facilitating closeness. Women, in turn, accommodate male friends in realizing that doing things together comprises a cardinal expression of friendship for them (Helgeson, Shaver, and Dyer, 1987).

Thus, shared activities are coded distinctly by males and females. For men, joint endeavors exhibit mutual liking, though they often include individualized displays of competence, competition, and the accomplishment of instrumental goals, all of which men highly value. For women, common activities are not enough to secure relational involvement; they appreciate indications of mutual and intrinsic concern, even while getting something done. Sustained surface engagements, though entertaining, are unfulfilling.

Finally, females and males view affection in friendship differently. Women appear to use similar criteria for evaluating the closeness of their relationships with both genders, and male friends are often not rated as caring or as close as female ones. Moreover, the sexual potential of relationships does not significantly confound females' views of friendship. In comparison, men seem to employ separate standards in assessing the emotional closeness of their friendships with men and women (Buhrke and Fuqua, 1987; W. Bukowski, B. Nappi, and B. Hoza, 1987). Basically, they seem to play down the caring exhibited in their male friendships while strongly emphasizing the affection displayed by their female friends (Bukowski, Nappi, and Hoza, 1987).

There are a few possible reasons for these inconsistent assessments. First, as female appraisals of male disclosure above imply, because men usually do not communicate affection as directly or sensitively as women, females' baseline expressions receive higher marks from men (Buhrke and Fuqua, 1987). Second, males confuse female friendliness with sexual attraction, view it differently, and rate it more positively than "mere" friendship with other males (Abbey, 1982). Third—and relatedly—males are more homophobic than females; they are more likely to fear being or being labeled homosexual (S. Morin and E. Garfinkle, 1978; R. Lewis, 1978). Such apprehension may lead to repressing feelings of affection for other men and emphasizing the sexual nature of the caring experienced with women (Rangell, 1963). Taken together, these double standards seem to reflect and reproduce traditional sex-role expectations within friendships (Rawlins, 1982).

CROSS-SEX FRIENDSHIP AS "BORDERWORK"

In her discussion of gender arrangements in elementary schools, B. Thorne (1986) uses the term "borderwork" to describe "interaction across, yet based upon and even strengthening gender boundaries" (172). Interestingly, she derives the idea from sociologist Robert Barth's "analysis of social relations which are maintained across ethnic boundaries without diminishing dichotomized ethnic status" (Thorne, 1986: 172). I argue that in pursuing cross-sex friendship, participants simultaneously engage in two forms of borderwork: (1) addressing the boundaries between sex-typed male and female behavior, and (2) addressing the distinctions between friendship and romantic love.

Traditional sex roles appear to influence significantly the possible trajectories of cross-sex relationships. As B. Hess (1972) observes, "The fusion of friendship with the sex role is so nearly complete through most of the life course that 'friend' in popular usage . . . generally refers to another of the same sex" (364). Cross-sex friendships often face the added exigencies of being perceived within and outside of the dyad as unconsciously or deceptively rehearsing, enacting, or obstructing romantic involvement and the normative adult path to selecting a spouse (Rawlins, 1982). As a result, the partners must rhetorically manage internal and external perceptions of the dyad as comprising "more than friendship" (Brain, 1976; Rawlins, 1982). These bonds also violate the "homosocial norm," which describes a tendency in our culture "for the seeking, enjoyment, and/or preference for the company of the same sex" (Rose, 1985: 63). Of course, sex-role expectations vary in precision and scope, and individuals differ in their degrees of internalizing or enacting stereotypical sex-role behaviors (J. Chafetz, 1974). Accordingly, the analysis below will link females and males with several ideal-typical trajectories for conducting cross-sex relationships. These gender alignments are based on modal patterns identified in the research literature. But all of these patterns must be relationally constituted in actual dyads, and any of the approaches described below could characterize either males or females in given cases.

Three other factors should also be considered. First, certain patterns considered below may be more indicative of the specific individuals' adherence to overarching cultural visions of romantic love or ideals of friendship than to specific gender-linked behaviors. Next, misunderstandings arising from expressing or repressing erotically charged feelings may develop within same-sex dyads as well (M. Werebe, 1987; Rangell, 1963). Finally, notions of romantic love or friendship may be subsumed by a utilitarian or instrumental conception of relationships whereby others in general are typically viewed as means to ends rather than as ends in themselves. This outlook may influence how a person conducts all his or her relationships, and cross-sex relationships simply comprise one example.

SCENARIOS OF CROSS-SEX BORDERWORK

As we have already discussed, males and females exhibit distinctive orientations to both same-sex and cross-sex relationships. Typically, males sharply distinguish between same-sex and opposite-sex relationships but view their associations with women rather uniformly. Same-sex bonds are sources of friendship, though many of these relationships are not particularly close or involving. Cross-sex bonds offer more disclosure, intimacy, and emotional involvement, which many males have difficulty interpreting as something other than precursors to romance. Males, experiencing competition and limited intimacy with other males, may therefore look to females as potentially loyal, caring, and supportive partners. But, informed by the socially conditioned alternatives of either friendship or romance, they often enact their cross-sex friendships as "not friendship," that is, as possible romances.

By contrast, females differentiate less markedly between same-sex and opposite-sex relationships, but make distinctions among their male partners. They are able to form close relationships with females and males. And they clearly distinguish between the males they consider friends and those they regard romantically. Even so, because their close same-sex friendships often involve jealousy and possessiveness, they view males as potentially easygoing and fun to be with as friends. Accordingly, their cross-sex friendships are typically enacted as "not romance," that is, as possible friendships.

In the ongoing management of cross-sex friendships, these outlooks counteract and complement each other in various ways that can reshape or reinforce stereotypical notions of appropriate male and female relational participation and their associated conceptions of friendship and romantic love. Let us consider five ideal-typical trajectories in negotiating cross-sex friendship.

1. When an individual's cross-sex "friendship as not friendship" approach meets with a similar cross-sex "friendship as not friendship" reaction from a potential "friend," the persons may play out a positive definition of the relationship as romance, *not* friendship, and being to behave according to the ideology of heterosexual romantic involvement. This trajectory affirms traditional sex-typed distinctions between the genders (especially when initiated by the male), and asserts that cross-sex friendships and romantic love occupy a teleological continuum, with the former relationship comprising an understudy or prelude to, and/or fallback for the latter. In this scenario, cross-sex friendships merely constitute what Freud called, "aim-inhibited sexuality or aim-inhibited love" (quoted in Rangell, 1963).

2. When a person's cross-sex "friendship as not romance" agenda receives cross-sex "friendship as not romance" responses from a desired opposite-sex partner, the individuals may negotiate a positive definition of the relationship as friendship, not romance, and begin to behave according to the ideals of friendship. This trajectory asserts more commonalities between the genders, even though role-typical behaviors may also persist, and emphasizes the distinctions between cross-sex friendship and cross-sex romantic love as options for continuing involvement between males and females.

3. When a male enacts a cross-sex "friendship as not friendship" approach and encounters a female's cross-sex "friendship as not romance" orientation, he may simply perceive rejection and decide not to be friends at all. Frequently, males are irritated at having to abandon an asymmetrical, future-oriented, means-to-an-end viewpoint of relationships. Romantic ideology calls for heightened experience of self's potentials, and exclusive possession and use of another person for one's own desires, including enhanced public status and sexual gratification (Rubin, Peplau, and Hill, 1980; Brain, 1976; Roberts, 1982). Ironically and regrettably, they return to only moderately supportive relationships with other males (unless they have a particularly close same-sex or cross-sex friend), and may try again for cross-sex "friendship as not friendship," or dating. This trajectory also reinforces gender distinctions and conceptions of cross-sex friendship as neither friendship, nor romantic love, but a stepping stone to the latter.

4. When a female enacts a cross-sex "friendship as not romance" approach and encounters a male's cross-sex "friendship as not friendship" orientation, she may simply perceive rejection and attempted exploitation and wonder if they were ever friends at all. Often, females are resentful or hurt by having to relinquish a symmetrical, present-oriented, end-in-itself conception of the relationship. This stance is consistent with the ideals of friendship as mutually expressive and beneficial. Still, they return to emotionally supportive relationships with females and consider other involvements with males on a case-by-case basis. This trajectory also sustains gender disparities and definitions of cross-sex friendship as neither friendship nor romantic love, but an ulterior version of the former and one-sided instance of the latter.

5. When one person's cross-sex "friendship as not friendship" or "friendship as not romance" outlook meets with mostly contrasting responses from an appealing other, neither party may experience their differences as either simple negations or simple affirmations of sex-typed behaviors, or of friendship or romance. Put simply, they may continue spending time together because they like and enjoy each other, yet without explicitly defining the nature of their relationship. However, there are few cultural guidelines or positive sanctions for conducting such a relationship.

Consequently, these relationships involve potentially unstable interplay between platonic and romantic communicative practices and activities

(Rangell, 1963; J. Block, 1980). Rangell (1963) notes that the exchange of tenderness in "friendship-love" is mutable, "conflict-laden, and vulnerable" (41). According to personal feelings, perceived injunctions to act out genderized scenarios and cultural visions of relational alternatives, and interpersonal events, the relationship may become friendship, romantic love or neither. Or the bond may persist as a mutually and dynamically contingent arrangement, which continually challenges while sometimes reflecting the pieties of sex-roles and the socially expected behavior between the genders.

CROSS-SEX FRIENDSHIP AS A RHETORICAL CHALLENGE

Persons participate in the greatest number of free-standing cross-sex friendships during young adulthood; these dwindle when people get married and continue to decrease across the rest of the life course (Booth and Hess, 1974; Adams, 1985; Rawlins, in press). By and large, cross-sex friendships reflect the traditional social order and sex roles. They tend to develop: (1) between males and females who work together; (2) between nonmarried men and women, since "friendship" can be viewed as a euphemism for dating and hence, a stage in the "natural" progression to publicly acknowledged romance and possibly marriage; and (3) if sanctioned by one or both friends' spouse(s) or romantic partner(s), thereby reinforcing the primacy of marriage and/or romance in heterosexual relations.

No neat conceptual category for cross-sex friendship exists because of its unusual and uncertain alignment with and threat to sex-type conceptions of opposite-sex bonds. Thus, such friendships potentially undermine the pieties of sex roles and the normatively constrained thoughts and behaviors socially constructing and perpetuating gender differences. Accordingly, such friendships are extremely vulnerable to labels of deviance. Further, because friendship can connote both attraction and love, a nuance of expression by a third party may suggest that two individuals are "really" lovers. Brain (1976) observes:

> We have been brought up as "dirty old men," assuming the worst when two men are constantly and devotedly together or when a boy and girl travel together as friends—if they share the same bedroom or tent, they *must* be lovers. We have imbued friendly relations with a smear of sexuality, so that frank enjoyment of a friend for his or her sake is becoming well-nigh impossible. (46)

Because of their unusual nature and subversive potential, many cross-sex friends experience ongoing judgments, insinuating remarks, and pressures from third parties.

In a frustrating cultural setting, cross-sex friends must orchestrate social perceptions of their relationship as well as develop a shared private definition (Rawlins, 1982). Thus, maintaining cross-sex friendship constitutes a rhetorical challenge, an ongoing array of predicaments requiring strategic management through communication with each other and with third parties. A rhetorical view of these relationships proposes a conscious supervision of interpersonal communication to achieve predetermined as well as emergent goals. Situational constraints include the degree to which sex-role expectations restrict individuals' behavioral options and the extent of social pressure experienced by the partners (Rawlins, 1982).

Often the rhetorical issues remain implicit in ongoing relationships for various reasons. First, unselfconscious cross-sex friends may be unconcerned with third party innuendos because they are innocent of, or less preoccupied with, the bases for them. Next, the "mystery" of unactivated or undiscussed sexuality may innervate a relationship without ever being overtly expressed. Finally, one or both members may want to preserve the possibility of a sexual relationship.

I hold that as long as sex-typed behaviors remain tacit concerns, cross-sex friends are especially vulnerable to similarly unspoken or subtle cultural injunctions. The friends may be following stereotypical relational paths without full awareness. As R. Laing (1972) notes in the family context, "Unless we can 'see through' the rules, we only see through them" (105). He argues further that commenting upon the unstated rules governing a given relationship reduces their power, thus the importance of explicit negotiation. J. Wood (1982) also advocates openly discussing relational definitions.

Because the development of friendship into romantic love or vice versa occupies an experiential continuum, there must be an expressive continuum for communicating or masking such transitions. I suggest a compendium of rhetorical issues and negotiated views of the other and of the relationship that avoids constraining, sex-typed choices and facilitates the maintenance of cross-sex friendship. The following discussion assumes that the friends' definition of their relationship will eventually affect how it is perceived by the social world at large.

CROSS-SEX FRIENDS' DEFINITION OF THEIR RELATIONSHIP

Several authors indicate that a mutual definition of a relationship is essential and unavoidable (J. Haley, 1963; Wood, 1982). In any friendship, and especially in cross-sex ones, a shared definition is necessary because there are few institutional guidelines for establishing such private cultures (G. Suttles, 1970; Brain, 1976; Wood, 1982). In defining their relationship, cross-sex friends must emphasize males' and females' commonalities more than their differences, and the friendship should be stressed as an end in itself. Regarding crucial definitional concerns such as the role of sexuality and equality, partners should clarify and demystify their positions. Verbal statements are congruently qualified by gestures, tone of voice and the context in which they occur (Haley, 1963). If sexually suggestive vocal tones or actions accompany discussions of the platonic nature of the bond, for example, then an incongruent definition of the relationship is being proposed (Haley, 1963). A pattern of such incongruent behavior may cause tension, promote second-guessing of the other's actions, and/or weaken confidence in the person's friendly overtures.

In general, romance is avoided. All friends communicate affection, but cross-sex friends monitor the behaviors that qualify such expressions because they can alter the interpretation of the message to include romantic intent. Basically, either friend might ask himself or herself, "How would I make this statement to a friend of my own sex?" or "Am I smuggling romance into this conversation?"

The activation or deactivation of sexuality is pivotal in most cross-sex friendships. Overt sexual behavior is liable to alter the definition of a relationship to something besides friendship (A. Booth and E. Hess, 1974; J. Block, 1980) or convert it to the unstable friendship-love. Brain (1976) remarks:

> The fact is that sex can be switched on or off as a situation demands—between brother and sister for example—and frequently this favors a more lasting friendship. We all know that sexual appetites once aroused are destructive of friendship, but they can and often do remain dormant. (46).

Thus, in friendship sexuality is deemphasized in favor of companionship (Bell, 1981). Of course, "sexual activity" can encompass a wide spectrum of behaviors with varying degrees of associated intimacy. And I do not deny that unexpected, romantically charged circumstances sometimes result in overt sexuality between male and female friends. Nevertheless, I argue that such actions usually reflect a change in the permissible behaviors of the friends that is negotiated by a series of rhetorical clues and cues subject to conscious management.

Cross-sex friends manage not only the presence or absence of sex in their relationship but the meaning that sexuality holds for them. The sex act can symbolize various things—from a relatively casual expression of affection or sharing of pleasure to the profound consummation of a love relationship. Developing a mutual view of sex that either upholds or opposes broader social conventions necessitates discussion. Talking about the significance of sexual involvement or non-involvement in the friendship may help relieve any residual feelings of guilt or inadequacy that might accompany a rejection of deeply internalized sex-typed injunctions.

Further, a spirit of equality pervades cross-sex friendship. Inequality and power plays suggest a different type of relationship—for example, a patron-client (R. Paine, 1969) or superior-subordinate one—and recall traditional social mores. Of course, there are friendships between individuals of different status, ability, attractiveness, or age, but often some facet in the friendship functions as a leveler (Brain, 1976). Stressing equality minimizes the risk of exploitation (M. Fiebert and P. Fiebert, 1969; S. Kurth, 1970). Though self-interest is part of any realistic bond, exploitation is not. Thus, considerations of equity as well as equality may mediate what is given and expected in the relational exchange (E. Walster, G. Walster, and E. Berscheid, 1978; E. Hatfield and J. Traupmann, 1981). Females and males must not extend the double standard into their friendships with each other though research data indicate this practice frequently occurs (A. Booth and E. Hess, 1974; Rawlins, 1992).

Finally, cross-sex friends relinquish exclusive claims to their friends; restricting freedom is antithetical to friendship (Rawlins, 1983). As von Hildebrand affirms, the special affection of friendship accentuates an intention of good over union (T. Owens, 1970). Lovers, not friends, tend to be possessive.

In summary, cross-sex friends manage several rhetorical issues within their relationship: (1) A mutual definition of the relationship as a friendship is sustained by consistently congruent messages. (2) Romance is avoided. (3) Overall, sexuality is deemphasized. (4) However, the meaning and possibility of overt sexuality, with its potential for altering the definition of the relationship, may require discussion. (5) Equality is fostered, and (6) Personal freedom is permitted.

SOCIAL DEFINITIONS OF CROSS-SEX FRIENDSHIPS

I have suggested that cross-sex friends embrace certain recurring rhetorical challenges in defining their relationship. Here I maintain that they may also need to adopt a strategic posture vis-à-vis those who would threaten the relationship with rumors and attributions. The friends' goal is to convince third parties that the friendship is authentic. This task is difficult because the defining features of cross-sex friendships are different from other opposite-sex bonds but are not always observable. What publicly distinguishes spiritual from sexual relationships if, in both cases, their most intimate moments are confidential? In short, the friends must manage the privacy and publicity of their actions.

Privacy is an important prerogative in all personal relationships. However, it poses an inherent threat to others' perceptions of a cross-sex friendship as legitimate. While both friends and lovers value privacy for sharing the unique features of their bond, with cross-sex friends privacy is seen to reflect the exclusiveness associated with love. Bell (1981) reports, "Frequently, a sexual relationship is assumed to exist between friends who keep their friendship private, whether or not it is actually the case" (105).

Thus, the visibility of the relationship comprises an ironic predicament: the more hidden and private the friends' actions, the more suspect; the more open and public, the more idiosyncratic behaviors may be compromised or restricted (R. Paine, 1969). Self-consciousness about "public performance" (Paine, 1969) may undermine the friends' natural inclinations for enjoyment of each other. Clearly, the rhetorical challenge implied here is discovering modes of interaction to interconnect the friendship's private and public spheres (Rawlins, 1989a; 1989b).

Unfortunately, it is difficult to recommend specific strategies for loosening the Gordian knot of societal reactions and attributions. Some friendships may become more public to preserve themselves while sacrificing much of their private moralities and proprietary norms. Others may adopt a rather defiant and self-righteous attitude and continue their relationship unchanged until others get their message, "This friendship is fundamentally not different from others though it is special to us. We will not compromise its essence." Such a policy stares "the smear of sexuality" square in the face by announcing that there is no sexual agenda and exploitation, simply an equitable and spiritual relationship. Given the intense socialization to experience cross-sex intimacy differently, it is interesting to consider how dyadic cultures can undermine the program by adopting a private morality.

ADVANTAGES OF CROSS-SEX FRIENDSHIPS

Acknowledging cross-sex friendship as a viable interpersonal option yields several advantages. For one thing it makes friendship possible with the other half of the persons comprising society (J. Chafetz, 1974; Bell, 1981). Next, cross-sex friendship allows individuals to see the world from the perspective of someone of the opposite gender (L. Sapadin, 1988). Participants may also expand their repertoires of friendship styles (Rawlins, 1992). Females may learn about and enjoy the prevailing agentic friendship style of men with its emphasis on activities and individual freedom. Males, in turn, may discover and practice the communal style of female friendships, emphasizing involved conversation, caring, and interdependence.

Moreover, persons learn about the pitfalls and vagaries of traditional sex roles as they attempt to transcend them in cross-sex friendships and treat each other more compassionately as particular individuals. Learning to value someone outside of materialist and sexist expectations is worthwhile in itself. It also enhances conceptions of personal worth by reducing objectification in viewing oneself and one's relations with others (Rawlins, 1991). Neither self or other is reduced to merely a role occupant or an object of self-gratification. Further, while kinship relations tend to perpetuate established patterns of interaction and keep an individual at a status quo, cross-sex friendship promotes personal experience in new modes (E. Douvan and J. Adelson, 1966). Thus, there is liberation from the constraints and expectations of ascribed relationships, an opportunity for independence and spontaneous actions (Dubois, 1974). Finally, cross-sex friendship breaches the image of love or affection as a "zero-sum game" (Chafetz, 1974). Chafetz advises: "Indeed, it is unlikely that any one individual can ever fill all of another person's emotional needs. To gain a full life and have a variety of their needs met, humans must develop deep emotional commitments to more than one individual in more than one way." (163).

Presently, stereotyped sex-role expectations appear to prevail in American cross-sex friendships (Rawlins, 1982; 1992). Ironically, friendships in general and cross-sex friendships in particular constitute privately negotiated contexts where sex-typed behavior may be ruled out. Yet such relationships are highly susceptible to scrutiny and attributions by third parties, especially if the friendship is perceived to threaten culturally sanctioned bonds like romantic or steady dating relationships, marriage, or kinship.

Cross-sex friendships are inherently ambiguous. Societal expectations, personal values, sexual orientations or motivations, third party pressures, and coordinated or clashing assumptions and perceptions all combine in shaping the dynamics of given relationships. Whatever occasions the shift, romantic involvement apparently alters cross-sex friendships. And the somewhat apologetic or defensive description of those dyads remaining "just friends" reflects the tendency throughout life to marginalize these bonds and to view them as precursors, threats or understudies to more institutionalized or socially endorsed romantic relationships (Rawlins, 1992).

Ultimately, the woman and man comprising such a relationship must negotiate its morality. This rhetorical challenge is twofold. On the one hand, the friends demonstrate to each other a commitment to maintain the relationship as a friendship free of over sexuality or exploitation. The friends must also convince third parties of the viability and authenticity of their bond. In doing so, they create a social context for the friendship that allows it to flourish.

NOTES

1. Portions of this chapter have previously appeared in William K. Rawlins (1982), "Cross-Sex Friendship and the Communicative Management of Sex-Role Expectations," *Communication Quarterly*, 30: 343–352, and in William K. Rawlins (1992) *Friendship Matters: Communication, Dialectics, and the Life Course*, Hawthorne, New York: Aldine de Gruyter. I thank these publishers for their permission to use this material.

REFERENCES

Abbey, A. 1982. Sex differences in attributions for friendly behavior: Do males misperceive females' friendliness? *Journal of Personality and Social Psychology* 42: 830–838.

Adams, R. G. 1985. People would talk: Normative barriers to cross–sex friendships for elderly women. *The Gerontologist* 25: 605–610.

Ashton, N. L. 1980. Exploratory investigation of perceptions of influences on best-friend relationships. Perceptual and Motor Skills 50: 379–386.

Bell, R. R. 1981. *Worlds of Friendship*. Beverly Hills, CA: Sage.

Berndt, T. J. 1982. The features and effects of friendship in early adolescence. *Child Development* 53: 1447–1460.

Bigelow, B. J., and J. J. La Gaipa. 1980. The development of friendship values and choice. In H. C. Foot, A. J. Chapman, and J. R. Smith, eds., *Friendship and Social Relations in Children*. New York: John Wiley, 15–44.

Block, J. D. 1980. *Friendship*. New York: Macmillan.

Booth, A., and E. Hess. 1974. Cross-sex friendship. *Journal of Marriage and the Family* 36: 38–47.

Brain, R. 1976. *Friends and Lovers*. New York: Basic Books.

Buhrke, R. A., and D. R. Fuqua. 1987. Sex differences in same- and cross-sex supportive relationships. *Sex Roles* 17: 339–352.

Buhrmester, D., and W. Furman. 1987. The development of companionship and intimacy. *Child Development* 58: 1101–1113.

Bukowski, W. M., B. J. Nappi, and B. Hoza. 1987. A test of Aristotle's model of friendship for young adults' same-sex and opposite-sex relationships. *The Journal of Social Psychology* 127: 595–603.

Caldwell, M. A., and L. A. Peplau. 1982. Sex differences in same-sex friendship. *Sex Roles*, 8: 721–732.

Chafetz, J. S. 1974. *Masculine/Feminine or Human?* Itasca, IL: Peacock.

Chodorow, N. 1976. Oedipal asymmetries and heterosexual knots. *Social Problems* 23: 454–468.

Davidson, L. R., and L. Duberman. 1982. Friendship: Communication and interactional patterns in same-sex dyads. *Sex Roles* 8: 809–826.

Douvan, E., and J. Adelson. 1966. *The Adolescent Experience*. New York: John Wiley & Sons.

Dubois, C. 1974. The gratuitous act: An introduction to the comparative study of friendship patterns. In E. Leyton, ed., *The Compact: Selected Dimensions of Friendship*. St. Johns: Institute of Social and Economic Research, 15–32.

Eder, D., and M. T. Hallinan. 1978. Sex differences in children's friendships. *American Sociological Review* 43: 237–250.

Feshback, N., and G. Sones. 1971. Sex differences in adolescent reactions toward newcomers. *Developmental Psychology* 4: 381–386.

Fiebert, M. S., and P. B. Fiebert. 1969. A conceptual guide to friendship formation. *Perceptual and Motor Skills* 28: 383–390.

Fischer, J. L. 1981. Transitions in relationship style from adolescence to young adulthood. *Journal of Youth and Adolescence* 10: 11–23.

Foot, H. C., A. J. Chapman, and J. R. Smith. 1977. Friendship and social responsiveness in boys and girls. *Journal of Personality and Social Psychology* 35: 401–411.

Fox, M., M. Gibbs, and D. Auerbach. 1985. Age and gender dimensions of friendship. *Psychology of Women Quarterly* 9: 489–502.

Furman, W., and D. Ruhrmester. 1985. Children's perceptions of their personal relationships in their social networks. *Developmental Psychology* 21: 1016–1024.

Gilligan, C. 1982. *In a Different Voice*. Cambridge, MA: Harvard University Press.

Ginsberg, D., and J. Gottman. 1986. Conversations of college roommates: Similarities and differences in male and female friendship. In J. M. Gottman and J. G. Parker, eds., *Conversations of Friends*. Cambridge: Cambridge Univ. Press, 241–291.

Gottman, J. M. 1986. The world of coordinated play: Same- and cross-sex friendship in young children. In J. M. Gottman and J. G. Parker, eds., *Conversations of Friends: Speculations on Affective Development*. Cambridge: Cambridge University Press, 139–191.

Green, S. K., and P. Sandos. 1983. Perceptions of male and female initiators of relationships. *Sex Roles* 9: 849–852.

Hacker, H. M. 1981. Blabbermouths and clams: Sex differences in self-disclosure in same-sex and cross-sex friendship dyads. *Psychology of Women Quarterly* 5: 385–401.

Haley, J. 1963. *Strategies of Psychotherapy*. New York: Grune and Stratton.

Hatfield, E., and J. Traupmann. 1981. Intimate relationships: A perspective from equity theory. In S. Duck and R. Gilmour, eds., *Personal Relationships 1: Studying Personal Relationships*. London: Academic Press, 165–178.

Helgeson, V. S., P. Shaver, and M. Dyer. 1987. Prototypes of intimacy and distance in same-sex and opposite-sex relationships. *Journal of Social and Personal Relationships* 4: 195–233.

Hess, B. 1972. Friendship. In M. W. Riley, M. Johnson, and A. Foner, eds., *Aging and Society: A Sociology of Age Stratification*. Vol 3. New York: Russell Sage Foundation, 357–393.

Horton, M. 1973. Alternatives to romantic love. In M. E. Curtin, ed., *Symposium on Love*. New York: *Behavioral Publications*, 107–121.

Hunter, F. T., and J. Youniss. 1982. Changes in functions of three relations during adolescence. *Developmental Psychology* 18: 806–811.

Johnson, F. L., and E. J. Aries. 1983. Conversational patterns among same-sex pairs of late-adolescent close friends. The *Journal of Genetic Psychology* 142: 225–238.

Karweit, N., and S. Hansell. 1983. Sex differences in adolescent relationships: Friendship and status. In J. L. Epstein and N. Karweit, eds., *Friends in School*. New York: Academic Press, 115–130.

Komarovsky, M. 1974. Patterns of self-disclosure of male undergraduates. *Journal of Marriage and the Family* 36: 677–686.

_____. 1976. *Dilemmas of Masculinity: A Study of College Youth*. New York: Norton.

Kon. I. S., and V. A. Losenkov. 1978. Friendship in adolescence: Values and behavior. *Journal of Marriage and the Family* 40: 143–155.

Kurth, S. B. 1970. Friendships and friendly relations. In G. J. McCall, M. M. McCall, N. K. Denzin, G. D. Suttles, and S. Kurth, eds., *Social Relationships*. Chicago: Aldine, 136–170.

La Gaipa, J. J. 1979. A developmental study of the meaning of friendship in adolescence. *Journal of Adolescence* 2: 201–213.

Laing, R. D. 1972. *The Politics of the Family*. New York: Vintage.

Lepp, I. 1966. *The Ways of Friendship*. New York: Macmillan.

Lever, J. 1976. Sex differences in the games children play. *Social Problems* 23: 478–487.

Lewis. R. A. 1978. Emotional intimacy among men. *Journal of Social Issues* 34: 108–121.

McAdams, D. P. 1985. Motivation and friendship. In S. Duck and D. Perlman, eds., *Understanding Personal Relationships: An Interdisciplinary Program*. London: Sage, 85–105.

Metts, S., W. R. Cupach, and R. A. Bejlovec. 1989. I love you too much to ever start liking you: Redefining romantic relationships. *Journal of Social and Personal Relationships* 6: 259–274.

Morin, S., and E. M. Garfinkle. 1978. Male homophobia. *Journal of Social Issues* 34: 29–47.

Olstad, K. 1975. Brave new man: A basis for discussion. In J. Petras, ed., *Sex: Male/Gender: Masculine*. Port Washington, NY: Alfred.

Owens, T. J. 1970. *Phenomenology and Intersubjectivity: Contemporary Interpretations of the Interpersonal Situation*. The Hague: Nijhoff.

Paine, R. 1969. In search of friendship: An exploratory analysis in "middle-class" culture. *Man* 4: 505–524.

Pleck, J. H. 1975. Man to man: Is brotherhood possible? In N. Glazer-Malbin, ed., *Old Family/New Family*. New York: D. Van Nostrand Co, 229–244.

Rangell, L. 1963. On friendship. *Journal of the American Psychoanalytic Association* 11: 3–54.

Rawlins, W. K. 1982. Cross-sex friendship and the communicative management of sex-role expectations. *Communication Quarterly* 30: 343–352.

————. 1983. Negotiating close friendships: The dialectic of conjunctive freedoms. *Human Communication Research* 9: 255–266.

————. 1989a. A dialectical analysis of the tensions, functions and strategic challenges of communication in young adult friendships. In J. A. Anderson, ed., *Communication Yearbook* 12. Newbury, CA: Sage, 157–189.

————. 1989b. Cultural double agency and the pursuit of friendship. *Cultural Dynamics* 2: 28–40.

————. 1991. On enacting friendship and interrogating discourse. In K. Tracy, ed., *Understanding Face-to-Face Interaction: Issues Linking Goals and Discourse*. New York: Lawrence Erlbaum Associates, 101–115.

————. 1992. *Friendship Matters: Communication, Dialectics, and the Life Course*. Hawthorne, NY: Aldine de Gruyter.

Richey, M. H., and H. W. Richey. 1980. The significance of best-friend relationships in adolescence. *Psychology in the Schools* 17: 536–540.

Roberts, M. K. 1982. Men and Women: Partners, lovers, friends. In K. E. Davis and T. Mitchell, eds., *Advances in Descriptive Psychology*. Vol. 2. Greenwich, Conn: AI Press, 57–78.

Rose, S. M. 1985. Same- and cross-sex friendships and the psychology of homosociality. *Sex Roles* 12: 63–74.

Rose, S., and F. C. Serafica. 1986. Keeping and ending casual, close and best friendships. *Journal of Social and Personal Relationships* 3: 275–288.

Rotenberg, K. J. 1986. Same-sex patterns and sex differences in the trust-value basis of children's friendship. *Sex Roles* 15: 613–626.

Rubenstein, C., and C. Rubin. 1984. Children's fantasies of interaction with same and opposite sex peers. In T. Field, J. L. Roopnarine and M. Segal, eds., *Friendships in Normal and Handicapped Children*. Norwood, N.J.: Ablex, 99–124.

Rubin, Z., L. A. Peplau, and C. T. Hill. 1980. Loving and leaving: Sex differences in romantic attachments. *Sex Roles* 6: 821–835.

Sapadin, L. A. 1988. Friendship and gender: Perspectives of professional men and women. *Journal of Social and Personal Relationships* 5: 387–403.

Seiden, A. M., and P. B. Bart. 1975. Woman to woman: Is sisterhood powerful? In N. Galzer-Malbin, ed., *Old Family/New Family*. New York: D. Van Nostrand, 189–228.

Smollar, J., and J. Youniss. 1982. Social development through friendship. In K. H. Rubin and H. S. Ross, eds., *Peer Relationships and Social Skills in Childhood*. New York: Springer-Verlag, 279–298.

Sprey, J. 1969. On the institutionalization of sexuality. *Journal of Marriage and the Family* 31: 432–440.

Suttles, G. D. 1970. Friendship as a social institution. In G. J. McCall, M. McCall, N. K. Denzin, G. D. Suttles, and S. Kurth, eds., *Social Relationships*. Chicago: Aldine, 95–135.

Thorne, B. 1986. Girls and boys together . . . but mostly apart: Gender arrangements in elementary schools. In W. W. Hartup and Z. Rubin, eds., *Relationships and Development*. Hillsdale, NJ: Lawrence Erlbaum, 167–184.

Walster, E., G. W. Walster, and E. Berscheid. 1978. *Equity Theory and Research*. Boston: Allyn and Bacon.

Werebe, M. J. G. 1987. Friendship and dating relationships among French adolescents. *Journal of Adolescence* 10: 269–289.

Williams, D. G. 1985. Gender, masculinity-femininity, and emotional intimacy in same-sex friendship. *Sex Roles* 12: 587–600.

Wood, J. T. 1982. Communication and relational culture: Bases for the study of human relationships. *Communication Quarterly* 30: 75–83.

Wright, P. H. 1982. Men's friendships, women's friendships, and the alleged inferiority of the latter. *Sex Roles* 8: 1–20.

Youniss, J., and J. Smollar. 1985. *Adolescent Relations with Mothers, Fathers, and Friends*. Chicago: University of Chicago Press.

CHAPTER 6

WHEN MYTHS ENDURE AND REALITIES CHANGE: COMMUNICATION IN ROMANTIC RELATIONSHIPS

AUTHOR   **Laurie Arliss, Ithaca College**

POINTS TO BE ADDRESSED

- Cultural messages about romantic interaction
- Traditions connecting love, sex, and marriage
- Unique aspects of romantic communication
- Linguistic forms used to refer to romance
- Impact of gender equality on romantic interaction
- Causes and effects of ambiguity in romantic interaction

There is little doubt that relationships we experience as most personal are usually very difficult to manage and even harder to label. Specifically, we struggle to label comfortably that special, cross-sex relationship that is neither a platonic friendship nor a family relationship. The formal marriage ceremony is accompanied by denotative labels used to refer to that special someone (husband, wife, spouse). Just before the marriage, the future partners often call themselves "engaged to be married" and refer to one another as "my fiance" or "my fiancee." Yet we have not coined an appropriate label for the relationship partner with whom future marriage is uncertain or unlikely or impossible.

Many simply refer to the person-in-question (usually of the opposite sex, chosen voluntarily and at least targeted for sexual/emotional involvement) as a boyfriend or girlfriend. But these are the same labels used by children and adolescents. And they are also used, at least by females, to refer to same-sex associates. Possessive pronouns may be used in conjunction with more adult words, although these terms tend to emphasize the exclusive ownership of the individual (this is "*my* guy" or "*my* woman"). Forward thinkers of the 1970s coined the term "significant other," a gender-neutral label that seems less possessive, although it, too, typically follows the pronoun *my*. This label is sufficiently broad enough to include most of the relationships we intuitively know belong in this category but too broad to be very informative about a particular pairing. It's difficult to imagine two individuals gazing at one another as they declare that they are now significant others. More realistically, they will probably declare (or discover) that they are lovers; assertive types at this stage frequently begin to refer to one another as such. But many relationships that belong in this elusive category do not have a sexual component and, even if the relationship is sexual, many individuals would find it difficult to disclose this status in social introductions.

Apologetically, no instantly logical and workable relationship label is proposed here. Deciding how to refer to one another comfortably is a task men and women will continue to deal with, particularly those who are not formally related but find themselves on a course toward intimacy. Scholars have had slightly less trouble identifying and naming these elusive pairs. They are typically called "romantic pairs" or "dating couples." The broad term "romantic relationships" is used to title this chapter, but there are frequent references to the social practice called "dating."

The emotional state experienced by participants in romantic relationships is often called "romantic love." This term may seem redundant, since romance is often believed to be synonymous with love despite the fact that many loving relationships are clearly not romantic. *The American Heritage Dictionary* equates the terms in one section and uses the more specific term "love affair" in another. But the primary listing that follows the word "romance" is as follows: "1. a. A medieval narrative telling of the adventures of chivalric heroes. b. A long, fictitious tale of heroes and extraordinary or mysterious events. c. A quality suggestive of the adventure and idealized exploits found in such tales." The fact that this definition is associated with the relationship under discussion points out the powerful, mystical, extraordinary adventure associated with the pursuit of an appealing mate in our culture.

ROMANTIC MYTHS: COMMUNICATION
ABOUT ROMANTIC RELATIONSHIPS

Our cultural mythology reserves a special status for romantic relationships. In a society dominated by the nuclear family, individuals are expected to select a singular suitable mate. But the practical aspects of this selection process are usually not explicitly acknowledged when we talk about courting or dating potential partners. On the contrary, our discussion of this highly significant male-female experience is dominated by the language of love. They mythology of romantic interaction has survived generations of retelling. Even in modern times, we continue to envision a sublime (albeit difficult to obtain) state of euphoria. Indeed, the content of our love stories has changed very little over time, despite the development of new technologies for marketing them. By the time we reach adulthood, images of true love are closely linked to our vision of life and to our understanding of ourselves as males and females.

CHILDHOOD NARRATIVES

Many of us are weaned on magical fantasies of daring heroes who rescue beautiful maidens. As children, we hear stories about Cinderella, Sleeping

Beauty, Snow White—all sweet, pure young maidens in the midst of terrible predicaments. Fortunately, they are rescued by strong, handsome, capable princes. Each helpless maiden is saved in a magic moment by a kiss or shoe that fits just right. The childhood characters that have survived intergenerational storytelling are aligned with the prevailing gender stereotypes: gentle, sweet, young women and strong, powerful, young men. The plot is equally traditional: the woman waits passively (often, she's asleep!) for the man to make the move that will ensure that they both live happily ever after. (Note: the gender dynamics of children's literature are far more complicated than this discussion suggests. Consider, for example, that it is usually an ugly, evil, powerful woman who causes the maiden's troubles.)

P. Smith and E. Midlarsky (1985) have argued that gender stereotypes are both embodied and perpetuated in fairy tale images and plots. These stories are commonly told to children who, according to experts, are just learning their own gender identity and seeking information about how to behave appropriately (M. Intons-Peterson, 1988). Children seek positive evaluations of their own gender, so it is not surprising that most young girls idealize the heroines. After all, these fictive maidens are beautiful and kind (although helpless and unbelievably gullible). It seems easy for little boys to emulate the heroes; they are capable, righteous, handsome, and usually of royal blood. Of course, children of both sexes appreciate the goodness of the opposite sex characters. But, S. Bem (1987: 265) explains that children are likely to "reject any way of behaving that does not match their sex." In the case of fairy tale images, this choice would have serious implications for young girls seeking to solve their own problems.

As children mature, so does their knowledge of romantic relationships. Children complement an increasing collection of romantic fictions with a number of firsthand observations. Most prominently in our culture, they learn about the institution of marriage, which may or may not explain the family relationships in their own lives but is an important cultural institution nonetheless. Even before children have a clear understanding of reproduction, they typically associate having a baby with being married and being married with positive feelings for a member of the opposite sex. Hence, it is not uncommon for a child to declare that he or she intends to marry his or her opposite sex parent, which demonstrates both the child's naivete about the conventions that eliminate partners and his or her wisdom that the marriage partner should be a special loved one of the opposite sex.

ADOLESCENT INTERACTION

As the child becomes an adolescent, the element of sexuality is added to the mix. At the onset of puberty, young people are physically capable of reproduction and, simultaneously, become interested in "the opposite sex," although they are commonly not well-versed in what is necessary to make the liaison. Therefore, despite the physical readiness, most cross-sex adolescent interaction is little more than a rough imitation of adult romance (J. Hill, 1982). Picture teenage boys and girls strategically planning social pairings, sharing secrets about the desirable aspects of the opposite-sex, and reflecting on the exhilarating emotions associated with young love. As you might image (or perhaps remember), the romantic adventures of adolescents seldom feature the sort of "extended, social interaction which might let (them) explore mutual interests and lay the foundation for a friendship" (Zick Rubin, 1980: 105).

In fact, Rubin (1980) speculates that romantic interest during this period does more to facilitate same-sex relating than cross-sex relating. Both boys and girls tend to converse more with same-sex peers about girlfriends or boyfriends than with the particular admired other. More often than not, they send messages and notes through same-sex confederates and arrange meetings in groups. The mystical nature of romance is largely created and preserved, in the midst of the adolescent's developing sense of himself or herself as male or female.

Given the adolescent's tendency to reflect on the success of various cross-sex experiences with members of the same sex, it might be argued that boys and girls develop values pertaining to all-important *heterosexual* interaction at a time when life is decidedly *homosocial* (L. Eggert and M. Parks, 1987). So, it is neither surprising nor comforting to realize that men and women leave adolescence with different expectations and impressions of romantic interaction. Girls tend to emphasize getting noticed by boys, often by one special boy. They may even begin to fantasize about true, lasting love. A good deal of time in female groups is devoted to the refinement of appearance through clothes, hairstyles, make-up, and the like (L. Rubin, 1986). Girls also devote time to various activities in which they provide support for male activity (Wilks, 1986). Being a cheerleader is often accorded a higher status than being a star athlete. Indeed, *who* you date may be the most important determinant of status. In line with stereotypic myths, athletes, social leaders, and those with material possessions are believed to be good catches.

Like their female counterparts, adolescent boys also attribute great status to sexual maturity, and they too are concerned with appearances, though they typically do not primp publicly. They tend to emphasize overt signs of maturity, strength, and athleticism as evaluated by male peers (Hill, 1982). Talk of athletic achievements dominates their conversations, but adolescent boys, like adolescent girls, also confide in friends about the opposite sex (L. Rubin, 1986). Seldom is true, lasting love a theme in their conversations. Rather, adolescent boys tend to emphasize sexual activity in their discussions. When they do talk about girls, boys tend to focus on the topic of sexual activity (J. Youniss and J. Smollar, 1985). Thus, *who* you date may be significant for boys as well as girls (although good catches are usually identified by their physical credentials), but *how you did* on the date is likely to be the most significant factor in gaining status.

The fact that sex differences continue to characterize perceptions of romantic interaction may disturb us, but should not surprise us. A recent study revealed that adolescents, particularly boys, continue to hold very rigid traditional images of men and women (M. Lewin and L. Tragos, 1987). Their experience with members of the opposite sex is not likely to be sufficient to challenge the traditional, stereotypic notions they adopted in childhood. Moreover, it appears that the nature of their same-sex interaction during adolescence does little to broaden their minds.

ADULT COMMUNICATION

The continued dominance of traditional gender images among today's children and adolescents may indicate that the heralded "age of gender equality" has not yet arrived. It could be argued that young people understandably oversimplify the world. If so, we would expect to see adult men and women, rich in experience and knowledge, portray more flexible images of gender in their communication about romance. We might expect college students to report a gender-neutral understanding of romantic interaction. But despite liberal attitudes about professional and legal issues, today's young adults continue to express conservative views of male-female interaction in personal relationships. Both sexes hold traditional values concerning dating relationships, especially about who should pay for the expenses, initiate sexual intimacy, and propose marriage (K. McKinney, 1987).

These expressed values represent talk *about* romantic interaction: the students by McKinney surveyed may or may not display more gender-neutral standards in their lived experience. But, if men and women are more traditional in their private cross-sex relationships than in their public cross-sex relationships, it might very well be because contemporary visions of love are not peopled with aggressive women and dependent men. That is not to say that these visions are not becoming more prominent, particularly in the media. But seldom do such couples "live happily ever after." Indeed the "emasculating female" has become nearly as prominent on daytime television as the "trusting, innocent maiden." Both characters are likely to be seen engaging in romantic interaction, but the virtuous, gentle female is more likely to find true love, despite interference from the jealous, aggressive female (M. Cassata, T. Skill, and S. Boadu, 1983). Our adult dramas seem to be very much like our childhood narratives in terms of the gender dynamics of romance.

Other media images of romance are equally traditional. Print images of men and women emphasize men engaged in activity, women just "looking pretty" (J. Umiker-Sebeok, 1981). Prime-time adventure shows portray physically attractive female characters supporting male protagonists. A few family programs, such as the popular *Cosby Show*, now include successful, happy career women (although usually not more successful than their men). Coincidentally, though, when the couple is portrayed alone, traditional images of romance often surface. Even our new "corporate woman," the subject of several recent movies, is not immune to traditional romance in the end. She may be tough at first, but softens at the smile or the touch of her true love. If she doesn't, she quickly fades from the role of heroine to that of villainess. Male characters are also pegged as "good guys" and "bad guys," although seldom are these attributions based on their willingness to be swept off their feet.

Their evaluations are derived from masculine myths, which emphasize participation in the public realm. Thus, they are evil or good based on whether they cause or solve problems.

Ultimately, as adults, we realize that neither media images nor fairy tales hold the truth about developing a steady and exclusive partnership. Nevertheless, individuals in our culture are pressured to find and win a desirable mate. *Courtship* in other cultures may amount to the negotiation of goods or the introduction of pre-assigned partners, but in our culture it involves identifiable *communication events*—attempts to appear attractive to members of the opposite sex, strategies to win the affections of desired individuals, and ultimately the negotiation of single, highly personal connection with a *significant other*, all events which are both a product of and an influence on each individual's self-image.

To the extent that one's self-image is a gender-specific image, romantic interaction will be understandably traditional. A dominant theme in this book is that future generations of men and women may consider themselves (and others) to be more gender-neutral than they do today. If so, traditions about romantic interaction may be challenged, but, according to J. DiIorio (1989), personal relationships between men and women have always been, and will continue to be, highly resistant to change.

NOT-SO-ROMANTIC REALITIES: COMMUNICATION IN ROMANTIC RELATIONSHIPS

Perhaps it is because we hold the mythology of love so dear that the realities of romantic interaction are so difficult to accept. The challenge of attracting a desirable person (preferably selected from a host of desirable alternatives) is one for which childhood lessons and adolescent rehearsal do not adequately prepare most of us. Even those who are considered successful at the sort of casual, short-lived entanglements typical among teenagers may find themselves ill-equipped to negotiate and sustain the singular intimate relationship revered in our culture.

Ironically, the aspects of romantic interaction that make it special are often the very causes of difficulty. To begin with, romantic relationships are voluntarily entered into in our culture. Each individual is expected to find a suitable life partner, one who is sufficiently similar to facilitate mutual decision making, yet also sufficiently dissimilar. If the relationship takes its full course, cultural norms predict that it will become legal and binding through the institution of marriage. According to the present legal system, the chosen marriage partner cannot be a family member and must be of the opposite sex, so the relationships that dominate youthful interaction are not likely to provide ready partners. In reality, finding a romantic partner amounts to negotiating a close relationship with a stranger.

Add to the mystical, adventurous nature of romance the expectation that romantic bonds are expected to become gradually more intense and more significant in our lives. Unlike the family relationships we experienced as children, which must become less intense in order to set us free to become adults, and friendships, which typically come and go, adult romantic pairings must either progress or be dissolved. Although adolescents "rehearse" these relationships, they are seldom sustained. It is difficult to state with certainty when these rehearsals become serious, but S. Duck (1988) suggests that "Typically, people seek a marriage partner most actively between the ages of about 16 and 26." This is probably a good estimate, since the median age of (first) marriage in the United States is currently 24.6 years for men and 22.8 years for women (National Center for Health Statistics, 1987: 64).

The romantic interaction typical between unmarried adults is especially significant in our culture because it is expected to be a precursor to marriage. This cross-sex interaction usually constitutes either a more complete and realistic rehearsal than that typical during adolescence or an extended interview in which individuals attempt to discern the suitability of one another as future marriage partners. Interaction between prospective partners used to be called "courtship" and, in past decades, was governed by established, gender-specific rules. There were proper and improper behaviors for males and females, "rules" commonly communicated by parental figures. During the 1950s, young adults rebelled against both the label "courtship" and the imposition of parental control. The term "dating" was coined, which, according to J. Pearson (1989), is now "dated."

New traditions emerged during the 1950s and 1960s to mark the development of romantic relationships. Communication events involving the exchange of promises and usually a symbolic gift for the female signified relationship states. Couples agreed to "go steady" or "get pinned." Female partners displayed their steadies' class rings or fraternity pins or school jackets to signify their status—*taken*. (Notably, the male partners seldom displayed any complementary token.) The obvious communicative markers that depicted relationship development helped the partners to clarify their increasing degree of intimacy. In turn, the relationship became progressively more exclusive, a characteristic of romantic pairings that is often a source of conflict.

According to a recent survey, young people today are questioning the utility of all these "new" traditions. Seventy-eight percent of the college-aged respondents prefer "informal meetings in social settings" to "formal dates." Dates are limited to formal occasions like proms, which are still in vogue and still very traditional. The "semantics of dating" have also changed. The most common way to refer to a nonplatonic male-female relationship is to note that the two individuals are "seeing each other" (R. Sacks, 1990) Although researchers have found it useful to distinguish "casual dating" from "serious dating" (J. Tolhuizen, 1989), many college students simply remark that they are "going out steady" or "not seeing others."

The new phrases are noticeably ambiguous. There are no clear-cut labels for relationship stages. This may be related to L. Baxter and W. Wilmot's (1985) finding that discussing the state of a close relationship is a taboo topic. Tolhuizen (1989) found that only about 29 percent of his respondents used "relationship negotiation" to intensify a dating relationship and even less (14 percent) offered verbal declarations of affection such as "I love you." W. Owens

(1987) data indicates that, in some cases, individuals use verbal declarations unilaterally and strategically to intensify a relationship, while in others, dating couples report simultaneously discovering that a relationship has grown closer. In a related study by P. Marston, M. Hecht, and T. Robers (1989), many subjects who identified themselves as involved in a heterosexual "love relationship . . . used *no* relational constructs in their definition of love" (390).

Along with relationship labels, relationship markers are also becoming less common. Only a small percentage of subjects in Tolhuizen's study (1989) reported giving tokens of affection, inviting partners to meet family or friends, or staging events to make partners jealous. Also, despite the fact that self report data indicates the prevalence of premarital sexual involvement (E. Grauerholz and R. Serpe, 1985; K. Woodward, 1990), it does not necessarily signify a desire to intensify the relationship (Tolhuizen, 1989).

It is interesting to speculate about the "new trends" in romance. Perhaps sex and love are no longer closely connected. Critics contend that the high divorce rate may be proof that love and marriage are not the "horse and carriage" they used to be (J. Footlick, 1990). The ambiguity that now characterizes romantic interaction is undoubtedly due to changes we generally regard as positive—the movement away from strict parental control and the questioning of traditional gender divisions. However, as the title of this volume suggests, with these changes come inherent challenges. Ambiguity is not necessarily comfortable. The prospect of negotiating male-female relationships in the absence of cultural traditions is at once exhilarating and frightening. It is a challenge that, like so many others, calls for effective communication. In the remaining sections of this chapter, several of the specific challenges inherent in romantic interaction are discussed.

INITIATION

As the discussion above suggests, if relationships are to progress, it is necessary for one or the other member to initiate that progress. Traditionally, when it came to romance, male partners were expected, even pressured, to do the asking, the proposing, and the like. Similarly, traditional images of physical interaction suggested that the man, not the woman, should "make the moves" that we know as precursors to sexual intimacy. D. Morris (1971) has argued that there is a predictable progression to the touches many think are spontaneously offered in intimate settings. At one time, females who asked men on dates or were too forward physically earned a "bad reputation." Of course, as gender restrictions become less rigid, partners should be expected to share the freedom and responsibility to initiate social and sexual activity.

However, recent studies suggest that young people are not altogether willing to abandon traditions when it comes to initiation in romantic pairs. Men are still far more likely to ask for a woman's company, move in for a kiss, suggest a more extended physical encounter and, ultimately, propose marriage (S. Green and P. Sandos, 1983). Women continue to occupy a relatively passive position in this relationship context, waiting and reacting, or perhaps taking indirect or subtle action. Young women do, however, report that they are willing to suggest social liaisons in platonic relationships (R. Buhrke and D. Fuqua, 1987). It seems that "let's get together" suggestions continue to be distinguished according to the nature of the relationship. But in potentially romantic relationships, male initiation continues to be the norm.

Sex-specific behaviors are being challenged in some dating relationships, according to J. DeLucia (1987). She points out that psychological gender orientation, a term coined by Bem to identify an individual's self perception that he or she is "masculine" or "feminine" or some combination thereof, is important in determining behavior in romantic interaction. Specifically, men who see themselves as "very masculine" and women who see themselves as "very feminine" are likely to conform to traditional standards. But those who see themselves as androgynous (possessing both male and female qualities) may cross the lines somewhat (DeLucia, 1987). Still, it is important to note that behaving "unfeminine" or "unmasculine" in romantic situations may be more costly than in professional or social situations.

It seems that the gender stereotypes "aggressive" and "passive" may take on special significance in romantic relationships with the potential for sexual intimacy. As Grauerholz and Serpe (1985) report, men continue to be sexually "proactive," while women continue to be "reactive." This boils down to greater freedom for men to *initiate sex* and greater freedom for women to *refuse sex*—both prerogatives that ideally should be available to either a male or a female in a free society. The researchers conclude that the proposed "single sexual standard does not yet exist" (Grauerholz and Serpre, 1985: 1049).

Sexual initiation is not the only significant form of initiation in romantic pairings. Men continue to be proactive in most aspects of relationship development. The practice of gift-giving as a symbol in male-female interaction continues to be dominated by male giving and female receiving. Florists still deliver most of their Valentine flowers to females and no widely accepted male counterpart of the engagement ring has emerged. The language of our wedding ceremonies has been revised so that the woman no longer has to "love, honor and obey," but a tender moment continues to be shared between father and daughter as he symbolically "gives her away" to the new husband. No such giving away is necessary for the groom.

Feminists have argued that women should take more initiative in our society, and many men and women have agreed, at least when it comes to legal and social reforms. However, according to feminist critiques, "efforts to equalize women's status through legal reforms guaranteeing equal rights and formal equality may be insufficient for creating true sex equality since in the private and intimate spheres of life . . . women still find themselves subordinate to their boyfriends, lovers and husbands" (DiIorio, 1989: 94).

The issue of subordination is not settled by simply citing that men tend to be proactive and women tend to be reactive. Young men might argue that it is the woman who holds the power in romantic relationships, because she can either accept or reject the advances of the man. Also, the receiving of gifts may constitute a superior position in some people's eyes. Both these arguments hinge on the proposed control of resources that are valuable in romantic relationships. In the next section, the control of such resources is examined.

CONTROL OF RESOURCES

Traditionally, researchers have defined power in male-female interaction as a function of controlled resources (McDonald, 1980). Thus, if the male partner initiates social action, provides necessary transportation, accepts responsibility for expenses, and so on, he may be assumed to be more powerful than the female. But, from another perspective, because the male partner is actually providing resources, giving of his own wealth and services to the female, he may be interpreted as subordinate to her. In fact, S. Sprecher (1985) found the latter interpretation to be more popular among both males and females currently involved in dating relationships. However, her interviews also suggested an interesting caveat. To the extent that the male dating partner perceived that he had "other options," the responsibility to initiate encounters and control the resources was seen as empowering. Conversely, when women have to "wait passively for someone else to show an interest," they perceive themselves as less powerful (Sprecher, 1985: 458). Apparently, perceptions of power in dating relationships may be based on the relative dependency of the partners on one another, but not necessarily in terms of monetary resources.

The above discussion of power in romantic relationships defines resources in traditionally male terms. But the power embodied in the dreaded "turn-down" has been identified as one of several "feminine resources." The same tradition that renders men in control of certain resources grants to women the control of resources associated with "love." In addition, women may control certain "services" that men want but cannot, or would rather not, buy (J. Carroll, K. Volk, and J. Hyde, 1985). It is interesting to note that nearly any service traditionally provided by women, even bearing and mothering children, can now be purchased for the right price.

Obviously, the resources labeled as "feminine" are valuable in romantic relationships, commodities that might be used for bargaining. But it is not difficult to imagine how, once contributed, these resources reduce the power of the giver. Research reveals that women who "give" a great deal in relationships tend to surrender power. They tend to become highly dependent on their male partners for the very same resources they formerly controlled, namely love and sex (Sprecher, 1985).

It seems that inequities continue to characterize male-female interaction when it comes to premarital romantic interaction. Unless men and women redistribute the resources so that both are free to initiate and pay for social encounters, and both are free to initiate and reject sexual advances, romantic relationships will continue to be dominated by traditional gender-specific guidelines. Borrowing traditions may be comfortable for many individuals when it comes to romance, but men and women will need to be open to a range of behaviors as these traditions are called into question.

EXCLUSIVITY AND POSSESSIVENESS

Questions about initiation and resources are most pressing in the early stages of romantic relationships. Other challenges emerge as couples attempt to negotiate progress toward exclusivity. It is illegal and immoral in our society to marry more than one person, and this norm also finds its way into premarital romantic pairings. But because no formal ritual designates a pairing as exclusive, the partners must negotiate their status.

Perhaps the most pressing issue is sexual exclusivity. According to ceremonial promise, marriage entails the "foresaking of all others," but to what extent does any given romantic relationship model this mandate? It seems worth noting that there may be different cultural standards for men and women when it comes to sexual exclusivity. The so-called "double standard" allows greater sexual freedom for men than for women, and may even regard many sexual partners for a man as a mark of social success. The negative image of women who engage in sex with many partners is evidenced in the words by which we refer to them, words that typically have no male complement. Our tendency to speak of women as "easy" or "loose" or worse, but not to refer to men in this way, demonstrates our understanding that women, at least stereotypically, are supposed to attach sex to emotional commitment, while men are expected to equate sex with pleasure, which can be separated from commitment.

In accord with these conceptualizations, a recent survey revealed that college women typically cited "emotional reasons" for engaging in sex, while college men cited "pleasure" far more often (B. Whitely, 1988). In a related study, this trend was one of the few correlated with biological sex—not psychological gender orientation—which means that even men and women who perceived themselves as "androgynous" conformed to gender-specific standards in explaining the reasons for sexual activity (DeLucia, 1987).

Regardless of the reason for engaging in sex, sexual exclusivity continues to be the norm in dating relationships. Both men and women expect their partners to be faithful, and feel that the failure to exclude other sexual partners threatens the romance (G. Hansen, 1985). But the issue of exclusivity in romantic relationships often extends beyond the bounds of sexual loyalty. Partners may struggle with the degree to which they are allowed other freedoms, such as time to spend with same-sex friends, family, and so on. Self-report data suggest that both men and women expect that certain outside relationships, particularly cross-sex friendships, will be subordinate to couple time, even during the early stages of romantic bonding (Hansen, 1982). However, females tend to believe that dating relationships mandate more devotion to one's partner than males do and tend to be more disturbed when their partners spend time with friends or family (Hansen, 1985).

Being a couple seems to create a situation in which time management can be a difficult issue. Couples have to negotiate about how to allocate social and work time, keeping in mind "each individual's need for privacy and intimacy" (Duck, 1988: 103). As if the internal pressures are not difficult enough, couples may be treated as a single unit by outsiders and pressured to decide together which social invitations to accept and which to decline (R. Cate and S. Lloyd, 1988). Attending separate social events may be evidence that the couple is either very secure about the relationship or not totally devoted, but such decisions are noticed in a couple-oriented social world.

VOLATILITY

One of the unique aspects of romantic relationships is their degree of volatility. Individuals who "fall in love" often experience intensely joyful moments, but they also experience moments of intense depression or anxiety. In some cases, the joy of finding one another and/or the threat of losing one another is felt so emotionally that individuals behave totally out of character. Consider the metaphors we use to describe this highly emotional condition: "crazy in love," "head over heels in love," "love-struck."

Researchers have verified that, just as the metaphoric language of love suggests, individuals may be literally overcome with the intense emotions they feel. It is not surprising that, as the degree of intimacy in a male-female relationship increases, so does the threat of violence. In one recent survey, nearly half of the respondents reported that they had experienced violence in a dating relationship. Both men and women revealed having made or received threats of physical abuse, witnessed violent destruction of inanimate objects and/or experienced "real violence" (J. Deal and K. Wampler, 1986).

Apparently, another expression, "you always hurt the one you love" is taken literally by some partners. Abuse may amount to little more than hurling violent profanities or expressions like "I could just kill you." Regardless of the severity of the remarks, however, it appears that expressions of anger are likely to be more intense and more frequent in romantic relationships than in nonromantic relationships. To complicate matters. cross-sex pairings are logically ill-equipped for interaction involving extreme negative emotions, because men and women deal quite differently with negative feelings. Men tend to "mask" sadness and fear with expressions commonly associated with anger, while women tend to "mask" anger with tears (G. Crester, et al., 1983; C. Ross and J. Mirowsky, 1984). Thus, confusion and frustration can result when invisible emotions are misconstrued based on visible behaviors.

Ultimately, words may fail to resolve love-sparked violence, and negative feelings may be expressed through physical separation or violence. Although separation seems preferable to violence, it can be just as threatening. "Breaking up" often embodies the ultimate threat. The thought that the relationship will be dissolved, and replaced by another, may be more than some can bear. Acts of violence against self and partner commonly follow threats or acts of separation.

The statistical reality of contemporary romance is that few who promise total, enduring devotion are able to fulfill their promises. The romantic relationships that "end" in marriage are, according to the fantasy, deemed successful, but other endings are associated with failure. A good deal is at stake in making these relationships last, but they are so fragile and so volatile that most do not succeed.

It is worth noting that today's young men and women seem to be deliberately postponing marriage. The rising median age of (first) marriage cited earlier indicates, according to one study, that romantic decisions are related to career decisions, which are undoubtedly related to freedom from gender prejudice (K. Baber and P. Monaghan, 1988). Devoting time to educational pursuits seems worthwhile regardless of subsequent marital status, but a commensurate lengthening of the dating years will be a side effect for which many individuals, both male and female, may not be prepared. Issues of initiation, exclusivity, and volatility, among others, will have to be addressed if these relationships are to be woven comfortably into the full lives young people hope to live.

Traditional assumptions about how many premarital relationships are acceptable, how long relationships can remain premarital, and the like, will also have to be reconsidered in view of the extended period of unmarried adulthood. Learning to manage and appreciate cross-sex relationships, complete with positive and negative emotions, has always been a challenge inherent in a free society. Coping with a diversity of conceptualizations of romance and gender is the special challenge of coming decades.

REFERENCES

Adelson, J., ed. 1980. *Handbook of Adolescent Psychology*. New York: Wiley.

Baber, K. M., and P. Monaghan. 1988. College women's career and motherhood expectations. New options, old dilemmas. *Sex Roles* 19: 189–203.

Baxter, L. A., and W. W. Wilmot. 1985. "Taboo topics" in close relationships. *Journal of Social and Personal Relationships* 1: 253–269.

Bem, S. L. 1987. Gender schema theory and the romantic tradition. In P. Shaver and C. Hendrick, eds., *Sex and Gender*. Newbury Park, CA: Sage, 251–271.

Buhrke, R. A., and D. R. Fuqua. 1987. Sex differences in same- and cross-sex supportive relationships. *Sex Roles* 17: 339–51.

Carroll, J. C., K. A. Volk, and J. S. Hyde. 1985. Differences between males and females in motives for engaging in sex. *Archives of Sexual Behavior* 15: 131–139.

Cassata, M., T. Skill, and S. Osel Boadu. 1983. Life and death in the daytime television serial: A content analysis. In M. Cassata and T. Skill, eds., *Life on Daytime Television: Tuning-in American Serial Drama*. (Norwood, NJ: Ablex, 47–70.

Cate, R. M., and S. A. Lloyd. 1988. Courtship. In S. W. Duck, D. F. Haley, S. E. Hobfoll, W. Ickes, and B. Montgomery, eds., *Handbook of Personal Relationships*. Chichester: Wiley.

Crester, G. A., W. K. Lombardo, B. Lombardo, and S. C. Mathis. 1983. Fer cryin' out loud—there is a sex difference. *Sex Roles* 9: 987–995.

Deal, J. E., and K. S. Wampler. 1986. Dating violence: The primacy of previous experience. *Journal of Social and Personal Relationships* 3: 457–71.

DeLucia, J. L. 1987. Gender role identity and dating behavior. *Sex Roles* 17: 153–161.

DiIorio, J. A. 1989. Being and becoming coupled: The emergence of female subordination in heterosexual relationships. In B. Risman and P. Schwartz, eds., *Gender in Intimate Relationships*. Belmont, CA: Wadsworth, 94–107.

Duck, S. 1988. *Relating to Others*. Chicago: Dorsey Press.

Eggert, L. L., and M. R. Parks. 1987. Communication network involvement in adolescents' friendships and romantic relationships. In *Communication Yearbook 10*. Newbury Park, CA: Sage, 283–322.

Footlick, J. K. 1990. What happened to the family? *Newsweek Special Issue*, Volume CXIV No. 27: 14–20.

Grauerholz, E., and R. T. Serpe. 1985. Initiation and response: The dynamics of sexual interaction. *Sex Roles* 12: 1041–1059.

Green, S. K., and P. Sandos. 1983. Perceptions of male and female initiators of relationships. *Sex Roles* 9: 849–852.

Hansen, G. L. 1982. Reactions to hypothetical jealousy producing events. *Family Relations* 31: 513–518.

————. 1985. Dating jealousy among college students. *Sex Roles* 12: 713–721.

Hill, J., ed. 1982. Early adolescence. *Child Development* 53.

Intons-Peterson, M. J. 1988. *Children's Concepts of Gender*. Norwood, NJ: Ablex.

Lewin, M., and L. M. Tragos. 1987. Has the feminist movement influenced adolescent sex role attitudes? A reassessment after a quarter century. *Sex Roles* 16: 125–135.

Marston, P. J., M. L. Hecht, and T. Robers. 1989. "True love ways": The subjective experience and communication of romantic love. *Journal of Personal and Social Relationships* 4.4: 387–408.

McDonald, G. W. 1980. Family power: the assessment of a decade of theory and research, 1970–1979. *Journal of Marriage and the Family* 42: 841–854.

McKinney, K. 1987. Age and gender differences in college students' attitudes toward women: A replication and extension. *Sex Roles* 17: 353–358.

Morris, D. 1971. *Intimate Behavior*. New York: Random House.

Owens, W. F. 1987. The verbal expression of love by women and men as a critical communication event in personal relationships. *Women's Studies in Communication* 10:15–24.

Pearson, J. 1989. *Communication in the Family: Seeking Satisfaction in Changing Times*. New York: Harper & Row.

Ross, C., and J. Mirowsky. 1984. Men who cry. *Social Psychology Journal* 47: 138–146.

Rubin, L. 1986. *Just Friends*. New York: Harper & Row.

Rubin, Z. 1980. *Children's Friendships*. Cambridge, MA: Harvard University Press.

Sacks, R. 1990. The Dating Game: An update on the rituals of courtship. *In View* 2.3: 16.

Smith, P., and E. Midlarsky. 1985. Empirically derived conceptions of femaleness and maleness: A current view. *Sex Roles* 12: 313–327.

Sprecher, S. 1985. Sex differences in bases of power in dating relationships. *Sex Roles* 12: 449–461.

Tolhuizen, J. H. 1989. Communication strategies for intensifying dating relationships: Identification, use and structure. *Journal of Personal and Social Relationships* 6.4: 413–434.

Umiker-Sebeok, J. 1981. The seven ages of women: A view from American magazine advertisements. In C. Mayo and N. Henley, eds., *Gender and Nonverbal Communication*. New York: Springer-Verlag, 209–252.

Whitely, B. E. 1988. The relation of gender-role orientation to sexual experience among college students. *Sex Roles* 9: 849–852.

Wilks, J. 1986. The relative importance of parents and friends in adolescent decision making. *Journal of Youth and Adolescence* 15: 323–334.

Woodward, K. 1990. Young beyond their years. *Newsweek Special Issue*, Volume CXIV No. 27: 54–60.

Youniss, J., and J. Smollar. 1985. *Adolescent Relations with Mothers, Fathers and Friends*. Chicago: University of Chicago Press.

FIRST MARRIAGE FAMILIES: GENDER AND COMMUNICATION

AUTHOR   Kathleen Galvin, Northwestern University

POINTS TO BE ADDRESSED

- The definition and status of first marriage families
- The influence of cultural norms on gender and communication in first marriage families
- The influence of family-of-origin experiences on gender and communication in first marriage families
- The gender-based patterns of marital interaction
- The gender-based patterns of parent-child interaction
- The changes in gender related communication patterns across family developmental stages

Near the close of many weddings, the new husband and wife approach the altar together. Each picks up one of two lighted candles, they jointly light a third central candle and then, stepping back, the bride and groom each blow out the two original candles—symbolically blowing themselves away. In this romantic and ritualistic way, the couple attempts to portray to assembled family and friends that two persons have now become one. Much of the mythology surrounding marriage supports the coming together of two halves to make a whole, the merging of oneself with another. Yet the lived marriage reflects a different reality, and for many persons, male and female, the candle ritual portrays neither reality nor a desirable dream.

The marriage vows incorporate phrases that contain the cultural expectations for adult life as a partner in marriage and family life. "With this ring I thee wed." With these five words a man and woman embark on a quest for a shared lifetime, the "happily ever after" that routinely concludes the fairy tales. Some expect to reach fulfillment simply through the marital declaration of commitment and legalization of the union, believing marriage itself is the desired end. Others may be less certain about the promise of predictable and lasting contentment. But each couple enters the ceremony hoping or praying that their marriage will be different from many others they have witnessed—but their marriage will be one that will continue "as long as we both shall live." For most couples this dream also includes forming a perfect family, "one that mirrors the image we carry around inside of us, and that will nurture and support us, and that we ourselves can create and mold, one that we feel comfortable in, one that will stretch our being to its full height" (M. Kolbenschlag, 1979: 155).

For most young people, the first marriage family is seen as the realization of that dream. The term "just marriage family" suggests a system created through the unbroken union of a man and woman and including their biological and adopted children.

At a time when issues of marital and family commitment are in a state of uncertainty, choosing to create a first marriage and family may be viewed as a courageous act on the part of a young man and woman. Although there are many perspectives one could use to examine the development of such a relationship, the twin lenses of gender and communication serve to shed light on the experiences of a committed long-term familial relationship. Gender and communication may be viewed as organizing principles of family life that influence structures, beliefs, meaning, relationships, and change (V. Goldner, 1989; L. Thompson and H. Walker, 1989; K. Galvin and B. Brommel, 1991). They undergird the development and maintenance of marital and family relationships, but may be taken for granted or ignored as crucial issues by persons in such relationships.

Although each couple intuitively understands that their marriage will be different from any other, what the bride and groom may not understand is that, just as there are two variations of human development, male and female, there are two marriages for each couple, "his marriage," and "her marriage." Their realities may be quite different (J. Bernard, 1972; M. McGoldrick, 1989). Today's young people, those who form the greatest percentage of first marriages, come to this union with more possibilities, more options, and more questions than their grandparents, yet once they are married, historical, familial, and cultural patterns emerge as powerful forces driving them toward the traditional and familiar.

This first marriage usually takes place during late adolescence or early adulthood. Current figures indicate the median age for first marriages in the United States is 24.6 years for men and 22.8 years for women. A sharp increase in age at first marriage has occurred over the last three decades— from 20 for women and 23 for men in 1955 to 24 for women and 26 for men in 1988. And for young couples, the transition to a family comes quickly; one-fifth of all children are conceived before marriage and many others are conceived within the first two years. Yet some couples, particularly dual-career couples, may marry later or postpone childbearing until their early to middle thirties. These first marriages have the potential to last close to half a century. In contrast to a century ago, when a typical couple lived together for thirty-one years before losing a spouse to death, today a life-long marriage lasts an average of forty-four years.

Currently about two-thirds of couples in first marriages are likely to divorce or at least temporarily separate st some point. Close to three-quarters of this group will remarry and begin a second family (P. Glick, 1989, 1990). Thus the words of the marriage ceremony "as long as we both shall live" apply only to the relatively small proportion of first marriage couples who will celebrate a forty-fourth anniversary. From these figures it is clear the family type known variously as the "nuclear," "intact," "first," or "traditional" family serves as a life stage for many couples and as a lifetime experience for a much smaller number.

Gender and communication in first marriage families may be viewed in light of the following:

1. The marriage incorporates the gender beliefs and communication patterns of each spouses' sociocultural traditions and their family-of-origin.

2. The spouses interaction patterns reflect significant male-female differences that affect both the marital and the parent-child relationships.

3. The marriage experience of gender and communication patterns will vary across family developmental stages and across cohort or peer groups.

MARITAL/FAMILY CULTURE: TRADITION AND CHANGE

"I take you to be my lawfully wedded wife/husband." Through the ages the wedding ceremony has served to initiate a man or woman into a new self-identification, husband or wife. Yet over the past decades, family life experience for males and females has been transformed. According to M. Bateson (1989), the process of creating a life has changed dramatically for men and women, but especially for women; "Today the material and skills from which a life is composed are no longer clear. It is no longer possible to follow the paths of previous generations (2)." Even within the flux of shifting gender roles and expectations, the weight of social and individual history presents itself in conscious and unconscious ways.

Couples in every culture make some sort of metaphysical bargain at the onset of their relationship, determining not only whether they will marry, but also setting the rules for the relationship (F. Walsh, 1989). These rules are constructed within an overall cultural frame that reflects tradition, and at the same time reflects the specific life experiences or particular family-of-origin experiences of the individuals involved.

Gender roles reflect centuries of consistent and predictable distinctions between, and expectations for men and women. These traditional distinctions are captured in the prescriptive characteristics contained in Figure 7.1 (L. Feldman, 1982, 355).

FIGURE 7.1
_____

PSYCHOLOGICAL DIMENSIONS OF THE FEMALE AND MALE ROLES

The female role. Women are expected to be (or allowed to be) the following:

1. Home orientated, child(ren)-oriented.

2. Warm, affectionate, gentle, tender.

3. Aware of feelings to others, considerate, tactful, compassionate.

4. Moody, high-strung, temperamental, excitable, emotional, subjective, illogical.

5. Complaining, nagging.

6. Weak, helpless, fragile, easily emotionally hurt.

7. Submissive, yielding, dependent.

The male role. Men are expected to be (or allowed to be) the following:

1. Ambitious, competitive, enterprising, worldly.

2. Calm, stable, unemotional, realistic, logical.

3. Strong, tough, powerful.

4. Aggressive, forceful, decisive, dominant.

5. Independent, self-reliant.

6. Harsh, severe, stern, cruel.

7. Autocratic, rigid, arrogant.

Traditional gender roles prepared husbands to distance themselves in the world of work and to function in a rational, judgmental manner, to suppress feelings and convey a sense of control. They prepared wives to take care of the home, children, and emotional concerns, to function in a dependent and sensitive manner, and to suppress strength or independence. These patterns were tied to common assumptions, such as the male being the "head" of the family household, the female role being to support the male, and marriage being more important to women while work was more important to men. The roles of husband and wife carried specified utilitarian functions; neither expected the other to meet extensive emotional needs or to serve as a best friend. Historically, male and female marital communication occurred within strongly segregated and highly predictable patterns. Men tended to maintain their closest relational ties in the male sphere outside the home while women interacted actively with other women within the extended family or community network.

Unique multigenerational family patterns combine with the sociocultural forces to influence new families. Multigenerational systems contain patterns that are shared, and eventually recreated in younger members; they affect new families because the husband's and wife's heritages reflect those family-of-origin influences (M. Hoopes, 1987). Families of origin provide blueprints for the communication of future generations because attitudes and rule-bound behaviors are transmitted from a family-of-origin to a newly forming system. Each spouse carries into the new marriage beliefs about what it means to be female or male, and what it means to be a wife/mother or husband/father. Such meanings reflect the transmission of culture across a number of generations. Issues of dominance, decision making, intimacy, emotional responsiveness, and conflict styles are bound to historical family gender patterns. A woman who comes from a family line of strong females, with a family theme "A woman must be able to support herself," will move to create a different marriage than a woman who witnessed generations of dependent females and learned, "You need to find a man to support you well." These familial patterns also reflect ethnic heritages that may embody specific strong gender beliefs (McGoldrick, J. Pearce, and J. Giordano, 1982).

These sociocultural and family-of-origin traditions counter-balance current forces that seek to release males and females from highly gender-bound structures. Contemporary young couples are attempting to work out non-traditional gender arrangements in their first marriage commitments, but find themselves struggling to create relationships for which there are few lifetime models. This reality leads to confusion and regular reinvention of the relationship. The following statement captures this tension well: "Even as women are rebelling against having responsibility for making family relationships, holidays and celebrations, they typically feel guilty for not continuing to do what they are expected to do" (McGoldrick, 1989: 200). These non-traditional marital relationships tend to be less prescriptive, less role bound, less predictable, and characterized by high levels of problem solving and negotiation. Males and females are attempting to create emotional partnerships—collaborative marriages—potentially quite different from those their parents or grandparents experienced.

The dual-career family serves as an example of the attempt to create a gender-flexible lifestyle. These collaborative marriages attempt to move beyond traditional gender expectations but still struggle with the issues of dominance and intimacy, especially as couples enter childrearing. Such marriages have to be renegotiated every time there is a move or major change; even daily crises require discussion and negotiation. Traditional gender patterns do not serve as predictable guides for behavior.

MARITAL/FAMILY INTERACTION PATTERNS

". . . in good times and in bad . . . to have and to hold." Such promises of presence and support undergird most marriage vows, although their actual meaning is determined by each couple. Contemporary couples expect to create a companionate marriage, a union with emotional connectedness at its core. Spouses are expected to be best friends or emotional partners as well as to serve instrumental or pragmatic roles. Expectations for a companionate marriage place extensive focus on communication, particularly nurturing or relational communication.

This emphasis on emotional substance in marriage appears to be related to enhanced well-being for both women and men but is especially important for women (D. Williams, 1988). Yet this expectation can place high pressure on men because their friendship history may not include this dimension. Currently, more men than women report their spouse is their best friend (L. Rubin, 1984), yet women are more likely to have a greater history of emotionally based same-sex friendships, and may have different definitions for "best friend." The communication and gender related assumptions underlying such first marriages are (1) that marital communication is the core of the system, (2) that the couple serves as the architect of the system, and (3) that each spouse's sociocultural and family-of-origin traditions will be reflected in the couple's interaction with each other and their children.

After studying a range of couple types, M. Fitzpatrick and J. Induik (1982: 696) reported that across couple types

> . . . the husbands perceived themselves as primarily instrumental in their communication behavior. Regardless of their normative orientations, the husbands in our sample perceived themselves as rarely nurturant, passive, or dependent, always dominant and task-oriented, and generally incapable of discussing or expressing their feelings. Consequently, it falls to the wives in these relationships to maintain some level of expressivity. . . . When wives cannot or refuse to be expressive, the relationship suffers. Wives may be said to bear the burden of expressivity in their marital relationships.

Wives and husbands tend to establish routine gender-specific everyday interaction patterns. Wives ask significantly more questions than their husbands do, questions that are used to engage their husbands in dialogue. The topics husbands introduce in a conversation are more likely to be discussed. Both partners seem to take for granted that any topic introduced by the husband is worth discussing (P. Fishman, 1978). In addition wives are more likely to use filler terms, such as "uh huh," to encourage men to keep talking, and are more likely to yield their turn to speak to their husbands (L. Stewart, et al., 1990).

Communication on a deeper level reflects the level of marital intimacy that has been developed. Marital intimacy involves the following characteristics: (1) a close, familiar, and affectionate or loving personal relationship, (2) a detailed and deep understanding of the other, and (3) sexual relations (L. Feldman, 1979). This is consistent with the depiction of intimacy as "a relational process with which we come to know the innermost subjective aspects of another, and are known in a like manner" (G. Chelune, et al., 1984). Feldman (1982) suggests sex role conditioning exhibits a negative influence on marital intimacy and problem solving by inhibiting the development of males' emotional expressiveness and empathy and inhibiting women's instrumental behavior or assertiveness. He suggests this conditioning may promote female use of nagging or pressuring and passive-aggression or violent behavior in some men, and affect the range of discipline or nurturing behaviors used by mothers or fathers. Therefore, certain gender-related communication skills are reinforced while others are given little ability to develop.

Wives are more likely to use a range of affective responses than are husbands. When discussing important interpersonal issues, wives' speech may be characterized by less neutral and more negative behavior and by greater emotional expressiveness (C. Notarius and J. Johnson, 1982). Studies of marital interaction during the discussion of relationship problems tend to underscore sex differences, with wives being more likely to express their negative feelings directly and to be more emotional. In general, wives appear to show a great range of affection while males demonstrate a lack of behavioral responses and expressivity (P. Noller and Fitzpatrick, 1990). Overall, women tend to be more expressive and affectionate than men in marriages (Thompson and Walker, 1989).

Males and females may differ in the ways they use or value relational currencies, in their ways of sharing affection. For example, although during courtship men are willing to spend intimate time with women, after marriage they tend to spend less and less time talking to their wives, often considering doing chores around the house to be an adequate demonstration of caring and intimacy. They feel mystified about what women want when they seek more contact in the marital relationship (McGoldrick, 1989).

Self-disclosure is a primary communication relational currency used to deepen and strengthen interpersonal relationships. Historically, spouses disclose more to each other than to anyone else, yet wives tend to disclose more than husbands. Recent studies suggest younger, more educated couples may be moving toward a pattern of more equal and intimate disclosure by both sexes. Disclosure is higher among men and women with egalitarian sex role attitudes. Women are also more likely to have same-sex confidants (L. Peplau and S. Gordon, 1985).

The nature of the message affects marital self-disclosure. For example, face honoring, face compensating, and face neutral emotions are disclosed more frequently and preferred more than face threatening disclosure. Overall, husbands and wives do not differ in their actual disclosure of emotions, but wives reported that they disclosed more emotions and that they value the disclosure of emotions more than husbands (S. Shimanoff, 1985).

Women tend to express a broader range of emotion in marriage with more tenderness, fear, and sadness. Many men tend to limit themselves to control anger (Thompson and Walker, 1989), a reflection of sociocultural and family of origin patterns that discourage softer emotions.

The quality of marital communication affects marital satisfaction. Williams (1988) suggests the beneficial effects of marriage are tied to the quality of dyadic communication between spouses: "It appears that it is the affective quality of the marital relationship rather than the marriage per se that is more important for the well-being of individuals" (465). In addition, there appears to be a relationship between marital satisfaction and the husband's ability to read nonverbal messages. In a study of married couples reading nonverbal clues, results indicated a positive relationship between marital satisfaction and nonverbal competence but only for husbands reading their wives' nonverbal cues. In comparison to male strangers, the husbands of satisfied wives were more able to read their wives' nonverbal cues, while the husbands of dissatisfied wives were less able to read them (J. Gottman and A. Porterfield, 1981). Fitzpatrick and D. Badzinski (1985) suggest a strong correlation between marital satisfaction and self-reports of communication in marriage; that is, the happily married believe they have good communication with their spouses.

These gender-related behaviors are carried into parenting. With changing norms men are expected to develop greater verbal and nonverbal nurturing communication. Yet historical patterns may work against this occurring easily. For example, children of both sexes tend to self-disclose more to their mothers than fathers; mothers receive more information—more intimate and accurate information—than fathers do (J. Pearson, 1989). The communication literature is filled with gender related parent-child differences.

Recent work reveals that changes in these patterns are tied to parent-child gender similarity or difference. Stewart, et al (1990) suggest that men's ability to embrace traditional feminine traits in parenting may be highly dependent on the sex of the child saying:

> For example, fathers who have sons exhibit fewer traditionally feminine [expressive] sex-role traits than men who have daughters, while mothers of sons exhibit more traditionally feminine traits. Fathers of daughters tend to retain their traditionally masculine traits but also acquire some of the traditionally feminine [expressive] traits in their parenting skills. Thus, sons seem to have a more traditional impact on parents' sex roles—fathers exhibit more traditionally masculine behaviors and mothers exhibit more traditionally feminine behaviors. (134)

Parenting tends to emphasize traditionally feminine behaviors, such as nurturing, sensitivity, and awareness of emotions; masculine traits such as dominance, competitiveness, and aggressiveness may not be a part of the typical parenting skills repertoire.

Such generalizations can be misleading, because each marriage and family is different. Recent work on marital and family typologies reveals similarities among groups or types of marriages and families. For example, Fitzpatrick's work (1988) on classifying couple types identifies three major types—independents, separates, and traditionals—plus mixed types. Independents accept uncertainty and change, do considerable sharing, and negotiate autonomy. They do not avoid conflict, value independence, and are more likely to support androgynous and flexible sex roles. Separates differ from independents in greater conflict avoidance, more differentiated space needs, fairly regular schedules, and less sharing. In relationships, they experience little sense of togetherness or autonomy. Separates usually oppose an androgynous sexual orientation. Traditionals uphold a fairly conventional belief system and resist change or uncertainty because it threatens their routines. Their high level of sharing leads to a high degree of interdependence and low autonomy. Traditionals will engage in conflict but would rather avoid it. Uncertainty and change in values upset them. Traditionals demonstrate strong sex-typed roles.

In their family-oriented work D. Kantor and W. Lehr (1976) identify closed, open and random family types. Closed families are characterized by high emphasis on authority, continuation of family values, and strong ties to traditions. Communication is predictable, controlled, and gender-specific. Open families value group consensus, flexibility, and a focus on the present. Negotiation is common and gender roles tend to be flexible. The random family is characterized by unpredictability, lack of social appropriateness, and constant change. As such, gender roles may be varied and unpredictable. These couple and family typologies demonstrate that gender must be viewed within many contexts and that gender roles and communication may vary across couple and family types.

DEVELOPMENTAL STAGES

"From this day forward as long as we both shall live . . ." This short phrase may describe a marriage of six months or sixty years. A developmental approach recognizes that marriage and family life is not a static reality; each life stage may appear different. In arguing for a life course perspective for understanding marriage, T. Cooney and D. Hogan (1991) suggest the patterning of the individual's life course is influenced largely by the interplay of changing historical conditions, social structures, and individual biological and psychological development. So too, the marital experience must be understood within this context as the experience of a marriage changes across time.

The developmental perspective is particularly effective for recognizing cultural shifts of the past two or three decades. Most persons who married twenty or thirty years ago set out to create a marriage and family that reflected strong gender role differences; contemporary young couples enter marriage with multiple options and different expectations.

Most models of family stages apply to the middle-class, intact American family life cycle. Historically, experiences such as untimely death or divorce placed those families outside the normal developmental patterns. Contemporary family theorists are beginning to call these "temporary interruptions," thus considering divorce as one normal stage for some persons and suggesting a "Y," or "fork in the road" model of development (D. Ahrons and R. Rodgers, 1987), (B. Carter and McGoldrick, 1988).

Traditionally, the first or intact family developmental model includes the following life cycle stages:

Forming the couple

Birth of the first child

Family with young children

Family with adolescents

Launching children

Couple in later life

Death of one spouse

(Carter and McGoldrick, 1988; K. Galvin and B. Brommel, 1991; McGoldrick, 1989)

This model presumes the couple will become parents. Although some couples will not move into parenting, this group remains a small minority.

Communication within intact family systems changes across the individual life span and family life cycle (R. Gilford and V. Bengston, 1979). Current researchers hypothesize that explicit verbal communication decreases, and implicit forms of communication increase over the marital career (A. Sillars and W. Wilmot, 1989). Concurrently, aging adults provide their spouses with less social support, particularly as perceived by women (C. Depner and B. Ingersoll-Dayton, 1985). In general, marital satisfaction appears to decline with the birth of the first child and increases after children leave home. The following overview of stages highlights some of the gender and communication issues.

FORMING THE COUPLE

This is a time of romance that eventually moves into reality. In the previous chapter, Laurie Arliss describes many of the romantic (happily ever after) notions likely to characterize views of first marriages. In the early relational stages, these views may be fed or fostered by media portrayals or fairy tale promises, yet they are characterized by male-female inequities even in terms of premarital interaction. In many marriage ceremonies the woman is "given away" by her father to another man; she wears a ring to symbolize the new affiliation, he may not. She may have attended showers while he attended stag parties, both of which reinforce traditional gender roles (E. Imber-Black, 1989). In the beginning, couples frequently make allowances for behavior that isn't quite acceptable because new spouses focus on what they are getting, and differences seem enhancing. Later, differences become annoying and call out for resolution (G. Lederer and T. Lewis, 1991).

These early stages of courtship and marriage involve the couple's attempt to create that "metaphysical bargain," setting the rules for communication and finding ways to deepen communication. The initial stage of first marriage is characterized by close monitoring of the relationship and more frequent and intense communication about the relationship than at any other stage (Sillars and Wilmot, 1989). Couples may negotiate such issues as the place of old friends, attachment to families-of-origin, time spent together or apart, closeness, and conflict. This is a time for investing in a relationship, engaging in high self disclosure, communicating sexual life, developing negotiation and conflict styles, and planning for future years. Young couples must resolve such issues as the initial integration of separate personalities and subsequent transformation from couple to family particularly dealing with gender role expectations and reality.

FAMILIES WITH YOUNG CHILDREN

The arrival of the first child irrevocably changes the couple's life. The pair becomes a threesome, with all the change in communication patterns such a shift implies. Pregnancy occurs relatively close to the wedding for most couples: although some couples, particularly dual-career couples, may marry later or postpone childbearing and have baby in early to middle thirties. No matter what the age, taking on a role of "father" or "mother" is a major life transition, with strong gender and communication implications.

Three factors influence couples during the transition to parenthood: their views on parental responsibilities and restrictions, the gratification childrearing holds for them as a couple, and their own marital intimacy and stability (R. Steffensmeier, 1982). Views on parenthood reflects sociocultural backgrounds. For example, middle-class mothers differ from lower-class mothers in their response to the stress of motherhood both during pregnancy and in the years following. Middle-class women take more time to adjust and feel fewer pressures than lower-class women, who must worry more about support and work roles (T. Reilly, D. Entwisle, and S. Doering, 1987).

Once men and women become parents they tend to do different things with and for their children, with mothers becoming more involved because "our culture still leaves women with primary responsibility for childrearing and blames them when something goes wrong" (McGoldrick, 1989: 200). Mothers appear to give more care, attention, response, and nonverbal comfort than fathers. They are more likely to spend long periods of time alone with a child. Yet fathers who are actively engaged in childcare may be as competent as mothers in providing attention, stimulation, and care; and as children grow older, fathers tend to be more directive and instructive than mothers (Thompson and Walker, 1989).

The birth of a first child appears to have a traditionalizing effect on the marriage. "There is likely to be some movement away from the degree of explicit communication and negotiation required by role sharing and greater implicit adjustment based on role delegation" (Sillars and Wilmot, 1989: 234). The major research on the transition to parenthood indicates that it is accompanied by a general decrease in marital satisfaction, a reversion to more traditional sex roles, even by dual-career couples, and a lowering of self-esteem for women (McGoldrick, 1989). Very few couples share household and children responsibilities equally.

Dual-career couples face the greatest challenge because, in the reorganization of their lives, "the wife typically assumes additional responsibilities at home, in most cases compromising her own career aims while her husband continues in full pursuit of his work goals. When she does continue to work outside the home, children arrangements are largely her responsibility and viewed as a 'womens issue' by the culture" (F. Walsh, 1989: 273).

Within this stage, the couple must deal with the following communication-related issues: (1) renegotiating the roles of husband and wife and assuming roles of mother and father, (2) transmitting culture and establishing a community of experiences, and (3) developing the child's communication competence. Such tasks are inevitably bound up with gender socialization of children.

The growth of the first child and births of subsequent children add complexity, if not chaos, to the couple's interactions. Time together seems to disappear and talk tends to focus on pragmatic child-centered concerns, including the gender socialization of the children. Given the increasing practical demands it is no wonder marital satisfaction declines.

Adolescents frequently add stress to the family system. Historically, this is a period when many young women struggle with self-identity and choose intimacy with a male as a way to find self-definition. Conventional gender values appear to be at an all-time high during adolescence (McGoldrick, 1989). The predictable teenage struggles with individuation, particularly in areas of sexuality, identity, and autonomy, may coincide with parental mid-life issues. Opposite sex parents and children may find a gulf between them as a response to the power of the "incest taboo." Parental conflict with teenagers may provoke husband-wife conflicts, although the adolescent schedule may provide more time for spouse interaction. Depending on the parental generation the life choices that are identified by their children may appear rewarding or may be viewed as a rejection of traditional gender values.

MID-LIFE COUPLES

Smaller families and greater life expectancy have given couples a more extensive midlife period. During this stable period, implicit role expectations should increasingly substitute for explicit communication, and couples may experience a blurring of personalities due to long-term interdependence (Sillars and Wilmot, 1989). There is a tendency for men and women to be going in opposite directions psychologically as their children move out into their own lives. Men may seek the closeness they missed during the career-building years, and women, usually done with childrearing by their early fifties, may feel more energized about developing their own lives (McGoldrick, 1989). They may become more assertive and focused on career development or individual fulfillment. Different generations may experience this quite differently—younger women may not have been gone from the work force for long, so this transition will be different for them. Equity in the tasks of cooking, homemaking, and providing economic support increases across the stages, with the greatest growth in the launching stage and middle years after the children leave home (R. Schaefer and P. Keith, 1981).

This period often involves grandparenthood, a role less complicated if the parenting couple has stayed together. In her review of related research, V. Downs (1989) reports women indicated higher satisfaction with the grandparent role than men, and greater socialization to the role. Both males and females report similar perceptions about their responsibilities for discipline or helping out with grandchildren. Some gender related communication patterns develop at this stage. Whereas grandmothers tend to discuss subjects of emotional or relational content with their grandchildren, grandfathers often communicate in terms of practical aspects and relate more to grandsons (G. Hagestad, 1985).

By this point the couple that has remained together expects contact with children and grandchildren, but not primary responsibility for their lives. Older couples with no children in the home are happier than those with children (J. Pittman and S. Lloyd, 1988). This is a time of redefinition and reinvigoration of the original couple relationship.

OLDER COUPLES

Couples who remain together and enter into the later life stages typically exhibit a commitment to the relationship, interdependence, and reasonably high marital satisfaction. Their self-disclosure tends to decline, or such communication becomes more implicit. This period often coincides with retirement, historically of the male, but increasingly of both partners. These couples may face issues of transition adjustment but most manage well. According to P. Zietlow and Sillars (1988), retired couples appear less analytic and more noncommittal, and they exhibit a remarkable passive and congenial style. A few exceptions of conflict-habituated couples do exist and this pattern appears to continue.

Retirement appears to be a period of more flexible male and female roles. Men appear to become more reflective, dependent, and affiliative, and females become more assertive. Retired men and women see themselves as having less normative pressures to either masculine or feminine things subsequent to parenting and retirement, so the sexes may become more similar and androgynous (Sillars and Wilmot, 1989).

These changes tend to bring about increased sharing and companionship. Satisfaction with an intimate relationship is related to life satisfaction and psychological well-being, especially for elderly women (T. Thompson and J. Nussbaum, 1988). For couples in good health, this stage may truly be the "golden years of communication."

DEATH OF ONE SPOUSE

At some point the couple faces the reality of the words "as long as we both shall live." Women are more likely to outlive their husbands—by an average of seven years. In cases where a woman dies first, the widower is at especially high risk of death and suicide for a year because of the loss, loneliness, and lack of caretaking (McGoldrick, 1991). Widowers and widows are faced with acknowledging the loss and openly grieving, learning to function physically and emotionally alone, and creating connections of interest and to a larger social network. The need for supportive communication especially from children and extended family is critical.

Life in first marriage families represents a long-term commitment to a life that involves the negotiation of gender issues and the development of communication patterns that create meaning in members' lives. When considering the candle-lighting ceremony of the marital ritual, importance of the lifelong two original candles should be clear.

According to B. Carter and McGoldrick (1988), "Marriage tends to be misunderstood as a joining of two individuals. What it really represents is the changing of two entire systems and an overlapping to develop a third subsystem" (15). Perhaps the candle lighting ceremony, described at the opening to this chapter, would come closer to the truth if three lighted candles were left on the altar, one for the man, one for the woman, and one for the marriage and family created by their union.

REFERENCES

Ahrons, O., and R. Rodgers. 1987. *Divorced Families*. New York: Norton.

Bateson, M. C. 1989. *Composing a Life*. New York: Atlantic Monthly Press.

Baruch, G., R. Barnett, and C. Rivers. 1983. *Lifeprints*. New York: McGraw-Hill.

Bernard, J. 1972. *The Future of Marriage*. New York: Gulliford Press.

Blumstein, P., and P. Schwartz. 1983. *American Couples: Money, Work, Sex*. New York: William Morrow.

Carter, B., and M. McGoldrick. 1988. Overview: The changing family life cycle—A framework for family therapy. In B. Carter and M. McGoldrick, eds., *The Changing Family Life Cycle*. 2d ed. Boston: Allyn and Bacon, 3–30.

Chelune, G. J., J. Robeson, and M. Kommer. 1984. A cognitive model of intimate relationships. In V.J. Derlega, ed., *Communication Intimacy and Close Relationships*. Orlando, FL: Academic Press, 11–40.

Cooney, T., and D. Hogan. 1991. Marriage in an institutionalized life course: First marriage among American men in the twentieth century. *Journal of Marriage and the Family* 53: 178–190.

Depner, C., and B. Ingersoll-Dayton. 1985. Conjugal social support: Patterns in later life. *Journal of Gerontology* 40: 761–766.

Downs, V. C. 1989. The grandparent-grandchild relationship. In J. Nussbaum, ed., *Life-span Communication: Normative Processes*. Hilsdale, NJ: Laurence Erlbaum, 257–281.

Feldman, L. 1979. Marital conflict and marital intimacy: An integrative psycho-dynamic-behavioral systemic model. *Family Processes* 18: 69–78.

————. 1982. Sex roles and family dynamics. In F. Walsh, ed., *Normal Family Processes*. New York: Guilford Press, 345–382.

Ferree, M. M. 1990. Beyond separate spheres: Feminism and family research. *Journal of Marriage and the Family* 52: 866–884.

Fishman, P. M. 1978. Interaction: The work women do. *Social Problems* 25: 397–406.

Fitzpatrick, M. A. 1988. *Between Husbands and Wives*. Beverly Hills, CA: Sage.

Fitzpatrick, M. A., and D. M. Badzinski. 1985. All in the family: Interpersonal communication in kin relationships. In M. L. Knapp & G. R. Miller, eds., *Handbook of Interpersonal Communication*. Beverly Hills, CA: Sage, 687–736.

Fitzpatrick, M. A., and J. Indvik. 1982. The instrumental and expressive domains of marital compressive domains of marital communication. *Human Communication Research* 8: 195–213.

Galvin, K., and B. Brommel. 1991. *Family Communication: Cohesion and Change*. 3d ed. New York: Harper/Collins.

Gilford, R., and V. Bengston. 1979. Measuring marital satisfaction in three generations: Positive and negative dimensions. *Journal of Marriage and the Family* 41: 387–398.

Glick, P. 1989. The family life cycle and social change. *Family Relations* 38: 123–129.

_____. 1990. Marriage and family trends. In *2001: Preparing Families for the Future*. Minneapolis: National Council on Family Relations.

Goldner, V. 1989. Generation and gender: Normative and covert hierarchies. In M. McGoldrick, C. Anderson, and F. Walsh, eds., *Women in Families*. New York: W. W. Norton, 42–60.

Gottman, J., and A. Porterfield. 1981. Communicative competence in the nonverbal behavior of married couples. *Journal of Marriage and the Family* 43: 817–824.

Hagestad, G. 1985. Continuity and connectedness. In V. Bengston and J. Robertson, eds., *Grandparenthood*. Beverly Hills, CA: Sage, 31–48.

Hoopes, M. 1987. Multigenerational systems: Basic assumptions. *American Journal of Family Therapy* 15: 195–205.

Imber-Black, E. 1989. Rituals of stabilization and change in women's lines. In M. McGoldrick, C. Anderson, and F. Walsh, eds., *Women in Families*. New York: W. W. Norton, 451–470.

Kantor, D., and W. Lehr. 1976. *Inside the Family*. San Francisco: Jossey-Bass.

Kohlenschlag, M. 1979. *Kiss Sleeping Beauty Good-bye*. Garden City, New York: Doubleday.

Lederer, G., and T. Lewis. 1991. The transition to couplehood. In F.H. Brown, ed., *Reweaving the Family Tapestry*. New York: W.W. Norton, 94–113.

McGoldrick, M. 1989. The joining of families through marriage: The new couple. In G. Carter and M. McGoldrick, eds., *The Changing Family Life Cycle*. 2d ed. Boston: Allyn and Bacon, 209–234.

_____. 1989. Women through family life cycle. In M. McGoldrick, C. Anderson, and F. Walsh, eds., *Women in Families*. New York: Norton, 200–226.

_____. 1991. A time to mourn: Death and the family life cycle. In F. Walsh and M. McGoldrick, eds., *Living Beyond Loss*. New York: W. W. Norton.

McGoldrick, M., J. Pearce, and J. Giordano. 1982. *Ethnicity and Family Therapy*. New York: Guilford Press.

Noller, P., and M. A. Fitzpatrick. 1990. Marital communication in the eighties. *Journal of Marriage and the Family* 52: 822–843.

Notarius, C., and J. Johnson. 1982. Emotional expression in husbands and wives. *Journal of Marriage and the Family* 44: 483–490.

Pearson, J. 1989. *Communication in the Family*. New York: Harper/Collins.

Peplau, L., and S. Gordon. 1985. Men and women in love: Gender differences in close heterosexual relationships. In R. O'Leary, R. Unger, and B. Washington, eds., *Women, Gender and Social Psychology*. Hillsdale, N.J.: Lawrence Erlbaum, 257–291.

Pittman, J., and S. Lloyd. 1988. Quality of family life, social support, and stress. *Journal of Marriage and the Family* 50: 53–67.

Raush, H. L., W. A. Barry, R. K. Hertel, and M. A. Swain. 1974. *Communication Conflict and Marriage*. San Francisco: Jossey/Bass.

Reilly, T., D. Entwisle, and S. Doering. 1987. Socialization into parenthood. A longitudinal study of the development of self evaluation. *Journal of Marriage and the Family* 49: 295–309.

Rollins, B., and H. Feldman. 1990. Marital satisfaction over the family life cycle. *Journal of Marriage and the Family* 32: 20–28.

Rubin, L. 1984. *Intimate Strategies: Men and Women Together*. New York: Harper & Row.

Schafer, R., and P. Keith. 1981. Equity in marital roles across the family life cycle. *Journal of Marriage and the Family* 43: 359–367.

Shimanoff, S. 1985. Rules governing the verbal expression of emotions between married couples. *The Western Journal of Speech Communication* 49: 147–165.

Sillars, A., and W. Wilmot. 1989. Marital communication across the life span. In J. Nessbaum, ed., *Life-span communication*. Hillsdale, N.J.: Lawrence Erlbaum.

Steffensmeier, R. H. 1982. A role model of the transition to parenthood. *Journal of Marriage and the Family* 41: 319–334.

Stewart, L., A. Stewart, C. Friedley, and P. Cooper. 1990. *Communication Between the Sexes: Sex Differences and Sex-role Stereotypes*. Scottsdale, AZ: Gorsuch-Scarisbrick.

Thompson, L., and H. Walker. 1989. Gender in families: Women and men in marriage, work, and parenthood. *Journal of Marriage and the Family* 51: 845–871.

Thompson, T., and J. Nussbaum. 1988. Interpersonal communications: Intimate relationships and aging. In C. W. Carmichael, C. H. Botan, and R. Hawkins, eds., *Human Communication and the Aging Process*). Prospect Heights, IL: Waveland Press, 95–110.

Walsh, F. 1989. Reconsidering gender in the marital quid pro quo. In M. McGoldrick, C. Anderson, and F. Walsh, eds., *Women in Families*. New York: Norton, 267–285.

Williams, D. G. 1988. Gender, marriage, and psychosocial well-being. *Journal of Family Issues* 9: 452–468.

Zietlow, P. H., and A. L. Sillars. 1988. Lifestage differences in communication during marital conflicts. *Journal of Social and Personal Relationships* 5: 233–245.

CHAPTER 8

COMMUNICATION IN NONTRADITIONAL FAMILY: TRANSITIONS BRING CHALLENGES

AUTHOR   Joyce Hauser, New York University

POINTS TO BE ADDRESSED

- Ending the traditional nuclear family: The divorce
- Reorganization after divorce
- The stepfamily—the new nontraditional family
- The problem of stereotyping
- Gender problems in stepfamilies

In the United States today there is an emerging American family, interwoven and complicated—two families, usually created by divorce, mingled and connected with new stepsisters or brothers, grandparents, aunts, uncles, and either one or two new stepparents. Even with the effort, fantasies, and dreams of being better this time around, more than one-half of second marriages end in divorce (Glick, 1989. Cited in Galvin and Cooper, 1990.).

There are 35 million stepparents in the United States and 1,300 stepfamilies are formed daily. Half of the children born during the 70s will experience broken families and most of these will become stepchildren. At least a tenth of the children will see their parents divorce, remarry, and redivorce before they have reached the age of sixteen (Einstein, 1982).

The family as a significant, evolving, and complex institutional structure has been studied extensively by many in a wide range of disciplines; however, the remarried family as a specific variant of the nuclear family has until recently received only occasional and limited investigation. One reason is the complexity and the uniqueness of the stepfamily. Questions about issues such as blending different lifestyles, defining the step role, forming new attachments while maintaining ties with the old, and achieving a new remarried family identity, must be addressed to gain understanding of the stepfamily. In many cases, the answers to these questions are closely linked to contemporary gender issues.

The Divorce

Noah's Ark has definitely sprung a leak! We are no longer a "two-by-two" society which is clearly reflected by the statistics on divorce over the past ten years. In America, we claim to value relationships, yet we toss them aside when they develop minor flaws (J. Hauser, 1988).

Divorce does not end the relationship between a husband and wife though—it transforms it. Even if no children are involved, civil law changes the rules and responsibilities involved, but it can not sever emotional bonds.

Every human being needs to be nurtured, and divorce is a period in which everyone involved is deprived, almost overnight, of important sources of nurturance. No wonder so many divorced people in the Kindred Spirit report (Hauser, 1988) said that they saw therapists or counselors before and after the decision to end the marriage.

The Divorce Mediation Research Project (1984), interviewed divorcing and/or divorced parents. During the first interview, most families were facing the problems of physical relocation of one or both parents, combined with financial stresses, and uncertainties about the future.

Professor L. Weitzman (1985) of Harvard University found that, on average, women with minor children experienced a 73 percent decline in standard of living during the first year after divorce whereas their husbands experienced a 42 percent increase in their standard of living. Weitzman predicts a two-tier society with women and children as an underclass.

In another study, J. Wallerstein and S. Blakeslee (1989) found a third of the divorced women and a quarter of the men, mostly the older ones, felt that life was unfair, disappointing, and lonely. According to Wallerstein, "Men who divorce undergo less psychological change than women in the wake of divorce. The male social roles tend to be defined by employment, whereas women tend to separate work and family roles. After divorce, a man's job, status, and contacts at work are relatively unchanged, so a major part of his life remains stable. Many women are completely different people ten years after divorce. Not so the men" (42).

R. Weiss (1975) believes that a person goes through two distinct phases in establishing a new identity: transition and recovery. The transition period begins with the separation and is characterized by separation distress and then loneliness. In its later stages, most people begin functioning in an orderly way again, although they still may experience periods of upset and turmoil. The transition period generally ends within the first year. During this time, individuals have already begun making decisions that provide the framework for new selves. They have entered the role of single parent or absent parent, have found a new place to live, have made important career and financial decisions, and have begun to date. Their lives are taking shape.

THE CHILD'S VIEWPOINT

One of the most unique, complex, and ambiguous relationships in contemporary America is that between ex-spouses with children. P. Bohannon (1971) points out that divorce does not end a relationship; it creates ex-husbands and ex-wives. If children are involved, divorce is only the beginning of new and often complicated relationships between former spouses (Furstenberg and Nord, 1985: 893–904).

According to J. Pearson and N. Thoennes (1984), many divorced parents feel overwhelmed and find it difficult to assess what their children are experiencing. In the words of one mother: "I didn't notice any immediate changes (in the children) but I might have been too busy trying to be competent and not fall apart myself, so I might not have noticed" (11:4). Around 20 percent of the parents in the study reported that their child seemed angry with at least one of the parents because of the divorce. Interviews with the children confirmed their anger with parents. The anger grew directly out of the divorce experience.

Loyalty conflicts are another key concern of children. A number of children indicated that they worried about having to take sides with one parent, putting them directly in the middle of the divorce. About 30 percent of the parents indicated the child's unwillingness to discuss the divorce. Interviews with children confirmed that for many the primary coping mechanism was avoidance. In the words of several children: "I don't think about it. That's how I handle problems"; "I don't think about them and they go away."

Most children have reconciliation fantasies and many blame the divorce on their own failures or limitations. Divorce changes how children think about and relate to parents. Children have difficulty deciding where they belong and articulating what their problems are and what can be done to alleviate them. Most professionals believe that parents must communicate the decision and the reasons for divorce and stress that the divorce is not the child's fault.

On a positive note, divorce does not necessarily have to have a deleterious effect on a child's growth and development. Ideally, a warm loving intact nuclear family is best, but when that is not possible appropriately managed divorce situations can be an alternative. Divorce covers many phases in the family's life: the predivorce family life, separation(s), a final separation, the legal divorce, the early post-divorce and the later post-divorce stages. The formation of stepfamilies intertwines at various times after the divorce.

EFFECTS OF DIVORCE ON CHILDREN

There is a growing body of literature that addresses children's response to parental divorce and remarriage. The studies, that follow, indicate that it is not equally disturbing for all children and that the child's response depends on their age and sex.

In California, Judith Wallerstein's (1989) team reported preliminary findings on a 10-year follow-up study of children from divorced families intended to determine which emotional issue was heightened at each development stage. This study looked at the effects of divorce on preschool, school age, and adolescent children.

Preschoolers

The youngest children at the time of the divorce regress at home and in nursery school during the first 18 months. They display a range of emotional disorders and serious learning problems, with boys being more severely affected than girls. These problems can be attributed to the child's sensitivity to change in the parents. Mother becomes more anxious and less available. Because the mother usually has custody, the child senses the loss of the father and panics at the idea that a parent is gone. This leads to the fear that the mother might leave as well, heightening the child's separation anxieties.

School-aged Children

Children ages 6–11 seem to cope the best. Their heightened sense of loss and sadness is significant but less extensive than that of the other age groups.

Psychiatrist J. Visher (1990), who works with many stepfamilies, questions the concept that a child's values are firmly established by age five or six. By showing the school-aged child what may be gained by change, rather than having a totally negative view of divorce, parents can increase the likelihood for change to be less debilitating. Moreover, when parents help the child work on the change, he or she will be more apt to live with these changes, with much less stress.

Adolescents

According to D. McLoughlin and R. Whitfield (1984) family life before separation seems to have an impact on how adolescents respond to their parents' divorce. In their study, 76 percent of the adolescents reported that there had been conflict in the marriage before separation. Sixty percent of the conflict was verbal, but 38 percent was both verbal and physical. In spite of the reported conflict, almost half of this group were surprised that their parents split up. They had come to view conflict as a normal part of marital life (McLoughlin and Whitfield, 1984).

According to B. Strong and C. DeVault (1979), adolescents usually experience immense turmoil but will protect themselves by separating themselves from the conflict. They may appear outwardly cool and detached. Unlike younger children, they rarely blame themselves, and are more likely to be angry with both parents, who they feel have upset their lives.

Also, adolescents often react dramatically to divorce because this is the period in their lives that is usually the most difficult in terms of change for them. The adolescent is groping, questioning, and evaluating the values that will guide him or her in life, and the problems of divorce only add to the confusion of the adolescent (Ackerman, 1958). Adolescence is the beginning of the struggle to resolve identification with two parents and to build from this identification a personal identity (N. Ackerman, 1958). If parents are unable to provide stability in the adolescent child's environment then the adolescent's instability is augmented (D. Curran, 1985).

One significant gender difference, according to E. Visher (1991), is in girls' heightened need for the father. Daughters from divorced homes often feel compelled to contact their fathers and share their closest feelings with them. This is especially the case when the child and the parent have had little contact over the years. The child's attempts at intimacy can be quite anxiety-provoking for the father, who may wonder why the child is only now willingly opening herself up.

Older Children

Long-range coping is often harder for children who are older at the time of divorce because they retain so many memories of their parents' struggles. Also, because they have lived for a longer period in an intact family, their sense of loss may be more profound. These children poignantly describe their sadness at recalling the fights and recriminations. For this group as well as for the adolescents, the divorce remains a central aspect of their lives and continues to evoke strong feelings.

Recent studies by individual child therapists following children and their families at different stages in their lives and during the divorce process reflect Wallerstein's findings. However, the resilience of children of all age groups, and how they manage to organize their lives around the difficulties that occur from divorce, is impressive.

REORGANIZATION

Social researchers have found that the remarriage family lacks the shared family experience, the symbols, and the rituals that help to maintain the psychic boundaries of the first marriage family. Interpersonal communication in the remarriage family, therefore, poses adaptation problems because there is no adequate role model like that the earlier nuclear family provided. Lacking symbols or model, each family is, consequently, left to devise its own solutions and rules in its relationships. We are a product of our family environment, and unless we stop, rethink, and readjust how we function in the new family, we are destined to make the same mistakes (Ackerman, 1958; Einstein, 1982).

Children's attitudes toward their fathers and the effects of the father's leaving has recently started to be studied as part of the divorce process. The changing and important role of fathers and how they can remain attached to their children even if their children don't live with them, is a question researchers are only now beginning to examine.

Preparing children for a new marriage more often than not isn't handled well. Children feel like unwanted baggage traveling from one parent's home to the other. Shuttling from their mother's house to the father's house, a set of clothes in one place and a different set in the other. The sleeping arrangements at each of the houses is different. Before the marriage perhaps the stepmother/father often do not consider the children an integral part of their future life. If a parent or stepparent did not pay too much attention to the child before the remarriage the tendency is to follow the same pattern or even resent the child. The painful fact is that stepfamily life is fragile (C. Jewett, 1982).

Children, according to Visher and Visher (1979), often have difficulty figuring out where they belong. If parents acknowledge children's fears regarding family reorganization, then they can be better prepared to attend to their needs. Concerns need to be expressed and feelings accepted, so that a clearer delineation of new roles can be successfully negotiated.

According to P. Bohannan and R. Erickson (1978), roles and boundaries in the new family have to be clearly spelled out as earlier roles from the former family are relinquished and/or redefined. Uncertainty breeds power struggles and manipulations. If there is to be a change of caretaker, for example, the child who is appropriately prepared for the change is given a chance to anticipate where she or he will live and who will keep her or him safe. Any of these experiences of sharing can help children complete their understanding of the changes occurring in their lives so that they can move on to new relationships with their self-esteem intact while continuing to care deeply about the lost family member.

Healthy mourning, according to A. Freud (1946), is achieved when a person accepts the changes in his or her external life, makes corresponding changes in this internal life, and finally makes the reorientation necessary to be able to feel attachment again. In the mourning process, after an acute period of denial, there usually comes guilt and anger, followed by despair or depression (Visher and Visher, 1979). It is important that parents anticipate this process in their children and that they allow grieving to occur in an environment that is supportive.

Remarriage is the last phase of the disintegration of the divorce. This step marks the beginning of a new phase in the lives of the stepfamilies' members.

THE FORMATION OF A NEW FAMILY

Romantics say love is better the second time around. When applied to remarriage, this idyllic notion of songs and movies fails to mention the "leftovers" from former family relationships: children, former spouses, child support and alimony, anger, guilt, jealousy, and fear (Einstein, 1982).

Remarriage is considerably different from first marriage in many ways. First, the new partners get to know each other during a time of significant changes in life relationships, confusion, guilt, stress, and mixed feelings about the past (Keshet, 1980). While they have great hope that they will not repeat past mistakes, they also fear the recurrence of the hurts they experienced in their previous marriage (McGoldrick and Carter, 1980). Effective communication skills are therefore especially important to the success of the remarried couple. Not only is it important for the new couple to be aware of communication problems between the two of them but, as mentioned earlier, if there are children from the first marriage, there are children that need to be considered. The ideal situation would be if stepparents could perfect their interpersonal skills with the children before the marriage with the children's biological parent. Sometimes a long courtship is advocated before the remarriage. The time before the marriage allows children to get to know the man/woman their mother/father is to marry. This period allows children to move into the relationship at a slow and stable pace. This time also allows the stepparent to get to know the children and create a history from singlehood to remarriage with adequate time for everyone to adjust to the new situation.

A tension may exist because of differences between the individual's need for maintaining a sense of personal identity and the need for the couple to maintain stability (Askham, 1976). Conflict is natural in intimate relationships. That is the paradox of love: the more intimate a couple becomes, the more likely they are to have differences. If this is understood, then the meaning of conflict changes for conflict will not necessarily represent a crisis in the relationship. David and Vera Mace (1979), prominent marriage counselors, observed that on the day of marriage, people have three kinds of raw material with which to work:

1. Things they have in common; the things they both like.

2. Ways in which they are different; these differences are complementary.

3. Differences between them that are seemingly irreconcilable.

How a couple addresses the differences between them will affect relationship satisfaction. As suggested, the period between dating and remarriage is the time to sort out feelings and weigh reactions under a variety of circumstances. A couple should determine when they will be stepping on each other's toes in questions of discipline, authority, money, relations with the other natural parent, modesty within the home, and social habits. It takes time to work through these issues, and it's best done *before* the final commitment. This period allows the couple to learn about the issues that are a potential source of conflict, and, how to deal effectively with these issues (H. Morton, 1977).

C. Chilman (1983) maintains blended families are significantly different from first-marriage nuclear families. Visher and Visher (1979) identify the following five characteristics that distinguish the blended from the intact family:

1. In blended families almost all members have lost an important primary relationship. The children may mourn the loss of their parent or parents, and the spouses the loss of their former mates. Because of this perceived loss, anger and hostility may be displaced onto the new stepparent.

2. One biological parent lives outside the current family. He or she may either support or interfere with the new family. Power struggles often occur between the absent parent and the mother or father which can lead to jealousy between the absent parent and the stepparent.

3. The relationship between a parent and his or her children predates the relationship between the new partners. Children have often spent considerable time and have grown accustomed to living in a single-family structure. A new husband or wife may be regarded as an intruder in the children's special relationship with their parent. A new stepparent may, therefore, find that he or she must compete with the children for a spouse's attention. The stepparent may even be excluded from the parent-child system.

4. Stepparent roles are ill-defined. No one quite knows what he or she is supposed to *do* as a stepparent. Most stepparents try role after role until they find one that fits.

5. Many children in blended families are also members of the noncustodial parent's household, living in one household and visiting the other. Each

home may have differing rules and expectations. When conflict arises, children may try to play one household against the other.

Researchers say it often takes from four to seven years for a new stepfamily to become stable, to work out a sense of "we." It starts with the fantasy "Oh, it's going to better the second time around. I'm going to be a better parent." Then come the chaos, confusion, and craziness stages, when the parent thinks he or she can't stand it. That's when many people give up, and marriages collapse. If one can get over that hump, the family begins to resolve problems and understands what it can and cannot be (J. Bernard, 1956; Hunt, 1966; N. Jones, 1977; Visher and Visher, 1979). Mutual acceptance, tolerance, and developing new family traditions are important strategies for bringing family members closer together.

Mutual acceptance means people accepting each other as they are, not as they would like each other to be. This is important at all the stages in transition—from the separation to remarriage. Marrying for the first time or remarrying with the idyllic notion that an insensitive partner will somehow magically become sensitive, for example, is an invitation to disappointment and divorce (Strong and DeVault, 1979).

There are other conflicts with stepchildren who have experienced parental loss through divorce. They are frequently hesitant to invest their feelings in a new person for fear of reexperiencing the pain. The parent who can be tolerant of the child's feelings and not insist on his or her liking the stepparent is off to a good beginning. The parent who can convey the attitude, "I know it takes time and you don't like your stepparent yet" is giving the child room to develop positive feelings. The parent who verbalizes that this new spouse does not have to displace the absent parent is recognizing the child's concern and need to hold back. The parent needs to understand just what message his or her child is saying (D. Cantor and E. Drake, 1983).

C. Jewett (1982) devised a way to help the child understand that he or she can have a parent-child relationship with more than one parent or set of parents. One helpful technique is what she calls the "candle ritual." As the child lights a new candle for each caretaker in his or her life, he or she can see vividly that the love and warmth once felt with earlier caretakers does not have to be "blown out" as new bonds are established, and as new candles are lit. The ceremony helps even the youngest children understand that new family constellations do not demand the death of old relationships.

THE PROBLEMS OF STEREOTYPES

Legally the prefix *step-* refers to a relationship by marriage rather than by biology. It comes from the Anglo-Saxon *astepan*, "to deprive." From this came stepchild, "a bereaved child or orphan." Part of the stepfamily's difficulty lies in this historical meaning. And when the word is used derisively, it reflects the stepfamily's second-rate status.

The term "step" carries such a negative feeling that sociologist Bernard (1956) avoided using the terms "stepchild," "stepmother," and "stepfather" in her classic study of remarriage, referring to them as smear words.

The "wicked stepmother" is a prominent character in many folk and popular fairy tales (for example, *Cinderella, Hansel and Gretel, Snow White*). Children in the United States are exposed very early to fairy tales; "wicked stepmother" tales, in fact, have always been favorites. These fairy tales often help perpetuate negative connotations about stepfamily members. Stepmothers, for example, often are afraid to discipline stepchildren or to engage in any meaningful interactions that might provoke conflict for fear of confirming their wickedness.

When a stereotype is negative, such as that of the "wicked stepmother," the stereotyped individuals may become the object of prejudice (N. Ehrlich, 1973; D. Schneider, et al., 1979). Prejudgments serve to increase social distance, and, therefore, maintain prejudices (M. Snyder and W. Swann, 1978). In the case of the stepmother, people may interpret a stepmother's behavior as negative, though it may not be, simply because negative behavior *fits* the image of the "wicked stepmother," thus maintaining the prejudice and stereotype.

Anecdotal evidence suggests that reading or hearing fairy tales colors children's images of stepmothers and stepfathers (Smith, 1953). Folklore about the step relationship is widespread. According to W. Smith, there are 345 variations of the Cinderella folk tale alone, and folk tales about step relationships are found in the cultural-historical lore in virtually every part of the globe.

Should the roles be reversed, with the family encompassing a stepfather and natural mother, a pattern of wicked stepfather may emerge, but that is not as likely. Generally, the stepfather is not asked to become involved with the stepchildren the same way as the stepmother. Consequently, his role as stepfather does not come under the critical scrutiny that faces the stepmother's position.

STEREOTYPING OF THE FAMILY

One study of stepfamily stereotyping designed to determine whether individuals perceive more negatively the concepts of "stepmother" and "stepfather" than they do "mother" and "father" (L. Ganong and Coleman, 1983) show there is abundant evidence for negatively stereotyping the stepfamily.

Within the family, negative stereotyping affects how the group members perceive and value themselves. They may interpret each others' behavior and subsequent interactions with each other, especially during the early phases of step family development, in the same prejudicial stereotypical way. For example, if children whose parents remarry expect their stepparent to be "wicked" and "cruel" the children may act in ways that will, in fact, elicit negative behavior from their stepparent. In such an instance, adjustment to family life becomes more difficult.

There is some evidence that children, too, are stereotyped on the basis of family structure. J. Santrock and R. Tracy (1978) found that teachers' perceptions of children varied according to family structure. After viewing identical videotapes of children playing, teachers who believed they were viewing a child from a divorced single-parent household rated the child as less happy, less emotionally well adjusted, and less able to cope with stress than a child whom they believed was from an intact nuclear home. A similar study of social workers, teachers, and lay persons also found that stereotypes of boys in single-parent households were more negative than stereotypes of boys believed to be in nuclear families (P. Fry and Addington, 1984).

THE REMARRIED DYAD

The formal and legal structure of marriage makes the male dominant, but the reality of marriage may be quite different. Sociologist J. Bernard (1972) made an important distinction between authority and power in marriage. Authority is based in law but power is based in personality. A strong, dominant woman is likely to exercise power over a weak, passive man simply by force of her personality and temperament. Accordingly, Bernard feels both men and women exercise power over the other and it is widely distributed in both sexes.

THE STEPMOTHER

Many of the women writing in Alice Neufeld's *Women and Stepfamilies* (1988) describe the trauma caused by trying to make the stepfamily an instant, traditional family. Women speak in voices laced with anger, bitterness, and unacknowledged hurt. A few women depict men as explicitly rejecting involvement because their notions of masculinity encourage authoritarian roles or distancing behaviors.

Even for women with the desire, opportunity, and skills to step out of their situation to reflect on it, the emotional urgency of negotiating the complexities of lives in stepfamilies can supersede intellectual understanding and feminine consciousness (Maglin and Schniedewind, 1988). What she knows and what she feels are at odds. Thus, insight—or any kind of reflective stance—while meaningful and clarifying, still may not match the power of the emotional experience.

The stepmother's relationship to her stepchildren is another puzzle. How does she maintain a relationship with the stepchild and with her own biological children without worrying about favoritism? The stepmother, in many cases, is haunted simultaneously by the images of the wicked stepmother and the perfect (biological) mother. We have learned that a woman is the nurturer, the emotional linchpin for family members, and that subsequently she has the primary responsibility for meeting others' needs. Many women try to succeed in stepfamilies by attempting to live up to these expectations. While some women have found this effort workable, most have found it painful or self-defeating.

Adapting to the role of stepmother is especially difficult because women know the reactions to things from their own children and not from their stepchildren. For children who live with their biological parent, the arrival of a stepparent (and children) may be regarded as an intrusion. Frequent complaints from stepmothers concern, among other things, how nasty children can be, indifferent husbands, and their own feelings of inadequacy. They want emotional support to help assuage these feelings of anger and self-doubt.

Being a stepmother is sometimes having all the responsibilities and none of the privileges of motherhood. The stepmother is faced with many troubling times especially at holidays. "On Mother's Day I made dinner for my stepchildren and then their natural mother picked them up to go for dessert," notes one stepmother. A stepmother raising someone else's child may get more than she bargained for. Being a stepmother to a child who doesn't accept you, or whose natural mother hates you, can be emotionally destructive. A stepmother can become very insecure with feelings that everyone is against her (A. Neufeld, 1988).

H. Deutsch (1973) explains the difficulties in the step relationship in the following manner. When the father remarries, the child loses an exclusive relationship with him that is often established after the break-up of the family. After the remarriage, the child must share the father with the stepmother. Although the father was originally shared with the natural mother, the prior positive nurturing of the mother toward the child and child's wish to maintain this relationship led to a positive identification with the mother, thus facilitating sharing the father. Because this "store" of love and nurturing is absent when the stepmother comes on the scene, the child has greater difficulty sharing the parent with the stepparent. Moreover, the sexual nature of the relationship between the father and the new wife stirs up "hate impulses" of children of both sexes against the stepmother. The child in the step situation has greater difficulty resolving the Oedipal conflict than when the natural mother is present. The natural mother continues to be "good" and is idealized, while the stepmother is cast in the role of the "bad" mother and is vilified. These unconscious phenomena feed the negative symbols and images of the "wicked stepmother" even when the behavior of the stepmother is not consistent with that image. Both the concepts of unresolved Oedipal conflicts and splitting of good and bad images have been useful to therapists in work with children in the remarried family.

Because negative emotions make us feel uncomfortable, many stepmothers come to believe that they are doing something bad or evil, and therefore, they do not feel good about themselves. If women are able to face the issues they will have to deal with in the stepfamily, they will enhance their ability to handle them effectively (J. Polenz, 1975).

Most of the women in Wallerstein's study (1979) brought children into the new marriage and were working outside the house. Because they did not want to burden their new husbands with problems, in a good percentage of these marriages these women readily accepted responsibility for caring for the home and family.

In their work with stepmothers Visher and Visher (1979) found nine common problem areas most stepmothers must face in relation to their role:

1. Expectation of instant love for and from stepchildren.

2. Tendency of stepmothers to rush in and come on too strong.

3. Difficulty in handling rejection from stepchildren.

4. Difficulties with the wicked stepmother myth.

5. Unsuccessful attempts to keep everybody happy.

6. Inability to achieve close family unity.

7. Anger, jealousy, and competition for love and affection from spouse.

8. Anger at ex-spouses.

9. Guilt generated by all of the above.

What can be done? For the wife, the issues in stepparenting are complex. To begin to make a success of this new role, women need to acknowledge the fact that stepparenting is a difficult task. Patience and sanity will be tested repeatedly. Overnight successes are rarely found. A stepmother should not demand instant love from stepchildren. She must recognize that love takes time to develop.

Many stepmothers start their second or subsequent marriage with the best of intentions. They are going to repair, undo, mitigate *all* the mistakes of her stepchildren's past. Everything is going to be perfect and the first thing she starts perfecting is the kids. The kids resist being perfected. They want to be accepted.

B. Carter (1989), a therapist at the Family Institute of Westchester, suggests individuals focus on the system that now exists—that of the father and his children. It is *that* system which should be the area of concentration, not having the stepmother fight her way into an already existing system. The father should be helped to clearly express the following message: "This is my wife. You will be courteous to her or you will answer to me." He should also explain to his children that he will also be doing things with his new spouse— activities that the couple will do alone.

Once the father's message has been clearly acted upon, time will allow the family to move on to stage two. It is during stage two that a relationship can be developed between the stepmother and the stepchildren. However, if the stepmother is made the heavy in stage one, the family may get caught up in stage one, never moving on to stage two: the new role of adult/friend.

THE STEPFATHER'S ROLE

The pre-divorce relationship between father and children is not necessarily a predictor of the post-divorce relationship. Attentive fathers before divorce can become distant, or, fortunately, closer. Fathers who have left the development of their children to the mother often become interested and involved, taking great pride in the newly active parental role. The noncustodial father remains a significant psychological presence regardless of his level of participation in the child's lives. It is rare for a stepfather to substitute for a father, although this tends to happen when the child is young at the time of the divorce and the stepfather is on the scene immediately. Children *need* to have a positive image of their parent in order to develop a strong self-esteem and will protect the image of the natural father even if he has been abusing or negligent (Ricci, 1980; Jewett, 1982; Wallerstein and Blakeslee, 1989).

Stepfathers seem to achieve better relations with their stepchildren than do stepmothers. L. Duberman (1973) studied 88 stepfamilies in which each adult in the family was interviewed and given an opportunity to rate familial relationships and to evaluate the closeness of the family. Neither sex nor age of stepchildren influenced stepfather relationships, but stepmothers had better relationships with stepchildren under the age of 13 than with teenaged stepchildren.

Although it may be assumed that stepfathers were as numerous as stepmothers, the focus of attention on the stepmother may be explained in terms of expected social roles. Families were organized along patriarchal lines of male domination, but men were out of the home for long periods of time in the role of provider. Meanwhile, women were the sole authority figures in the care of the home and of the children.

P. Bohannon and Erickson (1978) reported research that found that children in stepfather households got along as well with their stepfathers as children in natural households got along with their natural fathers. However, natural fathers rated their children as significantly happier than the stepfathers rated their stepchildren, and natural fathers rated themselves as significantly better fathers than the stepfathers rated themselves. Thus, stepfathers viewed themselves and their stepchildren as less successful and happy than did natural fathers, even though the stepchildren and their mothers did not feel that way.

One of the major differences between the stepmother's role and the stepfather's role is that, while the stepmother tends to fight actively for her place in the family, the stepfather tends to withdraw (Schulman, 1981). As a result, the relationship between a stepfather and his stepchildren tends to remain underdeveloped rather than negative. The stepfather's role in the family is poorly articulated—particulary in relation to discipline. In fact, discipline seems to create a great deal of difficulty for a stepfather, especially when each stepparent has unique methods of disciplining children. One father was very frustrated about his new stepdaughter, who was brought up in a household where there were very few rules and regulations about eating on time, staying out late, and so on. Major conflicts were created because his children had many restrictions, which created problems not only for the parents but for the stepsiblings.

Visher and Visher (1979) in their work with stepfathers indicate that seven general psychological tasks are faced by stepfathers in relation to their role:

1. Joining a functioning group and establishing a place for himself. (This is the reverse of the situation faced by the woman who marries a man who has custody of his children.)

2. Working out rules regarding family behavior.

3. Handling unrealistic expectations both on his part and on the part of the new family.

4. Dealing with feelings of guilt about his previous family.

5. Money.

6. Adoption, naming, and inheritance questions with reference to his stepchildren.

7. Sexuality in the stepfamily.

For the stepfather, everything wrong is bound to be intensified, especially when he has not had much experience raising a biological child. He may find out the hard way that he and his children have no connection to the stepmother or her children.

Everyone will need a good sense of humor and understanding if the family unit is to work. For example take the businessman who exclaimed, "I run a department of sixty people, worth upwards of 60 million dollars, and everything is pretty orderly. Then I go home and have to face this awful child who looks at me with such disdain that I wonder if this marriage wasn't a mistake. You would think that my wife would talk some sense into that spoiled kid of hers."

GENDER PROBLEMS UNIQUE TO THE STEPCHILD

In a recent study of remarried couples, L.K. White and A. Booth (1985) specifically identified the presence of stepchildren in the home as a principal source of strain in second unions. They report that couples in complex households, especially those in which both partners are remarried and have children, are more likely to say that they should not have gotten married. Apparently, having stepchildren in the home diminishes the satisfactions of family life.

For the majority of children their world has been turned upside down. The familiar "givens" are no longer present. An oldest child may no longer be the oldest child or youngest child the youngest. An only child may suddenly have two or three siblings; the mother or father now needs to give time and attention to three or four children rather than to one child.

For older children the displacement and confusion can be even greater. Imagine a teenage boy who has been the "man of the house" for several years suddenly being asked to relinquish this status to a stranger. No longer does the adolescent have the responsibility for cleaning the car, washing the windows, or carrying the heavy loads for his mother. Perhaps he complained bitterly about the tasks at the time, but he did have a recognized status in the home, which is now eliminated.

Or take the situation of a 16-year-old girl who did the housework and cooking for her father and younger brother for several years. Her father is planning to remarry a woman with strong motivation to be a super wife and mother, and is preparing for her new stepfamily. The stepmother-to-be is full of the very best of intentions, but the daughter who has been running the household feels upstaged, replaced and crowded into a very small corner (Wallerstein, 1989).

The diversity provided by having a membership in two households can eventually give children in remarried families additional role models and a wider variety of experiences from which to learn and grow. Many children, however, do not perceive the back-and-forth trek from one household to another in a positive light. They feel helpless and out of control. They seem to be faced with constant change which feels like complete "culture shock."

The sets of rules in the two homes may be quite different. Unless the children have some help in recognizing that there are many different acceptable patterns of living rather than a "right" and a "wrong" way, they may constantly battle at least one pattern. Without this mindset they can cut themselves off from one parent as well as from a richness of experience that is available to them (Ricci, 1980).

Some of the studies that have investigated the effects of remarriage on children have suggested that remarriage inflicts some degree of trauma on all children, regardless of gender. There are some differences, though. Stepsisters generally have a more difficult time with stepbrothers than stepbrothers do with stepsisters. Girls whose divorced mothers remarry may be particularly at risk, however, and young boys positively reacted to the entry of stepfather into the home, rapidly attaching themselves to him. Boys also benefit from having a stepfather more than girls. This could be part of the overall negative stress that girls experience in transition (Wallerstein and Kelly, 1980; C. Bowerman and D. Irish, 1962; C. Bitterman, 1968). Similarly, W. Clingempeel, E. Brand, and R. Ievoli (1984) found that girls in stepmother families did better the longer they lived in the remarried home. E. Heatherington, M. Cox, and R. Cox (1985) compared divorced families where the mothers had remarried with those where she had not, and with families that were not divorced. They found that boys showed more long-term problems when their mothers divorced and did not remarry, whereas girls showed more problems when their mothers remarried. However, improvement was found for the girls in later stages of remarriage over girls in the early stage, though stepdaughters continued to see themselves, and be seen by their stepfathers, as having more problems than girls in nondivorced families.

Most of the studies point out the life stresses in stepfamilies. Girls in stepfamilies reported more negative stress than either girls in nuclear families, or boys in stepfamilies. While girls in stepfamilies report more stress in their lives, their own self-concept and intellectual functioning does not seem to suffer. However, both mothers and stepfathers report that these girls exhibit more behavioral problems than do girls in nuclear families. It seems that girls in stepfamilies respond to the added stress by acting out and misbehaving, rather than feeling bad about themselves. The same is true for boys who seem to experience less negative stress than girls, but also act out and misbehave.

For the most part, the stepmother-stepdaughter relationship seems to be the most difficult of all step-relationships. This is particularly true when the daughter is an adolescent. Usually this is true because a girl's emotional development is more complicated than a boy's, in that a girl's feelings toward her mother are more intense than a boy's. The main problem seems to be that little girls want to be "Daddy's girl." Little boys outgrow the stage of wanting to be "Mama's boy" and being to emulate their fathers very early in development. The "Daddy's girl" syndrome lasts well into adolescence (Thompson, 1966).

Wallerstein's (1989) team reported on gender differences in their 10 year follow-up study of children from divorced families.

1. Boys from divorced families experience an intense, rising need for their fathers during adolescence—even if the divorce occurred ten years earlier. Before that time fathers were less important in their sons' lives.

2. Many of the girls in the study had problems with identification at adolescence. They were afraid to identify with a rejected mother, but they still wanted to be like her. They loved their mother but were afraid they too would be rejected. If she loved and admired her mother would she be cast away also?

3. In some cases a young woman may be fearful of surpassing her mother, of doing better in the world of love and marriage. She might have taken on many of the decisions and responsibilities for her mother, after the divorce, and it is difficult to leave that role and find her own identity. The fear of success had its roots in this young women's identification with her mother, she did not want to leave her mother behind by being better than her.

4. There was no conclusive evidence that one sex feels more or less pain, but girls were more inclined to readily express their feelings. The girls who denied their loss and pain experienced the "sleeper effect" in later years. Those repressed feelings were only placed on hold.

5. Boys were more apt to "shut out" their feelings to avoid the hurt and pain. These feelings create so much psychic energy that they had no energy to deal successfully with future relationships.

6. A whole group of young women in Wallerstein's study were attracted to older men. This was to avoid the emotional complications that they felt they would have with younger men.

Wallerstein's intent "was not to argue against divorce but rather to raise the consciousness of the community about the long-term effects of divorce on children. . . . The first step in solving a problem is to acknowledge it. Only then can we get at the complex tasks that lie ahead" (319).

Of utmost importance is that the stepchild must realize that while certain behaviors might be unacceptable, the child *is* important. This can be accomplished by explaining "I like you, but not some of the things you do." Deciding what is intolerable and what can be acceptable is important because in the long run, the more acceptance there is in the stepfamily, the more successful it can be (Visher and Visher, 1979).

Visher and Visher (1979) suggest viewing the stepfamily as a family in transition, almost like an immigrant family adjusting to a new culture. They outline the seven problems arising from the complexity of stepfamily characteristics:

1. There is a biological parent outside of the stepfamily unit and a same-sexed adult in the household.

2. Most children in stepfamilies hold membership in two households.

3. The role definition for stepparents is ill-defined.

4. The fact that "blended" families come together from diverse historical backgrounds accentuates the need for tolerance of differences.

5. Step-relationships are new and untested and not a "given" as they are in intact families.

6. The children in stepfamilies have at least one extra set of grandparents.

7. Stepfamily financial arrangements take on many emotional overtones.

Conflict in any remarried family requires a tremendous amount of sensitivity to the complexities of the newly formed family structure. Most studies have shown that stepfamilies have more crises than other families, and each crisis is more disruptive and dangerous to the relationship. The structure is more complex, the cast of characters includes at least a few unwilling members and perhaps unstable members as well, and there is usually less commitment to keeping things structurally stable. The financial complexity of remarried families can be so complicated as to lead to a major crisis. There can be rich kids and poor kids in the same household, and this can influence behavior, expectations and relationships. There are usually discrepancies in financial support: one father pays child support and another doesn't. Or one child can be lavishly subsidized by an absent father or a trust fund while the other stepchildren have none of those advantages.

A stepfamily departs from its forerunner, the "biological family," in several ways. Stepfamilies emerge through losses that are far from the minds of first-marrieds. It gives instant children to someone and a new parent role to kids who are probably desperate to keep those they've already got (Ackerman, 1958).

A very important consideration is where everyone lives and how. Most of the time a new house or apartment gets all family members off to a better start than staying put in one partner's place. A fresh space is "neutral" territory, free from memories that can keep children—and adults—living in the past. Planning the new home with the children gives a sense of togetherness. If a family must stay in one partner's home, redecoration can facilitate familial cohesiveness.

Each partner can also start to think about rules of the house. Will meals be scheduled or impromptu? Will the kids do chores? If so, what kind, how often, and what are the consequences of not doing them? It makes it easier to have a household work if everyone knows what they are responsible for (Hunt, 1977).

For even the best-prepared couples, the first year as a stepfamily will bring surprises, even shocks. Roles will be reevaluated, resolutions reformed and space shifted. Things will be chaotic. The family is called upon to function as if they had lived together for years, with all the things families develop over the years: discipline, traditions, and just living. It helps everyone to know that chaos is normal, not an indicator that something is wrong with the family or that the marriage isn't going to work.

Those who make the stepfamily a success are generally those who don't expect a "normal" family with Mom, Dad and kids gathered happily around the fireplace. Opening our minds to new definitions and structures of family can help build a reasonable new life for everyone involved. There's plenty of room for love and happiness in the stepfamily if one can accept it for what it is. The blending of different families can be a growing, exciting and challenging experience which can create marvelous relationships with new people (E. Einstein, 1982).

REFERENCES

Ackerman, N. 1958. *The Psychodynamics of Family Life*. New York: Basic Books.

Askham, J. 1976. Identity and stability within the marriage relationship. *Journal of Marriage and Family* 38: 535–547.

Bernard, J. 1956. *Remarriage*. New York: Dryden Press.

Bitterman, C. 1968. The multimarriage family. *Social Casework* 49: 218–221.

Bohannan, P. 1971. *Divorce and After*. New York: Doubleday.

Bohannan, P., and R. Erickson. 1978. Stepping in. *Psychology Today*, January.

Bowerman, C., and D. Irish. 1962. Some relationships of stepchildren and their parents. *Marriage and Family Living* 24: 113–121.

Cantor, D., and E. A. Drake. 1983. *Divorced Parents and Their Children*. New York: Springer Publishing Co.

Cherlin, A. J. 1981. *Marriage, Divorce, Remarriage*. Cambridge, MA: Harvard University Press.

Chilman, C. 1983. Parental satisfactions, concerns and goals for their children. *Family Relations* 29: 339–345.

Clingempeel, W., E. Brand, and R. Ievoli. 1986. Stepparent-stepchild relationships in stepmother and stepfather families: A multimethod study. *Family Relations* 33: 465–473.

Curran, D. 1985. *Stress and the Healthy Family*. Minneapolis, MN: Wilson Press.

Deutsch, H. 1973. *The psychology of women: Women: Motherhood; A Psychoanalytic Interpretation*. New York: Bantam.

Duberman, L. 1973. Step-kin relationship. *Journal of Marriage and the Family* 35: 283–292.

Ehrlich, N. J. 1973. *The social psychology of prejudice*. New York: Wiley.

Einstein, E. 1982. *The Stepfamily*. Boston: Shambhala Publications.

Freud, A. 1946. *The Ego and the Mechanisms of Defense*. New York: International Universities Press.

Fry, P. S., and J. Addington. 1984. Professionals' negative expectations of boys from father-headed single parent families: Implications for the training of child-care professionals. *British Journal of Development Psychology* 2: 337–346.

Furstenberg, F. Jr., F. Frank, and G. S. Spanier. 1985. *Recycling the Family: Remarriage after Divorce*. Beverly Hills, CA: Sage Publications.

Furstenberg, F. Jr., and C. Nord. 1985. Parenting apart: Patterns of childbearing after marital disruption. *Journal of Marriage and the Family* 47 (4): 898–904.

Galvin, K., and P. Cooper. 1990. Development of involuntary relationships, the stepparent-stepchild relationship. Paper presented at the International Communication Association Convention, Dublin, Ireland.

Ganong, L., and Coleman. 1983. Stepparent: A pejorative term? *Psychological Reports* 52: 919–922.

Glenn, N., and K. Kramer. 1985. The psychological well-being of adult children of divorce. *Journal of Marriage and the Family* 47 (4): 905–912.

Hauser, J. 1988. Divorce mediation: A growing field? *The Arbitration Journal* 43: 15–22.

Heatherington, E., M. Cox, and R. Cox. 1985. Long-term effects of divorce and remarriage on the adjustment of children. *This Journal* 24: 518–530.

Hunt, Morton. 1966. *The World of the Formerly Married*. New York: McGraw-Hill.

————. 1977. *The Divorce Experience*. New York: McGraw-Hill.

Jewett, C. 1982. *Helping Children Cope with Separation and Loss*. Harvard, MA: The Harvard Common Press.

Jones, N. 1977. The impact of divorce on children. *Consultations Courts Review* 15 (2).

Jones, E. E., A. Farina, A. H. Hastorf, H. Markus, D. T. Miller, R. A. Scott, and R. French. 1984. *Social Stigma: The Psychology of Marked Relationships*. New York: Freemen.

Kalter, N. 1977. Children of divorce in an outpatient psychiatric population. *American Journal of Orthopsychiatry* 47: 40–51.

Keshet, J. 1980. From separation to stepfamily. *Journal of Family Issues* 4: 517–532.

Mace, D., and V. Mace. 1979. *How to Have a Happy Marriage*. Nashville, TN: Abingdon Press.

Maglin A., and N. Schniedewind. 1988. Bauer and Schniedewind, eds., *Women and Stepfamilies*. Philadelphia, PA: Temple University Press.

McLoughlin, D., and R. Whitfield. 1984. Adolescents and their experience of parental divorce. *Journal of Adolescence* 7: 155–170.

McGoldrick, M., and E. Carter. 1980. The family life cycle. In F. Walsh, ed., *Normal Family Processes*. New York: Guilford Press.

Neufeld, A. 1988. M. Bauer and Schniedewind, eds., *Women and Stepfamilies*. Philadelphia, PA: Temple University Press.

Pearson, J., and N. Thoennes. 1984. *Divorce Mediation Project*. Denver, CO: Research Unit, Association of Family and Conciliation Courts.

Polenz, J. 1975. Children and divorce. Paper presented at the New York State Psychiatric Association Meeting, New York.

Ricci, I. 1980. *Mom's House, Dad's House*. New York: Macmillan.

Santrock, J., and R. Tracy. 1978. Effects of children's family structure status on the development of stereotypes by teachers. *Journal of Educational Psychology* 70: 754–757.

Schneider D., A. Hastorg, and P. Ellsworth. 1979. *Person Perception*. Reading, MA: Addison-Wesley.

Schulman, G. 1981. Divorce, single parenthood and stepfamilies: Structural implications of these transitions. *International Journal of Family Therapy* 9: 87–112.

Smith, W. O. 1953. *The Stepchild*. Chicago: University of Chicago Press.

Snyder, M., and W. Swann. 1978. Behavioral confirmation in social interaction: From social perception to social reality. *Journal of Experimental and Social Psychology*: 148–168.

Strong, B., and DeVault. 1979. Inside America's new families. *Family Life Educator* 1 (3): 9–11.

Thompson, H. 1966. *The Successful Stepparent*. New York: Harper & Row.

Visher, E. B., and J. Visher, 1979. *Stepfamilies: A Guide to Working with Stepparents and Stepchildren*. New York: Brunner/Mazel.

Visher, J. 1990. *Clinical Intervention with Stepfamilies*. Paper presented at the Annual Meeting of the American Association for Marriage and Family Therapy. Washington, D.C. Oct. 4–7.

Wald, E. 1981. *The Remarried Family—Challenge and Promise*. New York: Family Service Association of America.

Wallerstein, J., and J. Kelly. 1980. *Surviving the Breakup: How Children and Parents Cope with Divorce*. New York: Basic Books.

Wallerstein, J., and S. Blakeslee. 1989. *Second Chances: Men, Women and Children a Decade After Divorce*. New York: Ticknor & Fields.

Weiss, R. 1975. *Going It Alone*. New York: Basic Books.

Weitzman, L. 1985. *The Divorce Revolution: The Unexpected Social and Economic Consequences for Women and Children in America*. New York: Free Press.

White, L. K., and A. Booth. 1985. The quality and stability of remarriages: The role of stepchildren. *American Sociological Review* 50: 689–698.

COMMUNICATION AND GENDER IN THE CLASSROOM

AUTHOR   Pamela Cooper, Northwestern University

POINTS TO BE ADDRESSED
- The extent of sexism in curriculum materials
- The extent of sexism in classroom interaction
- The consequences of sexism
- Strategies for eliminating sexism in the classroom

In May Santon's book *The Small Room* (1961), Harriet Summerson asks Lucy Winters, "Was there ever a life more riddled with self-doubt than that of a female professor?" (29). What is it she doubts? She doubts the dominant forms of knowledge, the privileged ways of knowing and thinking and speaking. Why? Because, as M. Belenky and her associates (1986) suggest, women have cultivated and valued ways of knowing that have often been denigrated or neglected by the "dominant intellectual ethos of our time." The different voice by which women speak is often devalued in the educational system (Gilligan, 1982).

Women students now account for 54 percent of the total number of students enrolled in colleges in the United States (*Almanac*, 1990). Yet the dominant model for education is geared toward men. As Belenky and her associates point out, "Conceptions of knowledge and truth that are accepted and articulated today have been shaped throughout history by the male dominated majority" (5). This model stresses objectivity, separateness, competitiveness, and hierarchical structure. In contrast, women learn better in a model of education that emphasizes "connection over separation, understanding and acceptance over assessment, and collaboration over debate" (Belenky, et al.: 229) and one that accords "respect to and allows time for the knowledge that emerges from firsthand experiences" (Belenky, et al.: 229).

Perhaps the dominant model tenaciously holds on because the dominant sex in the academies is male. Recent figures reported in the 1990 *Almanac* published by the *Chronicle of Higher Education* indicate that the proportion of women faculty on U.S. campuses remains low. In 1989, only 29.3 percent of faculty at public institutions and 28.5 percent of faculty at private institutions were women (*Almanac*). The American Association of University Professors, (AAUP) Committee on the Status of Women (Committee W) reports even lower figures. The Report of Committee W 1990 shows that women represent only 27.4 percent of faculty. The report also indicates that women are employed in the greatest numbers at the lowest ranks, that they are the majority in untenured positions, and that they still are not being compensated equitably. The 1990 data show that salaries of female professors trail those of male professors by as much as 13 percent, primarily because women have less experience at the higher ranks and generally do not teach in the higher paid disciplines of science, law, and engineering.

According to the editors of *Educating the Majority: Women Challenge Tradition in Higher Education* (C. Pearson, D. Shavlik, and J. Touchton, 1989), an enormous amount of differential treatment, with regard to both the academic and social climate for women still exists in some form at all institutions (A. Wolpe, 1989). However, the circumstances that riddle female professors with self-doubt exist at all levels of education. Regardless of whether we examine the educational system historically, the differences in male/female occupational choices, the content of curriculum, or classroom communication patterns, we find that the educational system helps to mold the future dominant roles of males and channel females into less dominant roles. This sex-role stereotyping results in what has been termed girls' "below stairs" relationship to education (P. Mahony, 1983; N. Rubin, 1988). Sex-role stereotyping exists in both the content of educational materials and in classroom interaction patterns. Often this stereotyping is subtle. In this chapter, the extent and types of this sex-role stereotyping, the consequences of this stereotyping, and strategies for change will be examined.

CURRICULUM MATERIALS

TEXTBOOKS

Sex-role stereotyping in curriculum materials may be very subtle—so subtle, in fact, that we do not notice it at first. For example, more males than females are pictured in textbook illustrations. Researchers examining the most-used elementary textbooks in grades one through six found disturbing results (L. Weitzman and D. Rizzo, 1975). For example, in social studies textbooks, only 33 percent of the illustrations included females. In one series designed to teach reading, 102 stories were about boys and only 35 were about girls. J. Mliner (1977) examined elementary and junior high school math and science texts. In these textbooks, females were pictured as Indians, dolls or witches, or participating in activities such as skipping rope and buying balloons. Males are pictured as sailors, kings, bakers, circus performers, band members, and balloon sellers. The ratio of males pictured to females was 15:1. Lest these results seem out of date, A. Nilsen (1987), comparing three decades of science materials, found that artists are *still* drawing three times as many pictures of males as females. In addition, in the majority of books examined in this study, the word *man* is used to describe people in general, and few books depict women in scientific careers. J. Bazler (1989) examined the seven best-selling high school science texts and determined only one of the texts provided a balance of pictures of men and women. Calling for a change, Bazler says:

> If women do not see women in science, if their teachers are 95 percent men, and if textbooks are predominantly male, they won't go into science unless they're specifically out to break down those barriers (33).

Such discrepancies present negative images of females and reinforce sex-role stereotyped behavior. Thus, although more females may be taking math and science classes, curriculum materials still tend to reinforce traditional stereotypes.

Numerical discrepancies exist in other content areas as well. When women are discussed in history textbooks, for example, passages frequently include misleading words or phrases that detract from the significance of women and their accomplishments. For example, one text informs readers that no women were members of the Senate in 1972 when, in fact, Margaret Chase Smith served as a senator at that time (D. Kirby and N. Julian, 1981).

Discrepancies also exist in the number of male and female authors included in textbooks. In a survey of English literature anthologies, the 17 books that were examined included selections by 147 male authors and only 25 female authors (P. Arlow and M. Froschel, 1976). Another survey of 400 selections reveals 75 female authors and 306 male authors (Arlow and Froschel, 1976).

Generally, stereotypical roles can be found in all types of textbooks. In speech communication textbooks, for example, hypothetical applications of communication skills, such as a man arguing in court and a woman making an announcement at a PTA meeting, perpetuate sex-role stereotypes (see J. Sprague, 1975; P. Randall, 1985). Most anthologies dealing with speech communication feature speeches by men (Sprague, 1975). In math textbooks, men are depicted as active, alert, and scientific. Mathematics is typically seen as a masculine activity (Fennema, 1984). Males are more often pictured doing math, and most story problems are about males. Women are depicted as dull and insignificant, and are rarely involved in career situations.

In scientific textbooks, males control the action and females watch the action; boys perform experiments, girls clean up. In addition, adult women are almost never presented in scientific roles (Nilsen, 1987).

In economics textbooks, women are most frequently portrayed in stereotypical ways, and their socioeconomic experiences are treated as anomalous or deviant (S. Feiner and Morgan, 1987). In an analysis of 21 major introductory economics textbooks, the number of pages that make even a passing reference to economic topics salient to women is remarkably small, ranging from 2 to 22. The total pages of the texts ranged from 399 to 958 (Feiner and Morgan, 1987). Feiner and B. Roberts (1990) suggest that simply expanding the treatment of women in these textbooks would not solve the fundamental problem:

> We argue that two fundamental characteristics of neoclassical economics unavoidably bias its treatment of gender and race: its philosophical premises, including the positive-normative distinction, and the equilibrium structure of its analyses, which are based on deriving economic outcomes from the rational character of constrained individual choice (161).

In general, despite the adoption of nonsexist guidelines during the past decade, textbook publishers have made relatively few changes to increase the visibility of females and decrease the stereotyping of males and females. For example, in elementary school textbooks, stories about females are only included in one or two books in a series or added to a single grade level (M. deNys and L. Wolfe, 1985). The "nonbiased" material is sometimes added to the center or end of a text, without any attempt to integrate it into the overall format of the rest of the book.

CHILDREN'S LITERATURE

In addition to textbooks, educators are being encouraged to use other books to supplement basic curriculum (N. Aiex, 1988; B. Holmes and R. Ammon, 1985). A major supplement is children's literature. A plethora of research demonstrates that children's literature reflects and reinforces sex-role stereotypes. Numerical disparities and stereotyped behavior patterns and characteristics reflected in children's literature teach girls to undervalue themselves and teach boys to believe that they must always be stereotypically masculine.

Females are not included in children's books in numbers that reflect their presence in the general population. Several studies have examined how sex roles are treated in books that won the prestigious Caldecott Medal or the Newbery Award (Weitzman, et al., 1972; R. Kolbe and J. LaVoie, 1981; P. Cooper, 1989). From 1967 to 1972, the ratio of male characters to female characters in Caldecott Medal books was 11:1. From 1972 to 1979, the ratio of male characters in Newbery Award books was 18:1. Finally, from 1987 to 1989, the ratio of human male characters to human female characters in Caldecott Medal books was 2:1 and the ratio in Newbery Award winners was 6:1. From 1967 to 1987, only 14 books (out of a total of 97) depicted women working outside the home (see Cooper, 1991).

Although numerical disparities are decreasing in children's books, the role models presented for children have not become less stereotyped. The three studies cited above also examined the stereotyped behavior patterns and characteristics depicted in children's books. The 1967 to 1972 study showed that when females were illustrated, traditional sex-role characterizations were reinforced: girls were passive, boys were active; girls followed and served others, boys led and rescued others. Adult men and women in these books also were stereotyped: women were depicted as wives and mothers, while men held a variety of occupations. In the years from 1972 to 1987, sex-role stereotypes were still prevalent. From 1967 to 1971, all 18 Caldecott Medal books portrayed traditional sex roles; from 1972 to 1979, 17 out of 19 did; from 1980 to 1987, 22 contained traditional sex-role stereotypes. In a recent update of her 1989 study, Cooper (1991) examined the Caldecott and Newbery winners from 1980 to 1990. The ratios remained the same, as did the stereotypical role portrayal.

Stereotyped role portrayal does not occur only in Caldecott and Newbery Medal books. For example, Cooper (1987) examined the sex-role stereotypes in children's books concerning stepfamilies. She examined 42 books available in libraries in the Chicago metropolitan area and found many stereotyped sex roles in these books. Women worked, but in stereotyped occupations such as receptionist, secretary, or nurse. They were relatively passive and focused on their appearance. When women worked outside the home, they neglected their children or became aggressive. Men were depicted as lawyers and doctors who were inept at simple household duties. They were caring and sensitive, but only to a point—when problems were not resolved quickly, they became impatient.

S. Peterson and M. Lach (1990) examined picture books listed in the booklist in *The Horn Book* for 1967, 1977, and 1987. These researchers found that although the prevalence of stereotypes had decreased somewhat, the decreases in quantity and kind were not statistically meaningful.

Lee Barton (1984) suggests that the sex-role stereotyping of male characters in children's literature has been greatly ignored. The author analyzed over fifty children's books and found that books that depict a sensitive male role model do exist, but not in great numbers.

The concern with sex role stereotypes in curriculum materials stems from the fact that gender stereotypes influence a variety of cognitive processes, such as recall of material, clustering of learned concepts, inferences drawn from the material and comprehension (See C. Martin and C. Halverson, 1983; M. Signorella and L. Liben, 1984). Gender stereotypes also affect readers' perceptions of others' behavior, and their memory for that behavior as well as the inferences they draw from it (Berndt and Heller, 1986). As Peterson and Lach (1990) suggest, "It is clear that gender stereotypes affect not only self-concept, potential for achievement and perceptions of others, but a variety of dimensions of cognitive performance as well" (194). P. Campbell and J. Wirtenburg (1980) suggest that the amount of exposure children receive to gender-biased or to bias-free materials influences the effect these materials have—the longer the exposure to gender-biased material, the more gender-stereotyped their attitudes become and the longer these attitudes are retained.

CLASSROOM COMMUNICATION PATTERNS

A review of research for all educational levels suggests six major ways in which teachers communicate sex-role expectations to students (R. Hall and B. Sandler, 1982). First, teachers may call on male students more often than on female students. When female students are asked why they believe teachers call on male students more often, they indicate that teachers either do not expect them to know the answer or do not feel the answer would be correct or worthwhile.

Second, teachers often coach male students to help them work toward a fuller answer. Female students are not coached as often. For example, a teacher is more likely to say, "What do you mean by that?" or "Why do you believe that?" to male students than to female students. Coaching may communicate to males the expectation that, with a little help, they can succeed. The lack of coaching to females may communicate that their ideas are not important enough to probe further or that they are not intellectually capable of succeeding.

Third, teachers wait longer for males than they wait for females to answer a question before going on to another student. This may subtly communicate to females that they are not expected to know the answer and may communicate to males that they are more intellectually competent than their female counterparts. In addition, a male's silence following a question is often perceived as time used formulating an answer, while a female's is perceived as lack of knowledge.

Fourth, female students are more likely to be asked questions that require factual answers ("When was television invented?") and male students are more often asked questions that require critical thinking or personal evaluation ("How do you feel the concept of symbolic interaction affects communication?"). Teachers communicate expectations regarding the intellectual capability of each student—females are capable only of low-level cognitive processes; males are capable of high-level cognitive processes.

Fifth, teachers respond more extensively to male students' comments than to female students' comments. Thus, males receive more reinforcement for their intellectual participation than do females. In this way, a teacher communicates to female students that their comments are not as worthwhile or as interesting as those of male students.

Finally, teachers communicate sex-role stereotypes by their use of sexist language. V. Richmond and J. Gorham (1988), in their study of current generic-referent usage among 1,529 public school children in grades 3 through 12, found that the masculine generic usage is still prevalent. In addition, a heavy dependence on masculine referents were associated with self-image. Males used significantly more masculine referents than did females. Males who selected traditionally male careers used more masculine referents than did males who selected a gender non-specific career. Females selecting stereotypically feminine careers used the most feminine referents.

A great deal of research has explored the communication patterns which exist in the classroom in relation to sex of students and teachers. Generally, we know that differences exist in terms of initiation, discipline, and dominance (J. Stake and J. Katz, 1982).

INITIATION

Male students initiate more interactions with teachers than female students initiate (J. Brophy, 1985). In addition, the interactions between male students and teachers last longer (Hall and Sandler, 1982).

Teachers call on males more often and give them more positive feedback than they give girls. In addition, males are given more time to talk in class (P. Keegan, 1989).

J. Pearson and R. West (1991) examined 15 college classrooms and found that female students ask fewer questions than male students in courses taught by males.

In a recent study, the types of questions male and female students at various grade levels asked in mathematics and language arts classes were charted. The results suggest that, in advanced secondary mathematics classes, female students ask fewer questions than males. In addition, teachers subtly discouraged female students from participating (T. Good and R. Slavings, 1988).

Teachers explain how to do things to male students and simply do them for female students. Interaction time increases as a teacher explains how to set up lab equipment, work a math problem, or write a thesis sentence. If the teacher is "doing for" the female student, as is often the case, interaction time is decreased.

Teachers have suggested that males are more creative and fun to teach (M. Sadker and D. Sadker, 1985). Teachers may communicate this attitude to male students, who, in turn, may be more willing to initiate interactions because they feel more valued in the classroom.

DISCIPLINE

Classroom communication patterns differ in terms of how male and female students are disciplined. Criticism of female students focuses on their lack of knowledge or skill; criticism of male students focuses on disruptive behaviors. Male students receive more discipline than female students receive and are more likely to be reprimanded in a harsher and more public manner than female students (Brophy, 1985).

High-achieving male students receive more teacher approval and active instruction; low-achieving male students are likely to receive more criticism. However, high-achieving female students receive less praise than both low- and high-achieving male students (J. Parsons, K. Heller and C. Kaczala, 1980). Thus, although male students receive more disciplinary messages, they also receive more praise, in general, than female students receive, particularly for their intellectual ability. Boys believe they earn higher grades. Girls more often attribute their success to luck (See research reviewed in Cooper, 1990).

DOMINANCE

Male students often dominate classroom talk. They are given more opportunities to respond in the classroom, and teachers direct more attention (both positive and negative) toward them. In addition, teachers ask male students a higher proportion of product-and-choice questions (questions that require synthesis or analysis), thereby encouraging problem-solving behavior in male students to a greater extent than in female students (Brophy and Good, 1974).

Male students dominate more than just the conversation in the classroom; they also dominate nonverbal aspects of classroom communication (B. Thorne, 1979). In addition to dominating linguistic space, male students dominate the physical space of the classroom.

Boys may also emphasize their masculine dominance by using girls as a negative reference group. One researcher asked students, "Who would you least wish to be like?" All of the boys named girls (and only girls). The characteristic of girls most vehemently rejected by boys was their apparent marginality in classroom encounters. The term "faceless" was used repeatedly by male students (but by none of the females) to describe their female classmates, and seemed to sum up their feeling that silence robs female students of any claim to individual identity and respect (M. Stanworth, 1981).

Male students use several strategies to achieve dominance in mixed-sex classrooms. They deny female students' academic abilities, make negative remarks about females' appearances, and overtly resist females' adopting of nontraditional roles. Reay (1990) reports research that demonstrates that when girls' achievement levels were improved, boys became angry and resentful. As Sandler (1991) suggests:

> By giving men students the greater share of classroom attention, faculty unknowingly creates a climate that subtly interferes with the development of women students' self-confidence, academic participation and career goals (6).

Not only do teachers communicate differently with male and female students, but teachers also perceive male and female students differently. For example, D. Gold, G. Crombie, and S. Noble (1987) found that preschool girls whose behavior is in accordance with the compliant good student model are more likely to have their abilities perceived at a high level than girls whose behavior does not fit the model. Evaluations of boys' competence is not affected by teachers' perceptions of their compliance.

Classroom communication patterns differ in terms of how male and female students treat male and female teachers. A growing body of research indicates that male and female students treat female faculty differently than they treat male faculty (M. Ryan, 1989). L. Nadler and M. Nadler (1990), using a questionnaire measure of male and female perceptions of class-related communication behavior, found that male instructors were viewed as engaging in more dominant, controlling behaviors than female instructors. Female instructors were viewed as engaging in more supportive behaviors toward students than were male instructors. In addition, students rate their female instructors more harshly than their male instructors. A woman's voice, clothing, appearance, and form of address can, and often are, used against her (Sandler, 1991). The classroom climate is not only chilly for female students (Hall and Sandler, 1982, 1984), it's chilly for female faculty (Sandler and Hall, 1986).

The perceptions students have of instructors affect student communication in the classroom. Male and female students communicate differently with male and female instructors. When the instructor is male, male student interactions are three times more frequent than female student interactions. When the instructor is female, male and female student interactions are nearly equal (D. Karp & W. Yoels, 1976).

L. Rosenfeld and M. Jarrard (1985) examined how the perceived sexism of college professors affected classroom climate. They found that students who perceive their male teachers to be highly sexist describe their classes as less supportive and less innovative than those taught by nonsexist male teachers. In a follow-up study (Rosenfeld and Jarrard, 1986), the researchers examined coping mechanisms used by students in classes taught by sexist and nonsexist teachers. Coping mechanisms used by students in sexist male teachers' classes were passive (not doing what the teacher asked, hiding feelings) when students liked the class. If students did not like the class and perceived the male teacher as sexist, students used an active coping mechanism—forming alliances against the teacher. Generally, teachers in disliked classes were perceived as more sexist than teachers in liked classes. Also, male teachers were perceived as more sexist than female teachers.

CONSEQUENCES OF SEX-ROLE STEREOTYPING IN EDUCATION

As the research discussed in this chapter indicates, curriculum materials and classroom interaction patterns influence student sex-role stereotypes and behaviors. The question now becomes, "What is the effect of sex-role stereotyping in education?" Basically, sex-role stereotyping in education affects three areas: (1) the **self-concept** of students, (2) the **curriculum choice** of students, and (3) the **occupational choice** of students.

SELF-CONCEPT

E. Lenney (1977) reviewed the research concerning women's self-confidence in achievement settings and concluded that women's self confidence is not lower than men's when (1) the task is appropriate for females; (2) the information available on their ability at a specific task is clear and unambiguous; and (3) the emphasis placed on comparison to others, and evaluation by others is low. Generally, these three criteria are not met in achievement settings. Thus, women's self-confidence in the educational environment may be low and this low self-confidence may affect their self-concept.

P. McLaughlin (1991) reports results of a major research study by the American Association of University Women that found that at age nine, most girls were assertive, confident, and felt good about themselves. But by the time they got to high school, fewer than one third felt that way. A. Petersen (1987) also found that the achievement of girls declined from seventh to twelfth grades. M. Leonard and B. Sigall (1989) report that women's grades, career goals, and esteem decline over the four-year span of college.

In a recent major study, J. Earle, V. Roach, and K. Fraser (1987) studied female dropouts and concluded that the majority of female students who drop out are not pregnant, as had previously been assumed. The report, "Female Dropouts: A New Perspective," speculates that current school practices encourage girls to leave school by depressing their overall achievement. For example, studies have shown that teachers talk less to female than male students, counsel them less, and provide them with fewer directions and rewards. Also, schools provide limited opportunities for students to work cooperatively, though girls may perform better than boys in such situations. A recent report on girls' lower SAT scores, "Sex Bias in College Admission Tests: Why Women Lose Out" (reported by D. Carmody, 1987), suggests the long-term impact a lack of math and science background is having—a real dollar loss for females in later life. Females get less prestigious jobs, earn less money, and have fewer leadership opportunities. Male-dominated occupations are higher-paying, on average, than those dominated by females.

CURRICULUM CHOICE

The sex-role stereotyping in education also affects the course of study students pursue. Traditionally, female students have perceived math and science courses, spatial ability, and problem-solving as male domains (D. Goldman, 1987). Research examining differences in male/female math and science performance suggests that males are more likely to take higher-level math and science courses and that this is particularly true in physics, trigonometry, and calculus (C. Benbow and L. Minor, 1986; Boli and Coleman, 1987). The same is true in science. An analysis of 13 year olds reports no sex differences in science achievement. Yet females continue to move away from the sciences (F. Lawrenz and W. Welch, 1983). Thus, although achievement in science and math may not be different, when male and female students are exposed to the same material, female students tend not to take advanced math and science courses.

In terms of the influence of computer usage, B. Collis and L. Ollila (1990) found that despite daily participation in classroom computer activities over a period of 7 to 8 months, first grade children still perceived computer use as masculine. This coincides with the findings of research done with adolescents, in which adolescents also perceived computer use as masculine (J. Sanders, 1984; Collis, 1985; M. Lockheed, 1985). C. Hoyles (1988) suggests that while girls and boys might show a similar appreciation of the significance computers might have for their personal futures, boys tend to be more positively disposed than girls toward computers, are more likely than girls to take optional computer courses in school and to report more frequent home use of computers, and tend to dominate the limited computer resources that are available in school. Because educators argue that the computer should not be seen simply as an object of knowledge but should be integrated into the school curriculum as a resource to be used in all subjects when appropriate, the use of gender bias becomes extremely crucial. As Hoyles argues:

> If girls are in general less familiar with computers than boys are, or if children strongly identify computers with boys rather than girls, then the increasing use of computers across the school curriculum will have profound effects on the education of girls (32).

OCCUPATIONAL CHOICE

The choice of which curriculum to pursue is directly related to occupational choice. For example, math and science skills are critical in determining educational and occupational choices (Peng and Jaffe, 1979). Thus, when female students avoid science and math training, they preclude themselves from considering a wide range of occupations, not only in engineering and the natural sciences, but also in the social sciences and business administration (Carnegie Commission on Higher Education, 1973).

According to research cited in Fallon (1990), for the past 35 years, the wage differential between men's and women's salaries has defied eradication. A study conducted by the Women's Research and Education Institute revealed that for full-time female workers in 1988, the median income was 66 percent that of males—only a one percent increase over women's median income for the year 1955. Over a lifetime, a woman who holds a graduate degree will earn $1.3 million, while a man with only a high school diploma will earn more, $1.4 million.

It is well established that sex-typed labeling of school subjects is related to students' attitudes and achievement in those subjects (See research reviewed in Collis and Ollila, 1990). G Wilder, D. Mackie, and J. Cooper (1985) found that students at all grade levels, K through 12, saw writing as more appropriate for females than for males. Research reviewed in an article by Trepanier-Street and her associates (1990) reveals that elementary school boys at all grade levels and girls in grades 1 through 4 include significantly more male characters than female characters in their stories. The male characters are assigned more physical actions, emotions, physical and ability attributes, problem-solver roles, and occupational roles. Girls in the fifth and sixth grades assign more emotions, actions, and attributes to female characters. Examining the creative writing responses of third and sixth graders to either stereotypic (male mechanic and female nurse) or nonstereotypic (female mechanic and male nurse) occupational roles, Trepanier-Street and her associates found that students had the least difficulty maintaining a character in role when the character's gender did not match the occupational gender stereotype. The researchers conclude that gender-stereotypic thinking is "alive and well" at all levels of elementary education. In social studies classes, researchers (D. Gillespie and C. Spohn, 1987) examined junior and senior high school students' attitudes toward women in politics. Given adolescents' increased exposure to female political role models in the early 1980s, the researchers hypothesized that these students would hold positive attitudes toward women as political candidates. Adolescent girls had very positive and optimistic views of the role of women in politics; adolescent boys had more negative and pessimistic views.

STRATEGIES FOR CHANGE

Several researchers are suggesting strategies to change the present gender insensitive educational system to a gender sensitive one (See J. Wood and L. Lenze, 1991). Suggestions range from urging the inclusion of works by women in U.S. public address courses and as models in public speaking courses (K. Campbell, 1991) to using collaborative learning (D. Reay, 1990).

As most writers suggest, creating a gender sensitive classroom doesn't involve simply adding information about women to the curriculum. Ideological and pedagogical challenges abound. The "male-as-norm" conceptions of educational purposes, of students, of teachers, of curricula, of pedagogy, indeed of the profession of education, must be closely examined (M. Leach and B. Davies, 1990). To see the absence of women as a significant omission means to change civilization, to reform the disciplines, and thereby to change higher education (C. Gilligan, et al., 1990). M. Roth (1987), writing on teaching modern art history from a feminist perspective, speaks of her struggle in this endeavor:

> As mentioned earlier, I had found the piecemeal approach of addition (be it adding women artists of photography, American art, fold art, caricature, etc.) did not work. Rather, a wholesale revision of *all* material was necessary. Key in this is the examination of how gender together with class and race affect *all* artists, for to discuss the effect of gender only in the case of women artists places us yet again in the role of the "other" (a once-useful term/analytic structure that is now not only outworn but also pernicious). Thus, I am now radically changing the structure of both individual lectures and of entire courses. (23)

The goal, then, is to reach what E. Peterson (1991) describes for the field of speech communication as "Stage Five: Speech Communication Redefined to Include Us All." So, what has to be done to change the present educational system?

F. Maher and C. Rathbone (1986) suggest teachers need to be trained in choosing curriculum, classroom management techniques to equalize the classroom interaction, and teaching styles, particularly collaborative learning styles. E. Higginbotham (1990) outlines three tasks: (1) gather information about the diversity of female experience, (2) reconceptualize one's discipline in light of gender-based analysis, and (3) structure classroom dynamics that ensure a supportive climate for all students.

Several specific suggestions for accomplishing the goals of authors come to mind.

First, a feminist perspective to teaching/learning is needed. Why? Because, as Wood (1989) outlines, feminist pedagogy is good pedagogy because (1) feminism is inclusive so that topics representative of both sexes' experience and concerns are addressed; (2) feminism values diversity so that multiple ways of knowing are accepted and valued, (3) feminism values human relationships so that teaching becomes interactive rather than authoritative; (4) feminism values personal experience so that thoughtful consideration of how ideas/knowledge relate to personal experience is encouraged; (5) feminism emphasizes empowerment, not power, so that students have control over their own learning, and (6) feminism seeks to create change so that learners perceive themselves as agents of change. Such a feminist approach to pedagogy means that the instructor places an emphasis on such things as individual learning styles, variety in teaching strategies, student-student interactions, creating a collaborative learning environment, requesting and reacting to student feedback on course content and pedagogy.

Perhaps the most important aspect of feminine pedagogy is its emphasis on personal knowledge. The story with which each learner comes to the learning needs to be incorporated into the learning. Feminist pedagogy thus puts an emphasis on narrative. As J. Pagano (1988) suggests:

> The artistic medium of the teacher is the narrative; her teaching is a narrative enactment. When we teach, we tell stories. We tell stories about our disciplines, about the place of these disciplines in the structure of human knowledge. We tell stories about knowledge, about what it is to be a human knower, about how knowledge is made, claimed, and legitimated. The stories that we tell are stories built on other stories; they work to forge continuity between our stories and those of others, to confirm community among ourselves and others, and to initiate others into our communities. In educational theory, we tell stories of teaching, stories that at once reveal, constitute, and confirm the values that give significance to pedagogical acts. These are stories in which we represent those whom we teach in their relationship to ourselves and in which the nuances of the relationship, identity, power, and authority of individuals in their relationship to a community and its knowledge. (321)

So, too, the stories students tell are important to an understanding of how their personal experience relates (or fails to relate) to the content being discussed. When we deny, as we often do, students their stories, fearing the stories will take us too far afield from our all-important current topic, we deny students their ability to make the content real to their own experience. One of the most extensive lists of behaviors for nonsexist teaching is presented by Hall and Sandler (1982). Because research suggests that the classroom is a "chilly" climate for females, Hall and Sandler make the following recommendations for creating a climate that will encourage females to communicate:

1. Pay particular attention to classroom interaction patterns during the first few weeks of class, and make a special effort to draw females into discussion during that time. Participation patterns are likely to be established during this period that will often continue throughout the term.

2. Make a specific effort to call directly on females as well as on male students.

3. In addressing the class, use terminology that includes both males and females in the group.

4. Respond to female and to male students in similar ways when they make comparable contributions to class discussion by:

   a. crediting comments to their author ("as Jeanne said . . . ")

   b. "coaching" for additional information

5. Intervene in communication patterns among students that may shut out females. For example, if male students pick on each other's points, but ignore an appropriate comment offered by a female, slow the discussion, and pick up on the comment that has been overlooked.

6. Note patterns of interruption to determine if female students are interrupted more than males—either by yourself or by other students. Make a special effort to ensure that all students have the opportunity to finish their comments.

7. Ask females and males qualitatively similar questions—that is, ask students of both sexes critical as well as factual questions.

8. Give male and female students an equal amount of time to respond after asking a question.

9. Give females and males the same opportunity to ask for and receive detailed instructions about the requirements for an assignment.

10. When talking about occupations or professions in class discussion, use language that does not reinforce limited views of male and female role and career choices.

11. Avoid using the generic "he" whenever possible.

12. Avoid placing professional women in a "special category," for example, "woman" (or worse, "lady") doctor.

13. Make eye contact with females as well as with male students after asking a question to invite a response.

14. Watch for and respond to nonverbal cues that indicate female students' readiness to participate in class, such as leaning forward or making eye contact.

15. Use the same tone in talking with female as with male students (for example, avoid a patronizing or impatient tone when speaking with females, but a tone of interest and attention when talking with males).

16. Finally, eliminate sexist materials from your curriculum. (16)

Why is it the female professor, indeed, the female student doubts herself? The answer is obvious. The research reviewed in this chapter demonstrates she has been taught—through curriculum materials and classroom interaction patterns—to doubt her abilities, her goals, her very means of gaining knowledge. As long as strategies for changing the educational environment are not implemented, the question remains, "Was there ever a life more riddled with self-doubt than that of the female in the educational environment?"

REFERENCES

Adelman, C., and N. Alsalam. 1989. Number of Math Courses Taken Said Linked to Future Earnings. *Education Week*, 11 January: 9.

Aiex, N. 1988. Literature based reading instruction. *The Reading Teacher* 41: 458–461.

Almanac. 1990. *Chronicle of Higher Education* 5 Sept.: 3, 5, 13, 14, 18.

Arlow, P., and M. Froschel. 1976. Women in the high school curriculum: A review of U.S. history and English literature texts. In C. Ahlum, J. Fralley, and F. Howe, eds., *High School Feminist Studies*, Old Westbury, NY: Feminist Press, xi–xxviii.

Bazler, J. 1989. Chem text photos discourage women. *NEA Today* Nov.: 33.

Barton, L. 1984. What are boys like in books these days? *Learning* 13: 130–131.

Belenky, M., B. Clinchy, N. Goldberger, and J. Tarule. 1986. *Women's Ways of Knowing*. New York: Basic Books.

Benbow, C., and L. Minor. 1986. Mathematically talented males and females and achievement in high school sciences. *American Education Research Journal*: 23: 425–436.

Berndt, T. J., and K. A. Heller. 1986. Gender Stereotypes and social inferences: A developmental study. *Journal of Personality and Social Psychology*, 50: 889–898.

Brophy, J. 1985. Interactions of male and female students with male and female teachers. In L. C. Wilkinson and C. B. Marrett, eds., *Gender Influence in Classroom Interaction*, Orlando, FL: Academic Press, 115–142.

Brophy, J. E., and T. L. Good. 1974. The influence of the sex of the teacher and student on classroom interaction. In J. Brophy and T. Good, eds., *Teacher-Student Relationships: Causes and Consequences*, New York: Holt, Rinehart & Winston, 199–239.

Campbell, K. 1991. Hearing women's voices. *Communication Education* 40: 33–48.

Campbell, P., and J. Wirtenburg. 1980. How books influence children: What the research shows. *Interracial Books for Children Bulletin* 11: 3–6.

Carmody, D. 1987. SATs are biased against girls, report by advocacy group says. *The New York Times*. 17 April: B2.

Collis, B. 1985. Sex-related differences in attitudes toward computers: Implications for counselors. *The School Counselor* 33(2): 120–130.

Collis, B., and L. Ollila. 1990. The effect of computer use on grade 1 children's gender stereotypes about reading, writing, and computer use. *Journal of Research and Development in Education* 24: 14–20.

Cooper, P. 1983, October. *The Communication of Sex Role Stereotypes: The Image of Stepparents in Children's Literature.* Paper presented at the Sixth Annual Communication, Language and Gender Conference, New Brunswick, NJ.

_____. 1984, November. *Sexism in Children's Literature: Extent and Impact on Adult Behavior.* Paper presented at the meeting of the Speech Communication Association, Chicago.

_____. 1987. Sex role stereotypes of stepparents in children's literature. In L.P. Stewart and S. Ting-Toomey, *Communication, Gender, and Sex Roles in Diverse Interaction Contexts*, Norwood, NJ: Ablex, 61–82.

_____. 1989. Children's literature: The extent of sexism. In C. Lont and S. Friedley, eds., *Beyond Boundaries: Sex and Gender Diversity in Education*, Fairfax, VA: George Mason University Press, 233–250.

_____. 1991. *Speech Communication for the Classroom Teacher.* 4th ed. Scottsdale, AZ: Gorsuch-Scarisbrick.

_____. 1991, April. *Women and Power in the Caldecott and Newbery Winners, 1980–1990.* Paper presented at the meeting of the Central States Communication Association, Chicago.

deNys, M., and L. Wolfe. 1985. Learning her place: Sex bias in the elementary classroom. *Peer Report* 5: 1–10.

Earle, J., V. Roach, and K. Fraser. 1987. *Female Dropouts: A New Perspective.* Alexandria, VA: National Association of State Boards of Education.

Fallon, J. 1990, November. *Challenges to Women Students: Overcoming the Barriers.* Paper presented at the meeting of the Speech Communication Association, Chicago.

Feiner, S., and Morgan. 1987. Women and minorities in introductory economics textbooks: 1974–1984. *Journal of Economic Education.* 10: 376–92.

Feiner, S., and B. Roberts. 1990. Hidden by the invisible hand: Neoclassical economic theory and the textbook treatment of race and gender. *Gender and Society* 4: 159–181.

Fennema, E. 1984. Girls, women and mathematics. In E. and M. J. Agers, eds., *Women and education.* McCutchens Publishers, Berkeley, CA, 137–164.

Gillespie, D., and C. Spohn. 1987. Adolescents' attitudes toward women in politics: The effect of gender and race. *Gender and Society* 1: 208–218.

Gilligan, C. 1982. *In a Different Voice.* Cambridge, MA: Harvard University Press.

Gilligan, C., W. Lyons, and T. Hanmer. 1990. *Making Connections* Cambridge, MA: Harvard University Press.

Gold, D., G. Crombie, and S. Noble. 1987. Relations between teachers' judgment of girls' and boys' compliance and intellectual competence. *Sex Roles* 16: 351–358.

Goldman, D. 1987. Girls and math: Is biology really destiny? *New York Times Educational Life,* 2 Aug.: 42–46.

Good, T., and R. Slavings. 1988. Male and female student question-asking behavior in elementary and secondary mathematics and language arts classes. *Journal of Research in Childhood Education* 3: 5–23.

Gray, M. 1990. *Report of Committee W 1990.* Washington, DC: American Association of University Professors.

Hall, R., and B. Sandler. 1982. *The Classroom Climate: A Chilly One for Women?* Washington, DC: Association of American Colleges Project on the Status and Education of Women.

_____. 1984. *Out of the Classroom: A Chilly Campus Climate for Women?* Washington, DC: Association of American Colleges Project on the Status and Education of Women.

Higginbotham, E. 1990. Designing an inclusive curriculum: Bringing all women into the core. *Women's Studies Quarterly* 18: 7–23.

Holmes, B., and R. Ammon. 1985. Teaching content with trade books: A strategy. *Childhood Education* 61: 366–370.

Hoyles, C. 1988. *Girls and Computers: General Issues and Case Studies of Logo in the Mathematics Classroom.* London: University of London.

Karp, D. A., and W. C. Yoels. 1976. The college classroom: Some observations on the meanings of student participation. *Sociology and Social Research* 60: 421–439.

Keegan, P. 1989. Playing favorites. *New York Times*, 6 Aug.: Section 4A, 26.

Kirby, D. F., and N. B. Julian. 1981. Treatment of women in high school U.S. history textbooks. *Social Studies* 72: 203–207.

Kolbe, R., and J. C. LaVoie. 1981. Sex role stereotyping in preschool children's picture books. *Social Psychology Quarterly* 44: 369–374.

Lawrenz, F. P., and W. W. Welch. 1983. Student perceptions of science classes taught by males and females. *Journal of Research in Science Teaching* 20: 655–662.

Leach, M., and B. Davies. 1990. Crossing the boundaries: Educational thought and gender equity. *Educational Theory* 40: 321–332.

Lenney, E. 1977. Women's self-confidence in achievement settings. *Psychological Bulletin* 84: 1–13.

Leonard, M. M., and B. A. Sigall. 1989. Empowering women student leaders: A leadership development model. In C. S. Pearson, D. L. Shavlik, and J. B. Touchton, eds., *Educating the Majority: Women Challenge Tradition in Higher Education,* New York: ACE/Macmillan, 230–249.

Lockheed, M. E. 1985. Women, girls and computers: A first look at the evidence. *Sex Roles* 13(3/4): 115–122.

McLaughlin, P. 1991. *Hiding Places. Chicago Tribune,* 10 March: Section 6, 5.

Maher, F., and C. Rathbone. 1986. Teacher education and feminist theory: Some implications for practice. *American Journal of Education* 94, 214–235.

Mahony, P. 1983. How Alice's chin really came to be pressed against her foot: Sexist processes of interaction in mixed-sex classrooms. *Women's Studies International Forum* 6: 107–115.

Martin, C. L., and C. F. Halverson. 1983. The effects of sex-typing schemas on young children's memory. *Child Development* 54: 563–574.

Mliner, J. 1977. *Sex Stereotypes in Mathematics and Science Textbooks for Elementary and Junior High Schools: Report of Sex Bias in the Public Schools.* New York: National Organization for Women.

Nadler, L., and M. Nadler. 1990. Perceptions of sex differences in classroom communication. *Women's Studies in Communication* 13: 46–65.

Nilsen, A. P. 1987. Three decades of sexism in school science materials. *School Library Journal* 33: 117–122.

Pagano, J. 1988. Teaching women. *Educational Theory* 38: 321–339.

Pallas, A. M., and K. L. Alexander. 1983. Sex differences in quantitative SAT performance: New evidence on the differential coursework hypothesis. *American Educational Research Journal* 20: 165–182.

Parsons, J.E., K.A. Heller, and C. Kaczala. 1980. The effects of teachers' expectancies and attributions on students' expectancies for success in mathematics. In D. McGuigan, ed., *Women's Lives: New Theory, Research and Policy*, Ann Arbor: University of Michigan Center for Continuing Education of Women, 373–380.

Paulsen, K., and M. Johnson. 1983. Sex role attitudes and mathematical ability in 4th, 8th, and 11th grade students from a high socio-economic area. *Developmental Psychology* 19: 210–214.

Pearson, C., D. Shavlik, and J. Touchton. 1989. *Educating the Majority: Women Challenge Tradition in Higher Education.* New York: ACE/Macmillan.

Pearson, J., and R. West. 1991. An initial investigation of the effects of gender on student questions in the classroom: Developing a descriptive base. *Communication Education* 40: 22–32.

Peng, S., and J. Jaffe. 1984. Women who enter male-dominated fields of study in higher education. *American Educational Research Journal*, 16, 285–293.

Petersen, A. 1987. Those gangly years. *Psychology Today*, Sept.: 28–34.

Peterson, E. 1991. Moving toward a gender balanced curriculum in basic speech communication courses. *Communication Education* 40: 60–72.

Peterson, S., and M. Lach. 1990. Gender stereotypes in children's books: Their prevalence and influence on cognitive and affective development. *Gender and Education* 2: 185–197.

Randall, P. R. 1985. Sexist language and speech communication texts: Another case of benign neglect. *Communication Education* 34: 128–134.

Reay, D. 1990. Girls' groups as a component of anti-sexist practice—One primary school's experience. *Gender and Education* 2: 37–48.

Richmond, V. P., and J. Gorham. 1988. Language patterns and gender role orientation among students in grades 3–12. *Communication Education* 37: 142–149.

Rosenfeld, L. B., and M. W. Jarrard. 1985. The effects of perceived sexism in female and male college professors on students' descriptions of classroom climate. *Communication Education* 34: 205–213.

————. 1986. Student coping mechanisms in sexist and nonsexist professors' classes. *Communication Education* 35: 157–162.

Roth, M. 1987. Teaching modern art history from a feminist perspective: Challenging conventions, my own and others. *Women's Studies Quarterly* 15: 21–24.

Rubin, N. 1988. Math stinks! *Parents*, June: 132–136, 207–208, 210.

Ryan, M. 1989. Classroom and contexts: The challenge of feminist pedagogy. *Feminist Teacher* 4(2/3): 39–42.

Sadker, M., and D. Sadker. 1985. Sexism in the schoolroom of the '80s. *Psychology Today*, March: 54–57.

Sanders, J. S. 1984. The computer: Male, female or androgynous? *The Computing Teacher* 11(8): 31–34.

Sandler, B. 1991. Women faculty at work in the classroom, or why it still hurts to be a woman in labor. *Communication Education* 40: 6–15.

Sandler, B., and R. Hall. 1986. *The Campus Climate Revisited: Chilly for Women Faculty, Administrators, and Graduate Students*. Washington, DC: Project on the Status and Education of Women, Association of American Colleges.

Santon, M. 1961. *The Small Room*. New York: Norton.

Signorella, M. L., and L. S. Liben. 1984. Recall and reconstruction of gender-related pictures: Effects of attitude, task difficulty and age. *Child Development* 55: 393–405.

Sprague, J. A. 1975. The reduction of sexism in speech communication education. *Speech Teacher* 24: 37–45.

Stake, J. E., and J. F. Katz. 1982. Teacher-pupil relationships in the elementary school classroom: Teacher-gender and pupil-gender differences. *American Educational Research Journal* 19: 465–471.

Stanworth, M. 1981. *Gender and Schooling: A Study of Sexual Divisions in the Classroom*. London: Women's Research and Resources Centre.

Thorne, B. 1979. *Claiming Verbal Space: Women, Speech and Language in College Classrooms*. Paper presented at the Conference on Educational Environments and the Undergraduate Woman, Wellesley College, Wellesley, MA.

Trepanier-Street, M., J. Romatowski, and S. McNair. 1990. Development of story characters in gender-stereotypic and nonstereotypic occupational roles. *Journal of Early Adolescence* 10: 496–510.

Weitzman, L. J., D. Eifler, E. Hokada, and C. Ross. 1972. Sex role socialization in picture books for preschool children. *American Journal of Sociology* 77: 1125–1150.

Weitzman, L. J., and D. Rizzo. 1975. Sex bias in textbooks. *Today's Education* 64(1): 49–52.

Wilder, G., D. Mackie, and J. Cooper. 1985. Gender and computers: Two surveys of computer-related attitudes. *Sex Roles* 13(3/4): 215–223.

Wolpe, A. 1989. *Within School Walls. The Role of Discipline, Sexuality and the Curriculum.* London: Routledge.

Wood, J. 1989. *Feminist Pedagogy in Interpersonal Communication Courses.* Paper presented at the Speech Communication Association, San Francisco.

Wood, J., and L. Lenze. 1991. Strategies to enhance gender sensitivity in communication education. *Communication Education* 40: 16–21.

COMMUNICATION IN CORPORATE SETTINGS

AUTHORS   Lea P. Stewart, Rutgers University
Dianne Clarke-Kudless, Rutgers University

POINTS TO BE ADDRESSED

- Current business practices
- Impact of gender on interpersonal communication
- Impact of gender on corporate communications
- Effects of gender on leadership dynamics
- Application of gender to specific business activities
- Challenges, issues, and workplace dynamics of the future

Imagine that it is the year 2000. You are working for a large corporation. What is your job like? What does your workplace look like? Who are your co-workers? How will you handle conflicts between family responsibilities and the demands of your job? Will your company offer flexible work schedules so that you can choose your working hours, depending on other obligations in your life? Does your company have a good history of promoting women into higher levels of management? Are there opportunities for alternative career paths within the company? If your company makes a product, does it strive to maintain gender-neutral product packaging and promotion? All of these questions are relevant to the issue of gender in corporate settings and have been considered by researchers in this area.

Based on current research on the future nature of the workforce, it is safe to assume that the workplace of the future will be somewhat different from the workplace as we know it today. The Hudson Institute's Workforce 2000 report documented the fact that the workforce of the future will be dramatically more diverse in terms of both gender and ethnic background (L. Duke, 1991). According to the Bureau of Labor Statistics, by the year 2000 only 30 percent of the new entrants into the workforce will be white males. Thus, issues of gender have a particular importance for today's corporations attempting to meet the needs of the future.

But how are today's corporations responding to the issues presented by Workforce 2000? Unfortunately, in terms of gender issues, the answer is not very positive. In 1988, 39.3 percent of the people employed in the United States in managerial, executive, and administrative occupations were women (U.S. Department of Labor, 1989). Yet women held less than 2 percent of senior executive level jobs (U.S. Department of Labor, 1989). *Fortune* magazine examined the 1990 proxy statements of 799 of the largest U.S. public industrial and service companies. They found 19 women (less than 1 percent) in the 4,012 people listed as the highest paid corporate officers and directors (J. Fierman, 1990). When *Fortune* magazine looked at the annual reports of 225 major companies, they found a total of 9,293 corporate officers (including corporate secretary and other positions traditionally filled by women) listed—only 5 percent were women (Fierman, 1990).

Of course, most men do not achieve the highest levels of corporate life; but how do women in other jobs fare in comparison to men? According to a report by the Women's Research and Education Institute, American women who work full time have average annual earnings that are about two-thirds as high as those of men. The report predicts that it may take 75 to 100 years to overcome the inequities in hiring, promotion, and other aspects of employment (S. Rich, 1990).

Women and men still perceive a very different workplace. For example, according to a survey of 134 male and female middle managers and executives at Fortune 500 companies and some small businesses, half of the men believe that men and women are working well together, but only 34 percent of the women agree (C. Hymowitz, 1989).

The changing nature of the workforce is a fact, and we must be ready to respond to it. Although this chapter primarily focuses on issues of gender in the workplace, it is important to be aware of issues raised by multiculturalism and the aging of the workforce, too. Many of the issues of gender bias discussed in this chapter are also relevant to older workers and to people from diverse ethnic groups. Noting parallels with these groups can expand ones' perspective on the effects of the changing workforce and the communication issues raised by these changes.

Many businesses today have begun the transition into the Workforce 2000 era. Public opinion concerning gender bias in the workplace has resulted in legislation, landmark court cases, and public action groups and lobbying efforts to counter bias. Progress has also been made in the internal workings of corporate practices such as hiring, performance appraisals, promotion policies, and corporate social activity. For example, job applicants are rarely asked questions about marriage plans, desire for children, or childcare arrangements. Such obviously irrelevant questions are unlawful and generally avoided in professionally conducted interviews. In terms of corporate social activities, most companies no longer pay membership fees for corporate officers who belong to male-only clubs. In another example of current changes, a knowledgeable company representative would not begin a speech with a joke that offends a multicultural audience.

Individuals are also affected by Workforce 2000 issues. Family composition, sexual preference, educational background, language fluency, and cultural background have changed interaction in the community. Volunteer associations, such as the Girl Scouts of the USA, have introduced new programming and recruitment efforts to attract a more diverse adult and child population. Government social service agencies find their services demanded more than ever by distressed families, including those suffering from abuse, alcohol and/or other drug problems, or financial difficulties. In addition, single parent families are increasing in number due to the growing incidence of separated and divorced family units. Some religious groups have revised their positions on such basic doctrines as sexual preference, family composition, and leadership in order to reach out to this changing community composition. Today's corporations must face the challenges caused by these societal changes.

The above discussion has provided a brief overview of the corporate, community, and interpersonal issues raised by Workforce 2000. Obviously, corporate communication will be affected by these changes. In the next part of this chapter, we review these issues and discuss the business work experiences that have been specifically affected by gender issues. In the rest of the chapter, we will address the impact of gender issues on interpersonal communication in the corporation, leadership, business practices, and opportunities for the future. More extensive discussions of other communication issues affecting men and women in organizations can be found in G. Fairhurst (1986), G. Powell (1988), and L. Stewart et al. (1990).

CURRENT BUSINESS PRACTICES

The business practices that have been affected by the issues raised by Workforce 2000 can be grouped into three categories: (1) legal, (2) economic, and (3) public.

LEGAL ISSUES

Legal issues that affect gender relations in the workplace include affirmative action and equal opportunity legislation, sexual harassment, revised job qualifications, and modified training programs.

Since 1964, most companies have been required by the Federal government to follow affirmative action and equal employment guidelines that prohibit discrimination on the basis of race, color, religion, sex, or national origin. More current additions to this legislation include age, physical disability, pregnancy, childbirth or related medical conditions. Some local communities have also included sexual preference in their anti-discrimination laws. These laws are designed to give all members of the workforce equal access to opportunities for jobs and to prevent employees from unnecessary harassment. As is evident from the previous discussion, however, these laws do not guarantee that all people progress through the organizational hierarchy at an equal rate.

One area of legal policy that has received a great deal of attention and communication-based research is sexual harassment. Sexual harassment has been defined by the Equal Employment Opportunity Commission as:

> unwelcome sexual advances, request for sexual favors, and other verbal and physical conduct of a sexual nature . . . when (1) submission to such conduct is made either explicitly or implicitly a term or condition of an individual's employment, (2) submission to or rejection of such conduct by an individual is used as the basis

for employment decisions affecting such individuals, (3) or such conduct has the purpose or effect of unreasonably interfering with an individual's work performance or creating an intimidating, hostile, or offensive work environment. (G. Mastalli, 1981: 94)

From a communication perspective, sexual harassment is an exchange between two people in which one exhibits sexual approach behaviors, the other counters with sexual avoidance behaviors, and the first subsequently exhibits additional sexual approach behavior (S. Simon and B. Montgomery, 1987). Sexual harassment behavior often appears in ascending stages. In other words, the harasser may begin with more subtle behavior, such as joking, which escalates to a more extreme behavior, such as physical touching (M. Booth-Butterfield, 1986). One survey (P. Loy and Stewart, 1984) found that approximately half the reported incidents of sexual harassment concerned verbal commentary (sexual messages delivered through innuendo or off-color jokes). Thirty-six percent of the incidents reported in this survey involved physical contact, such as unwanted touching or groping. Verbal negotiation (explicit requests to exchange sex for economic or career benefits) occurred 10 percent of the time. Three percent of the reported incidents involved actual physical assault. Companies are responsible for their employees' behavior and can be held legally liable for the negative consequences suffered as a result of this behavior (R. Sandroff, 1988).

Two other areas of legal concern that affect gender relations in the corporation are revised job qualifications and modified training programs. Many job qualifications have been modified to accommodate women applicants. For example, in many communities, the physical test required to become eligible to be a firefighter has been modified to identify qualified applicants without discriminating against women because of their smaller size and weight. In addition, many on-the-job training programs have been designed to prepare women as well as men for jobs that have traditionally been held by men. When you see a woman doing telephone repair you are seeing an example of the effects of this type of program.

ECONOMIC ISSUES

Because businesses are economic enterprises, many of the changing business policies are economic in nature. For example, many businesses have set aside special funds to promote minority (including women-owned) business development. Changes in government contracting criteria encourage minority-owned and women-owned businesses. International competition has encouraged businesses to improve both the pricing and the quality of their products. Although it may be difficult at first to see how economic policies are affected by communication, communication processes are being used to meet economic challenges. For example, innovations to improve quality include listening more to employees who have direct contact with the product and encouraging employee suggestions, both strategies identified with a more feminine communication style.

PUBLIC ISSUES

Public issues affecting current business practices include responding to legal violations and moral issues, changing purchasing demographics, and legislative influence (national candidates, lobbyists, and legislative action). Thus, public communication, such as public speaking and public relations campaigns, influences current business practices.

IMPACT ON BUSINESS FUNCTIONS

Corporations are responding to the changing workforce, including gender issues, in a variety of ways. For example, in terms of structural changes, organizations are adding new functions, such as AA/EEO Officer, cultural diversity teams, or Women in Sales Task Force groups. Existing parts of the organization also have been greatly affected. The role of the Human Resource Department has changed dramatically to address the obligations in corporate AA/EEO legislation. Today, human resource specialists act as watchdogs for corporate compliance and also serve as counseling sources to reduce stress and confusion when employees and management differ on compliance issues. Training programs have been changed to reflect the diverse populations in the workforce and to eliminate bias in content and presentation of programs. For example, it is no longer acceptable to use sexist language or all-male terminology in case study materials (such as referring to "salesmen," or assuming that all machine operators are male or that all secretaries are female) or to use visual media that portray women and minorities only in support roles and men only in decision-making roles.

Some companies have expanded their employee services by adding child care support, flexible work schedules, and special interest groups to promote a more uniform benefit structure and address the needs of a more diverse employee population. For example, a recent survey found that 56 percent of 259 major employers offer some type of child care aid, 56 percent allow flexible scheduling, and 42 percent grant unpaid parental leave (Fierman, 1990).

As mentioned previously, employment interviewing is another area that is receiving increased attention in terms of preventing gender bias in organizations. Changes in interviewing practice include advertising, recruitment, interview structure, decision making, and record-keeping requirements. Job advertisements often contain a statement such as "We are an affirmative action/equal employment opportunity employer," designed to encourage women and minority applicants. Companies often conduct outreach recruitment efforts designed to recruit a more diverse college population. The structure of the interview is carefully planned to include the job description, hiring criteria, and assessment of the applicant's qualifications. Decision making is based on multiple contacts and clear documentation. In addition, companies must keep accurate records that contain non-discriminatory applicant profiles and clearly specify the results of the interviews.

The following questions can help an applicant in an employment interview to identify signs of gender bias:

1. Did you feel comfortable? Were treated with courtesy and respect?

2. Did you experience any direct examples of discrimination (questions, jokes, social references)?

3. Does the company have a public image of fair action? Look for a corporate mission statement or code of ethics.

4. What are the results of fair action? Does the management team, leadership, and recruitment/promotion activity substantiate their commitment?

5. What opportunities for training and advancement are available? Does your performance affect your consideration?

6. Are there special group activities, benefits, and projects that are of interest to you?

7. Do the company's references and referrals check out? Some companies are recognized for their progress on gender issues. Review the annual report and product literature and talk to customers.

The more you understand about the company, the better you can evaluate the opportunity for you.

Once an applicant is hired, performance appraisals are also being modified to prevent gender bias. Modifications have occurred in the structure and scheduling of performance appraisals, in the training and decision making of the appraiser, and in improvement programs used as follow-ups to the appraisal. Appraisals should be performance-based and results-oriented. They should be evenly distributed throughout the work year and routinely administered. Appraisers must be trained to eliminate bias in delivering feedback to employees, and their decisions may be subjected to third-party review. In addition, improvement programs based on weaknesses identified in performance appraisals should be multi-step to encourage systematic, gradual change resulting in progressive action.

INTERPERSONAL COMMUNICATION IN ORGANIZATIONS

Traditionally, organizations have emphasized productivity, competition, self-reliance, independence, and success (J. Grant 1988). Thus, much of the formal communication in organizations is based on a traditionally masculine model of interaction. According to I. Devine and D. Markiewicz (1990), "organizations pride themselves on their creation of rational structures based primarily on a male perspective of interaction. Workers are expected to set aside interpersonal behaviors that do not directly contribute to task performance" (333). Workers have traditionally been expected to focus on competition, strategy, and "bottom-line results." This type of thinking has occurred because "organizations have traditionally been established and managed by men. Rational structures were consciously created where decision-making processes, communication patterns and norms of interaction were based on normative male experiences of relationships and approaches to work" (333). Yet, "as more women enter organizations at managerial levels, they bring with them their own norms of relationship, friendship and interaction" (333).

According to Devine and Markiewicz:

> The importance of relationships for women is reflected in such tendencies as (1) women's emphasis on assisting others to achieve the others' goals; (2) the emphasis on establishing the security of intimate relationships prior to consideration of personal achievement; (3) women's tendency to define themselves in relation to others; (4) women's inclination towards self-disclosure and the development of close relationships with others. (333)

Related themes in men's lives include:

> (1) relationships (for example, mentor, spouse, friends) as instrumental to attaining one's career goals or "dream"; (2) the emphasis on succeeding in one's career during early adulthood; (3) the importance of work and achievements in defining male identity; (4) men's tendency to avoid self-disclosure and to develop few, if any, close relationships with co-workers. (333)

Grant believes that "women's greater ease with the relational world could help make organizations places in which affiliation, friendship, connection, and personhood could also be valued in a more integrated manner" (60). She criticizes organizations for creating "she-males"—women who have moved up the organizational hierarchy of success and who strongly identify with the male model of managerial success. Of course, the "she-male" is often negatively perceived by her male peers. For example, one consultant notes, "the most common lament of top management men is 'She's too shrill. She's too aggressive. She's too hard-edged'" (Fierman, 1990: 46). Women often feel trapped by these attitudes. If their communication style is "too feminine," they are perceived as too soft; if they adopt a more "masculine" style, they are seen as abrasive (Fierman, 1990).

Although we have come a long way from the "power-pumps era" of the 1970s and 1980s in which many women believed that to win the corporate game required a poker-faced mentality and an imitation of men's behavior (D. Oldenburg, 1990), working closely with women continues to make many male executives uncomfortable (Fierman, 1990). Ellie Raynolds, a partner at Ward Howell International, notes:

> Corporate males still don't know how to deal with women. They are afraid to yell at them or to give them negative feedback. It's as though they think they are yelling at their mothers or their wives. Men often worry women will run from the room in tears, or worse yet, yell back. They're not really sure the women will come through for them. They don't trust them as much as the guys with whom they talk football (Fierman, 1990: 42).

To find out how men and women in organizations actually communicate with each other, A. Statham (1987) surveyed a matched sample of women and men in management jobs and interviewed their secretaries. The managers worked for three diverse organizations—a financial institution, a manufacturing firm, and a technical institute. The female managers described themselves as both "people" and "task oriented." The male managers focused more on the importance of their jobs (called "image engrossment" by Statham). Statham concluded that the women used their people orientation to accomplish tasks while the men valued autonomy in their jobs. This difference in managerial style was most clear in the area of delegation. Women felt a need to be involved with their subordinates while men believed that good management entailed *not* being involved in what their subordinates were doing. These styles were often resented by employees of the other sex. For example, women perceived male managers' autonomy as neglect, and men felt women managers' need to be involved was an indication that women managers were not confident in their male subordinates' ability to carry out a task. Statham differentiates between the male ethos of "give everybody space to do their jobs" and the female desire to "look over their shoulders" (422). Although Statham acknowledges several exceptions in which women were concerned about autonomy and men were more involved, she concludes:

> Men managers leave women subordinates to struggle on their own because they believe this is the "best way to manage." Men subordinates resent women managers who "stand over their shoulders" because this signals to them a lack of confidence, while the woman believes she is demonstrating her "concern for the employee." And women resent men who "dump the work" onto others or who in other ways are perceived as not contributing as much as women (425).

Thus, as noted earlier, men and women in organizations see the same behavior and perceive it quite differently.

LEADERSHIP DYNAMICS

As mentioned earlier in this chapter, more women are moving into leadership positions in organizations. It is important, therefore, to discover how these women are being perceived. In general, women have a more positive attitude than men toward women as managers, but people who have worked with or for a woman manager have a less traditional view of women as managers than those who have not had this type of work experience (V. Wheeless and C. Berryman-Fink, 1985). Thus, as more women become managers and more people have experience working with women managers, attitudes toward them may change.

Women managers appear to be more open in terms of communication than men are. For example, N. Josephowitz (1980) reports that women managers are on the average twice as accessible to their subordinates as male managers are. Thus, women may be expressing their communication style by listening to subordinates more than other managers do.

In addition to interpersonal differences in communication behavior, the type of organization may influence attitudes toward women in leadership positions. Companies that deal with high technology products and small start-up companies are often more accommodating to women managers. Because new industries are less likely to be run by the old boys' network (Fierman, 1990), they allow women to maximize the benefits of their own communication style.

Although perceptions of women in leadership positions are beginning to change, there is still a lack of women in the very top managerial levels of corporations—the so-called "glass ceiling effect." Researchers at the University of California at Los Angeles Graduate School of Management and Korn/Ferry (a corporate recruiter) surveyed approximately 700 top executives and found that since 1979 neither women nor minorities have increased their ranks at the level of senior vice president or above by more than 2 percentage points (L. Silver, 1990). They conclude that there has been little progress after ten years of growing awareness of the importance of promoting women and minorities. All of the respondents in one study (male and female managers as well as their secretaries) mentioned a "point beyond which women could not go" (Statham, 1987).

According to a report by the Women's Research and Education Institute, the lack of women at the top of corporate hierarchies cannot be explained solely by their recent entry into those professions. Women have not reached the top of the corporate hierarchy in part because of the sex-role stereotype held by many corporate decision makers that women do not have the personality characteristics necessary for top leadership roles (S. Rich, 1990). *Fortune* magazine recently polled 1,000 CEOs to determine why women are not progressing into the highest levels of corporate management. Of the 241 respondents to the survey, 81 percent attributed the problem to stereotyping and preconceptions (Fierman, 1990). As one authority notes, "it's a little bit surprising that there hasn't been more breakthrough [for women and minorities]. There're barriers imposed if you don't share the same interests or follow the same football teams" (quoted in Silver, 1990).

CHALLENGES FOR THE FUTURE

As one can see from the discussion presented above, many challenges face workers as we move into Workforce 2000. According to N. Colwill and M. Erhart (1985), "education, attitude change, the establishment of women's networks, and improved communication between men and women [are] catalysts for sex-role change "in organizations" (30).

Thus, one of the best communication strategies for women to use to overcome barriers in the workplace is networking. As noted previously in this chapter, although women are entering management in increasing numbers, their progress up the corporate ladder is often blocked by barriers, such as gender bias, that limit the advancement and compensation of female executives. Colwill and Erhart (1985) found that women who used networks such as membership in private clubs or on corporate boards were more successful than women who did not have these contacts. Networking can be through formal information channels such as head-hunting firms or informal channels such as family and friends (R. Bartlett and T. Miller, 1985). These networks are often successful because over 40 percent of managerial jobs are discovered by word of mouth (M. Corcoran, L. Datcher, and G. Duncan, 1980).

Prospects for better pay for women are also increasing. According to one authority, "a shrinking labor force is expected to force employers to compete for workers and that is expected to mean better pay for women" (J. Mann, 1990). Hopefully, this change in the workforce will also help to eliminate the glass ceiling effect. As noted in a recent article by Fierman, "our best hope for the future is women who don't see the ceiling but the sky" (62).

In addition, many corporations are introducing programs to help their employees deal with and manage the increasing diversity of the workforce. Managing diversity means that managers' performances will be judged on their ability to manage a diverse work force (Duke, 1991). Also, as managing culturally diverse programs becomes more popular, men are being challenged to confront their own negative stereotypes about people who are different from themselves (Duke, 1991). These changes should also contribute to the increased understanding between men and women and to the increased success of women in organizations.

REFERENCES

Bartlett, R. L., and T. I. Miller. 1985. Executive compensation: Female executives and networking. *AEA Papers and Proceedings* 75: 267–270.

Booth-Butterfield, M. 1986. Recognizing and communicating in harassment-prone organizational climates. *Communication Quarterly* 9: 42–51.

Colwill, N. L., and M. Erhart. 1985. Have women changed the workplace? *Business Quarterly*, Spring: 27–31.

Corcoran, M., L. Datcher, and G. J. Duncan. 1980. Most workers find jobs through word of mouth. *Monthly Labor Review* 103: 33–35.

Devine, I., and D. Markiewicz. 1990. Cross-sex relationships at work and the impact of gender stereotypes. *Journal of Business Ethics* 9: 333–338.

Duke, L. 1991. Cultural shifts bring anxiety for white men. *Washington Post*, 1 Jan.: A1, A14.

Fairhurst, G. T. 1986. Male-female communication on the job: Literature review and commentary. In M. McLaughlin, *Communication Yearbook 10*, Newbury Park, CA: Sage, 83–116.

Fierman, J. 1990. Why women still don't hit the top. *Fortune*, 30 July: 40–62.

Grant, J. 1988. Women as managers: What they can offer to organizations. *Organizational Dynamics* 16(3): 56–63.

Hymowitz, C. 1989. Gender gap is how you perceive it. *Wall Street Journal*, 16 Feb.: B1.

Josephowitz, N. 1980. Management of men and women: Closed vs. open doors. *Harvard Business Review* 58(5): 56–62.

Loy, P. H., and L. P. Stewart. 1984. The extent and effects of the sexual harassment of working women. *Sociological Focus* 17: 31–43.

Mann, J. 1990. The shatterproof ceiling. *Washington Post*, 17 Aug.: D3.

Mastalli, G. L. 1981. Appendix: The legal context. *Harvard Business Review* 59(2): 94–95.

Oldenburg, D. 1990. Cracking the ceiling with a smile. *Washington Post*, 29 Oct.: B5.

Powell, G. N. 1988. *Women and Men in Management*. Beverly Hills, CA: Sage.

Rich, S. 1990. Women's pay still far behind men's, group reports. *Washington Post*, 26 April: A9.

Sandroff, R. 1988. Sexual harassment in the Fortune 500. *Working Women*, Dec.: 69–73.

Silver, L. 1990. Few women, minorities at the top. *Washington Post*, 14 Aug.: A1, A5.

Simon, S., and B. M. Montgomery. 1987, May. *Sexual Harassment: Applying a Communication Perspective*. Paper presented at the meeting of the Eastern Communication Association, Syracuse, NY.

Spruell, G. 1985. Making it, big time—Is it really tougher for women? *Training and Development Journal*, July: 30–33.

Statham, A. 1987. The gender model revisited: Difference in the management styles of men and women. *Sex Roles* 16: 409–429.

Stewart, L. P., A. D. Stewart, S. A. Friedley, and P. J. Cooper. 1990. *Communication Between the Sexes*. Scottsdale, AZ: Gorsuch Scarisbrick.

U.S. Department of Labor. 1989, December. *Facts on Working Women*, Women's Bureau No. 89–4. Washington, DC: U.S. Government Printing Office.

Wheeless, V. E., and C. Berryman–Fink. 1985. Perceptions of women managers and their communicator competencies. *Communication Quarterly* 33: 137–148.

COMMUNICATING IN LEGAL SETTINGS

AUTHOR   Cindy Rhodes Victor, Attorney-at-Law,
Howard & Howard Attorneys, P.C.

POINTS TO BE ADDRESSED:

- Recognition of gender differences in legal communication
- Communication with gender-based and gender-biased terminology
- Gender differences in communication in law school and professional development
- Gender communication in the practice of law and specific areas of practice
- Gender communication and client relationships

The practice of law, perhaps more than any other profession, illustrates the challenges and changes in gender communication. The legal setting has long been exclusively or predominantly male-dominated. In 1970, only three percent of lawyers were women. As late as 1988, the figure had risen to just twenty percent (Gellis, 1991: 941). Accordingly, communication in legal settings has historically been male-centered, without any regard for the differences in how women communicate among themselves or with men. However, the number of women entering law schools has risen dramatically. Women now constitute more than forty percent of law school students, a tenfold increase in ten years (MacCrate, 1989: 993). As more and more women enter the profession, discussions of gender communication issues—such as gender-based terminology, law school education, differences in training and development that senior attorneys provide to newer lawyers, gender differences in litigation and other legal settings, and client development and service—of necessity become more important.

RECOGNIZING GENDER DIFFERENCES
IN LEGAL COMMUNICATION

Because of its historically male-dominated nature, the law has been slow to recognize gender differences in communication, even in situations in which one of the parties—as client, litigant, crime victim, employee—was female. Yet, as experts agree, gender differences do exist. As Leslie Bender (1989) points out:

Our general experiences as women and men suggest that there are also non-physical differences between our sexes that affect the ways in which we understand the world, our roles in it, and our relationships to other people. These differences are learned from birth as we are socialized into the dominant ideological systems of our culture. The culture/social construction and attribution of qualities to different biological sexes is called gender. (946)

While Bender recognizes the controversy among scholars as to the origin of gender differences, she states:

Regardless of whether gender differences are biological or cultural or mixed, they are real and they matter in the world as it currently functions. (946)

Bender contends:

There are two gender cultures, one for women and one for men, each with its own accepted customs, norms, practices, behaviors and rituals. We need not suppose that there are any universal, ahistorical, acultural gender traits that are the essence of womanhood or manhood. Even though different cultures may have different gender expectations, and even though socially assigned gender traits are not universally applicable within sexes or even between them, each culture presumes distinctions between men and women that broadly apply within that culture. (947)

Bender describes "gendered selves" as "dialectic relationships between free will and the structures of our gendered cultures" (948, n. 26). One acquires gender through observation, positive and negative reinforcement by those in authority, and copying the social roles that exist in "families, schools, religions, media and workplaces" (948). Once there is a gender culture, and people have become acculturated within an assigned gender, the experiences of one gender differ greatly from those of the other gender. Notwithstanding the plethora of differences among women, they have one common experience—being treated as women within their particular culture. According to Bender,

If we deviate from the cultural construction of gender, then we are deemed to be "more like men" or less like "true women". This is not a matter of physical sexuality, but social construct. If there were no characteristics culturally assigned to the concept of women, the idea of a biological female not being a true woman would be inconceivable. (948)

Carol Gilligan (1982), a professor of education at Harvard University, contends that there are distinct male and female modes of thought. Based on the differences in the gender identity development identity between boys and girls—"relatedness" (with their mothers as caretakers) of girls and "separateness" of boys (who distinguish themselves from their mothers)—Gilligan asserts that men and women have different concepts of ethics and morality. According to Gilligan, women have an ethic of "caring" and men, an ethic of "rights" (164). The objective of the male ethic of rights is the preservation of separateness and autonomy. Under the male ethic, when competing and conflicting rights of autonomy occur, the conflict is resolved by balancing the competing rights on the basis of a rational system of values (164). The female ethic of caring, on the other hand, has as its goal the preservation of relationships. Women accordingly resolve conflicts through a duty of caring for particular people in specific contexts. (28, 32). Gilligan suggests that the law should recognize and encourage the differing ethics of men and women.

A number of authors have extended Gilligan's system to legal settings. For example, Patricia Wald (1983), Chief Judge of the United States Court of Appeals for the District of Columbia, believes that more women should act as judges, not only for the sake of gender equality, but because the societal experiences of *both* men and women should serve as the bases for dispute resolution since the law resolves conflicts arising between people—whether male or female (48–49). Kenneth Karst (1984), a law professor, has argued that the substantive law must incorporate the female ethic of caring before it can be truly fair to all people. According to Karst, the constitutional rights of liberty, equality, due process and property are solely based on and interpreted by reference to the male ethic of rights (480–86).

There are, however, scholars and practitioners who disagree with Gilligan's conclusions, contending that the focus should be on differences among individuals regardless of gender (Ginsburg, 1986: 144–46), that men and women are more alike than they are different (Greeno and Maccoby 1986: 315), or that equality will be realized only by deemphasizing gender differences (Finley, 1986: 1119). Yet these authors differ only on the emphasis that should be given to gender differences, not on the fact that differences exist, in whatever degree, between men and women. Although, as Robert MacCrate (1989), a partner in the law firm of Sullivan & Cromwell, New York City, observes:

> The quest for gender equality must become a central objective of the legal profession if we are to be faithful to the professional ideal of opposing all forms of discrimination, and if we are to achieve full integration and equal participation of women. (990)

it is clear that, as legal theorist Catherine MacKinnon (1989) points out, "to look for the place of gender in everything is not to reduce everything to gender" (xi). Judith Kaye (1988), associate judge of the New York Court of Appeals and former partner in a Wall Street law firm, points out:

> I am particularly drawn by the debate focused on the significance to be given to women's differences—their biological and cultural differences from men, as well as differences that have been identified in their sense of self, their sense of morality, their relationships with others. Some adjure all talk of differences, remembering that women's differences once served as the basis for laws that circumscribed their lives. But today there is a growing voice for the view that recognizing differences is essential to true gender equality. (118).

Gender differences are particularly marked in the law as a profession. To succeed as a lawyer, particularly in a large, well-established law firm, women traditionally believed that they had to eschew feminine characteristics and modes of thinking, and instead "act like a man." Bender (1989) posits that to be a woman in any specific culture means "having to acquire some of [the] gender attributes [of men] to succeed in traditional male-created institutions and professions, like law" (949). The influx of women into the profession has not always succeeded in bringing the female gender culture into the culture of the legal profession. Bender determines:

> The parts of our daily activities that reflect our gender culture are specifically excluded from and deemed inappropriate to our professional environment. As a consequence, in our professional communities, and, in particular, in the world of high-powered law firms, gender inequality predominates. (949)

Feminist scholars have proposed two different models for the elimination of gender inequality in the legal profession. The first model is based on the premise that women can do the same tasks as men as well as men do, if given equal opportunity, access to positions, and treatment (see Ginsburg, 1975). According to Bender:

> The goal of this model of feminism was getting women accepted into the big law firms based on traditional criteria of merit, competing on existing terms, and being treated equally to, that is, the same as, men. (950).

The second model holds that in situations in which women are biologically different from men, such as pregnancy, women should be accorded special treatment and not be disadvantaged by these physical differences, so that they can compete equally with men (see Littleton, 1987; Finley, 1986; Williams, 1984-85). But neither model permits the entry of what has been described as female gender culture traits. Both models attempt to recreate women as men in the profession, the first model by treating women no differently in any aspect, however large or small, even when there are situations in which men and women do differ. This model may be illustrated by the idea of a man and woman engaged in a wrestling match, with no regard for who had greater physical strength, more training and encouragement in development, and more chances to wrestle on a daily basis. The second model attempts to recreate women as men by giving women special treatment to put them on the same level as men. This model can be illustrated by the idea of a man and a woman wrestling, with the man having one arm tied behind his back. Yet neither model suffices, because they attempt to *recreate* women as men in the practice of law. More preferable is a profession in which both men's and women's behavior are accepted and valued. This model can be illustrated by asking the question, Why is there a need to wrestle at all? —Wrestlers and non-wrestlers, that is, men and women, should be accepted in the profession equally.

However, the practice of law does not presently accept gender culture differences. The accepted modes of thought and behavior are still for the most part masculine, especially in communication. As Rand Jack and Dana Crowley Jack (1989) determined in their study of the changing values of men and women lawyers:

> Not only must care-oriented lawyers face the puzzle of integrating their moral perspective into a rights-oriented system, but women attorneys have the additional

task of accomplishing this in an atmosphere of discriminatory attitudes and structures. Beginning in law school, women learn that feminine ways of participating are not always welcome. Given that qualities learned by women at home in play make them vulnerable in a predominantly male profession, one solution women have attempted is to eradicate feminine characteristics. For example, a female partner in a large firm advises: "Don't think of yourself or allow anyone to think of you, as anything but a hard-driving, capable lawyer." The safest way to succeed is emulation of males, even to the extent of learning to "speak louder and lower," and "actively becoming an intimidator." Even clothes, a worldwide symbol of gender difference, are to be homogenized to the male mode. "Dress and talk in a conservative and professional style. Avoid wrap-around skirts, casual shoes or hair color changes. Dress like a lawyer, in a conservative suit. Don't chew gum." (935–936).

Thus, particularly in issues of communication, women are told, expressly or otherwise, "Forsake the law or forsake the self" (Jack and Jack, 1989: 935–36). Even the presence of more women in the profession has not eradicated this dilemma. Instead, we have that which Bender (1989) describes as "the infamous 'add women ad stir' model of reform":

Even though we add more and more females to the quotient of persons doing the job, women who demonstrate aspects of the gendered women's culture are discouraged, badly evaluated, and seen as unfit. We add members of our sex to a profession, but we do not add "acceptance" of gender differences. Those women who can make themselves act [and] think most like the gendered male culture succeed. (950–951)

Yet, gender differences still make women suspect in the profession. As one of the women lawyers whom Jack and Jack (1989) interviewed stated:

While most male lawyers are assumed to be serious and to be embarking on a life-long career, females still are viewed as question marks who may quit to stay home and raise children. Each woman, therefore, must establish herself as a committed and competent professional and convince each judge and opposing counsel that she means business and is in the profession to stay. (936)

Women thus have had to accept male gender culture differences or adopt them as a role-playing to succeed as lawyers. If a woman rejects the sex role norm, she is labeled as "too feminine" and not tough enough for the profession. Yet, as Bender suggests:

It is not gender equality for women to assume characteristics of the male gender or to attempt to take a male perspective and then do those jobs. Just because we are talented enough to assimilate male characteristics for the business world does not mean that that is what we want or what is best. Getting inside the law firm is a start, but if the only women who succeed and achieve the power to change the institutions are the women who are most like men and least gender-identified, then gender inequality continues unabated. (951)

However, women are less and less willing to accept presence and success in the profession solely on masculine terms. As a number of female and minority law students at Yale Law School observed in a 1984 open letter to the law school community:

> The voice that troubles us is the monolithic, confident voice of "insiders" who see themselves as the norm and who have (often unconsciously) little tolerance for our interest in diversity and difference. This voice, tone, style is often defended as "the way lawyers speak." . . . To the extent that this is the way lawyers speak, we must conclude that we cannot be lawyers—or that we cannot be ourselves. (Jack and Jack, 1989: 938)

As this chapter explains, these gender differences in voice exist in all areas of the profession, from gender-based and -biased legal terminology to the treatment of women as litigators, negotiators, and service providers. Recognition of gender differences in legal communication is the first step toward acceptance of these gender differences in legal settings.

GENDER-BASED AND GENDER-BIASED LEGAL TERMINOLOGY

A discussion of gender communication in legal settings must begin with an examination of the language of the law. As Lucinda Finley (1989) says, "Language matters. Law matters. Legal language matters" (886). While this might appear, as Finley herself terms it, just "a clever syllogism," the nature of legal reasoning and the language through which this legal reasoning is expressed clearly is of consequence.

Unlike in many other professional fields, language and communication in legal settings are made significant by the fact that the law itself is a "language, a form of discourse, and a system through which meanings are reflected and constructed and cultural practices organized" (Finley, 1989: 888). As Finley (1989) describes it:

> Law is a language of power, a particularly authoritative discourse. Law can pronounce definitively what something is or is not and how a situation or event is to be understood. The concepts, categories, and terms the law uses, and the reasoning structure by which it expresses itself, organizes its practices, and constructs its meanings, has a particularly potent ability to shape popular and authoritative understandings of situations. Legal language does more than express thoughts. It reinforces certain world views and understandings of events. Its terms and its reasoning structure are the procrustean bed into which supplicants before the law must express their needs. Through its definitions and the way it talks about events, law has the power to silence alternative meanings—to suppress other stories. (888)

Because of this power that the law as a language holds, participants in legal institutions—particularly lawyers and judges—must recognize that gender biases exist in legal terminology and must learn to accommodate and accept gender differences in communication.

The language of the law—"the way lawyers speak"—has traditionally been male-based and -biased, because the profession was until recently almost exclusively male-dominated. Since men "created" legal terminology, it reflects one gender's experiences and understanding of the world and of the other gender. Because women have only recently been entering the profession in significant numbers, male-based legal language has had few challenges, and accordingly has enabled its users to claim that legal language is not gender-specific or gender-biased, but is instead objective and neutral (Finley, 1989, 1987; MacKinnon, 1982, 1983). Yet a review of the historical underpinnings and development of the language of the law—and the language itself—demonstrates its bias.

> Legal language is a male language because it is principally informed by men's experiences and because it derives from the powerful social situation of men, relative to women. Universal and objective thinking is male language because intellectually, economically and politically privileged men have had the power to ignore other perspectives and thus to come to think of their situation as the norm, their reality as reality, and their views as objective. (Finley, 1989; 893).

Although many women have become skilled in employing legal language, this does not transform it into a gender-neutral language. Rather, "it simply means that women have learned male language, as many French speakers learn English" (Finley, 1989: 894).

This inculcation into "male language" begins in law school, where professors teach men and women students from texts, called "casebooks," which reflect and perpetuate gender bias and gender-based terminology. While this chapter discusses gender communication in legal education in more detail below, it is important to note here that the authors and editors of these casebooks generally demonstrate a male bias in the language they employ in books. For example, masculine pronouns are used almost exclusively to refer to generic persons. In one leading contracts law casebook, analyzed in great detail by New England School of Law professor Mary Jo Frug, the editors selected cases where judges used masculine pronouns in their decisions, even though the parties to whom the decisions applied were female (Frug, 1985: 1094). Frug also points out instances in that casebook in which the editors chose to include scholarly articles that exclude women as readers or participants in legal institutions. Most importantly, Frug found that the editors did not modify *their* own language to include feminine pronouns:

> Of the nine problems which the editors have created for the casebook, . . . in those instances where the editors do not describe the figures in the problem neutrally, they refer to them by male pronouns, with the sole exception of one question (out of six, in the fourth problem), in which the editors refer to a shopper interested in purchasing an alligator bag as "she." Using a feminine pronoun once, and then only in conjunction with the stereotypical women's role of mindless consumer, hardly compensates for the many instances in the casebook where women were not recognized because of historical custom. Instead, a reader's overwhelming impression is that the casebook is not addressed to, nor does it contemplate, women. (Frug, 1985: 1095–1096)

The editors' failure to address women in the casebook from anything other than a male-biased and stereotypical-laden viewpoint becomes even more egregious when one considers that the editors state in the preface to their book that their goal in developing that casebook was to pass on not only "substantive knowledge and analytical skills," but more importantly, "a language and a culture" (Dawson, et al., 1982: xvii). Frug points out that the only gender-neutral terminology that the casebook editors use is at the beginning of each case, where the decision's authors are denominated by a first initial and a last name or just a last name. Because of the focus of the book, students could easily assume that the authors of all the cases the book includes were male, even though women actually wrote several of the opinions (the term for the written decision in a case) (Frug, 1985: 1096). Such an error did in fact occur in a class Professor Lucinda Finley taught at Yale Law School. A casebook included an opinion by Justice Marie Garibaldi of the New Jersey Supreme Court, but the author of the opinion was designated only by "Garibaldi, Justice." At least one student believed from this that Justice Garibaldi was a man:

> When Finley kept referring to the justice as "she," one male student complained, "You're carrying this he and she stuff too far," the student told Finley. "You're turning it into a political rap." (Moss, 1988: 52)

An examination of substantive areas of the law likewise shows the presence of gender-based and -biased language. For example, in tort law, the definition of the scope of injuries and measurement of the compensation that should be awarded for these injuries are based primarily on a male perspective of what people are worth. Under this system, a 45-year-old man who earned $200,000 per year before suffering injury is worth more than a 45-year-old woman who works in the home caring for her family. A determination of injury in the area of employment discrimination law is predicated upon the "reasonable person" standard (until recently called the "reasonable man standard"), even where the victim of discrimination is female. Thus, in a sexual harassment case, the standard for determining whether or not a woman was subjected to a sexually harassing hostile work environment would be whether a "reasonable person" would have believed that the conduct of which she complains was sexually harassing. Under this standard, if an employer subjected all its employees to a sexually harassing work environment, then this environment could be considered the workplace norm. A woman bringing suit for sexual harassment might lose in court because she could not show that she had been treated *differently* from others, even though in actuality all the company's employees might have been forced to work under demeaning and sexually hostile conditions.

Efforts to minimize and remove gender basis and bias from legal terminology are complicated by the "conservatism" of the legal language. The structure of our legal system gives little credence to "new" ideas and theories. Decisions are almost always made by referring back to case precedent, that is, to decisions that previous judges and tribunals rendered in cases presenting similar issues. If one party can support its position by citing decisions made by the same tribunal in analogous cases (even though the analogy might be stretched considerably), and the other party cannot, then the party relying on case precedent will most likely prevail. Indeed, if the adjudicator does not follow precedent, the written decision must clearly state either that (1) the precedential authority on which one party relies can be "distinguished" from the facts of the current case, or (2), in rare instances, that the adjudicator has rejected the previous decisions by "overturning" them in favor of new legal statements.

Yet there has been some progress in changing legal discourse. For example, at least two state courts have determined that the issue of whether sexual harassment in the workplace existed must be viewed from a "reasonable woman" standard—did the victim believe that she was being sexually harassed? However, even with some progress, legal language is still replete with gender-based terminology and bias. Practitioners accordingly must recognize and remain aware of this bias and perspective when communicating in legal settings.

GENDER AND COMMUNICATION IN LEGAL EDUCATION AND PROFESSIONAL DEVELOPMENT

Indoctrination into the skills of communicating within the language of the law begins in law school, whose purpose is to teach students to think "like lawyers." Yet, as discussed above, thinking "like a lawyer" usually means thinking only from a male perspective.

Law professors employ predominantly the "Socratic method," which is based on conflict and argumentative reasoning as a means of teaching class, to the virtual exclusion of consensus building or group problem-solving. A number of studies have concluded that women students as a group participate in classroom discussions and answer questions in less time than do male students (see Adams, 1988; Taber, et al., 1988; Weiss and Melling, 1988). One survey by the University of Tulsa College of Law professor Tawnya Lovell Banks, found that 16.7 percent of women law students never volunteer in class, as opposed to only 9 percent of the male law students. Indeed, women become more reluctant to volunteer in class the longer they are in law school. In the first year of law school, 13.3 percent of the women never volunteer. By the third (and final) year, this figure rises to 25 percent (Moss, 1988). Likewise, in a survey of all 764 living female Stanford Law School graduates and an equal number of male alumni, the staff of the Stanford Law Review determined:

> One explanation is that women speak less frequently than do men because they feel less comfortable talking in class or because professors call on women less often than they do on men. We can also interpret this observed gender difference in terms of Gilligan's theory. Women may feel perfectly comfortable speaking in class but simply choose to do so less often. Women may be less interested in dominating classroom discussions and more concerned with furthering collegial cooperation. (Taber, et al., 1988: 1242)

In the report of the study conducted by the Stanford Law Review, the authors noted:

> Other investigators have examined women's experiences with the Socratic and case and instructional methods. For example, James Elkins, a professor of law and psychiatry, argues that women have trouble adjusting to law school because "[l]egal education is a man's world and reflects the traditional array of 'masculine virtues'." He has stated that women are not silenced by overt sexual discrimination, but are silenced by subtle aspect of traditional legal education that deny the importance of their personal feelings and beliefs. Elkins' studies suggest that many professors may not respond favorably when women point out the social ramifications of legal holdings. It is also possible that the Socratic method may be less congruent with the way in which women, as contrasted with men, think about legal problems. (Taber, 1988: 1220)

The Stanford study proposes that "lower rates of class participation may reflect women's withdrawal from . . . the law school experience because the Socratic method 'denigrates' the high value many women place on avoiding conflict and competition" (Adams, 1988: 4).

Similarly, the casebooks that professors use to teach law school subjects reflect the profession's male gender-bias. For example, as discussed in the previous section, a popular and widely-used contracts casebook contains numerous examples of male-gender-based, and -biased, communication. The presence of this bias in law school communication is important, for, as Frug (1985) points out:

> gendered aspects of a casebook affect readers' understanding of the law and of themselves. . . . The editorial choices within a casebook determine how many readers think about the law of a doctrinal area, about lawyering in that field, about clients, and about legal reasoning. (1065, 1069)

In fact, as Frug notes, because this contracts casebook may be one of only five books a first-year law student reads, it may have enormous influence upon students' views.

In this casebook, the editors use communication devices other than gender-based terminology that reflect gender bias. First, as characters in the cases, men overwhelmingly outnumber women:

> readers who notice gender differences are likely to be sensitive not only to the marginal representation of women in the casebook, but also to any sex role stereotyping within the decisions. Moreover, the cumulative impression provided by similarities among the women parties could provoke readers somewhat disinclined to notice gender to observe the casebook's links between women and ideas about gender. (Frug, 1985: 1077)

In the cases in which they do appear, women have legal problems arising from the "limited activities typically associated with their sex, and the jobs they have are the most stereotypical forms of women's work" (Frug, 1985: 1077–78). Women are often shown in "stereotypical and unflattering" ways. The effect of this portrayal is that:

the cases in the book confirm, rather than challenge, the generalization that women and men mostly do different things, and that women's opportunities are drastically more limited than men's. Most women who read the casebook do so to prepare for a career that historically has been predominantly male, and they may be concerned about the effect gender will have on their legal careers. (Frug, 1985: 1080).

Likewise, in a study of seven most widely-used criminal law casebooks, Ohio State University College of Law Professor Nancy Ericson found that only two had any discussion concerning battered spouses, and of the two, only one had a paragraph that stated that a husband could no longer legally beat his wife. According to Ericson:

> The criminal law casebooks trains people to be very good defense attorneys for male defendants. . . . They are terrible in discussing defenses that can be used for female defendants, whether the female is a battered woman who strikes back at her batterer, whether the woman is a battered woman who fails to protect her children, or whether the woman is suffering from premenstrual syndrome or postpartum depression. (Moss, 1988)

The written materials on which students rely thus can perpetuate and enforce gender bias, thereby making women believe that only male-based communication is acceptable. This acceptance of the male mode of communication also appears in the way in which men and women verbally express themselves in the classroom. According to Beatrice Sandler, director of the Project on Status and Education of Women for the Association of American Colleges, women are trained to speak with more hesitancy, ending in a request for agreement or confirmation. However, as Sandler states:

> in law school, the forceful way of talking is the valued way of speech. . . . those speaking more hesitantly are more likely to be viewed as less intelligent, less sure of themselves. (Moss, 1988).

Thus, women in law school receive through different media the message that "women's communication" has no place in the law. Yet, as Sandler points out, the female mode of speaking may bring people into a discussion, and encourage people attorneys are interviewing to speak more openly and at greater length.

Gender differences continue in development after students leave law school and enter the profession. Less experienced lawyers learn from observing, working, and being trained by senior attorneys, and through formal training programs. Yet, gender has an impact on communication in this setting. Noted legal trainer Joel F. Henning (1984) advises law firm managers to look closely at gender issues when planning both formal and informal training programs. With respect to who gets trained, according to Henning, professional men are twice as likely as professional women to be given time off from work for training:

> if the female lawyer's supervisor perceives the firm's training investment in her is less likely to yield maximum dividends than the same investment in a male counterpart, that female lawyer may get fewer opportunities for formal training. (Henning, 1984: 15)

Henning also points out gender issues relating to how lawyers are trained, and recommends that training programs should take into account gender differences in communication:

> Women, I believe, can teach their male peers how to be better interviewers and counselors, how to listen better, how to elicit all the information that clients should reveal, how to develop a more empathetic relationship with their client. They can also teach male lawyers a lot about efficiency and management. Similarly, men can teach women about the "game" of negotiating: how to keep personality out of it, how to distinguish reservation price from principle, how to focus on common goals rather than differences.
>
> Whether or not I am right about the relative strengths of men and women regarding these particular skills, it seems certain that training programs should be designed with sensitivity to gender issues. (15)

By training all attorneys in the communication styles and strengths of both genders not only is the validity of the female mode of communication recognized, but attorneys of both genders, and the profession, benefit as well.

To ensure that formal continuing legal education programs take into account both male and female communication differences, it is important that both men and women conduct the training sessions. In addition, as Henning points out, "traditionally, teachers have been important role models for their students" (15).

Gender differences in communication also affect informal training, in which more senior attorneys instruct and guide junior attorneys through work assignments and supervision. Some male lawyers may be concerned that working with members of a different gender will be perceived as more than a professional relationship. Others may feel uncomfortable supervising junior female lawyers because "they find it harder to relate to them in the traditional good-old-boy coach-to-player style" (Henning, 1984: 15), and may provide little or no feedback on work assignments and performance. In a survey conducted by the Indiana State Bar Association, almost twice as many women (25%) as men (13.1%) reported that they were dissatisfied with feedback from their firms or employing organizations. When asked whether "inadequate feedback has been an obstacle to your success as a lawyer," almost three times as many women as men answered "yes" (Gellis, 1991: 950–51).

It is clear that lawyers in supervisory roles must be trained to eliminate different treatment and communication to of subordinate men and women:

> Lawyers can be taught how to be better assignors of work, supervisors and deliverers of negative and positive feedback. To the extent that they are so trained, their firms will become better managed and better able to serve their clients. In the process, women lawyers in the firm will also be better served and consequently better able to serve the firm. (Henning, 1984)

At least one firm, Graham & James (with 150 lawyers in its San Francisco and Palo Alto offices), has adopted such a training program, specifically designed to handle issues of gender differences and bias:

In two sessions already, junior associates and senior partners have switched positions in role-playing exercises and have been taught about differences in the ways men and women communicate. (Morris, 1991: 2)

According to managing partner David Gross, the goal of the training sessions is to sensitize lawyers to gender-biased behavior and "to open the lines of communication" (Morris, 1991: 2). Adoption of this program was part of the firm's emphasis on developing supervisory skills. The training program includes a session specifically on the differences in the way men and women communicate, which Gross and others particularly found to be "an eye-opener," and which they believe will affect their communication with lawyers of the other gender in future interactions. Through adoption of such a training program, negative aspects of gender differences in communication, and gender bias, can be minimized, and female modes of communication integrated into the legal workplace. As Robert MacCrate (1989) correctly stated:

> Only as the distinctive viewpoint of women directly influences the culture of the legal workplace can we accommodate the differences that matter to both women and men. True equality in legal employment will be achieved only when the perspective of women becomes an integral part of law firm culture. (990)

GENDER AND COMMUNICATION IN THE PRACTICE OF LAW

Gender perceptions and differences do not occur only in the way men and women are trained to be lawyers and in the way they interact within a law firm or other employing organization. Gender and communication issues arise within the practice of law, as women attorneys handle matters involving litigation, negotiation, and other professional matters.

GENDER PERCEPTIONS AND DIFFERENCES IN LITIGATION

The practice of litigation, perhaps more than any other area, demonstrates the existence of gender issues in legal communication. Traditionally there have been few women litigators (White, 1967). As Gellis suggests,

> Men perceived women as not suited to litigation and barred their entry, believing women could not handle the rough and tumble of trial work. (964, n. 40).

However, as more and more women engage in practices that include litigation, gender perceptions, and differences in communication among litigators, litigants, judges, and juries come into focus.

At least 24 state courts and bar associations have organized committees and task forces to study gender issues in the courts. These studies have found similar attitudes and practices concerning communication in which one or more of the participants—as attorney, judge, litigant, witness, or juror—are female, and conclude that men communicate with each other differently than they do with women.

The area in which most attention has been focused is the communication that occurs between judges and attorneys, particularly in cases in which the judge is male and one of the attorneys appearing before him is female. The Michigan Supreme Court Task Force on Gender Issues in the Courts held pubic hearing and conducted written surveys, and found as a result that women litigators had been subjected to:

patronizing language, improper forms of address, references to appearances and marital status;

verbal and physical actions which exclude women or ignore their presence;

questions, comments and behavior related to whether women are "real" attorneys;

"bullying" and intimidation;

sexual harassment and innuendo against women, including jokes, sexual references, physical touching, and implied or overt pressure for sexual favors;

tolerance and encouragement of behavior in male attorneys which is not valued in female attorneys, such as aggressive/assertive behavior and failure to meet the "feminine" ideal;

less attention and credibility given to female attorneys' statements than to male attorneys' statements; and

judges' greater impatience with and criticism of female attorneys than male attorneys. (Michigan Supreme Court Task Force, 1989: 85).

In an incident reported in the *American Bar Association Journal*, Susan Tone Pierce, then a 27-year-old attorney in Chicago, appeared before Judge Arthur Cieslik for a pretrial conference on a rape case. When Pierce came before him, Judge Cieslik announced:

I am going to hear the young lady's case first. They say I'm a male chauvinist. I don't think that ladies should be lawyers. I believe that you belong at home raising a family. Ladies do not belong down here. . . . What does your husband think about you working here? (Blodgett, 1986: 48).

Fearing judicial reprisal, Pierce remained silent. While this clearly is a blatant example of gender bias, other more subtle situations regularly occur, such as judges' complimenting women attorneys on their clothing while not saying anything similar to their male counterparts; calling women attorneys "honey," "sweetie," or other gender-related terms; or inquiring about marital status. This behavior toward women lawyers has been accepted, while similar conversations between judges and members of their same sex would be quite suspect.

In studying the ways in which these types of gender-biased communications between attorneys and judges can be eliminated, many have suggested such gender bias will dissipate only when more women become judges, bringing to the litigation process different modes of communication and conflict resolution. As Professor Carl Tobias points out:

> Much evidence suggests that numerous female judges have different attitudes, experiences, points of view and approaches to judging than many male jurists and that these attributes will improve the federal judicial process. Considerable data indicate that there is widespread gender bias in the federal justice system which the services of additional women as judges will reduce. The appointment of more female judges could correspondingly help persuade fellow citizens of the neutrality of the justice system. Justice Christine Durham of the Utah Supreme Court recently observed that female judges "bring an individual and collective perspective to our work that cannot be achieved in a system which reflect the experiences of only a part of the people whose lives it affects. (Tobias, 1990: 177).

Professor Elaine Martin contends that the different perspectives and mode of communication that women have could produce other benefits as well. The presence of more women in the judiciary could alter the sexist demeanor of some male litigators, increase the employment of women in law clerk positions, and foster collective action, such as participation in such projects as gender bias task forces (Martin, 1990: 208).

Gender differences in communication in litigation settings are not limited to interactions between women lawyers and male judges. To win a trial, a lawyer must convince a jury panel of six or more people that his or her client is right and the opposing party's version of the facts is wrong. If, however, the jurors have preconceived ideas about the roles persons of each gender are to play, this can have a negative effect on cases litigated by women attorneys. As Professor Leonard Cavese bluntly put it:

> Having a woman represent a client can affect the outcome of the case. . . . The outcome of a case depends upon the presentation as much as its merits. If an audience is prevented from receiving a presentation for what it's worth, this will affect the outcome.

> A woman cannot raise the issue of her gender at a trial and be done with it. These sexist attitudes start at birth. She cannot say: "Don't pay attention to the fact that I don't look and sound as you want me to." Some people see women in a more traditional, provincial way. If those people are jurors, women lawyers will have a more difficult time winning a case. (Blodgett, 1986: 48).

Gender can also play a role in perceptions of the litigants themselves. In one study, male jurors judged attractive female criminals less harshly and gave them lighter punishments than their less attractive counterparts (Efran, 1974). In other studies involving defendants accused of rape, female jurors were more likely to convict defendants and give them longer sentences than were male jurors, (see Jacobson, 1981; Rumsey and Rumsey, 1977; Calhoun, Selby, and Warring, 1976).

Gender differences in communication can likewise occur within the jury panel itself. In studies that analyze and determine how jury deliberations are conducted, researchers have found that juror gender correlates with the rate of participation in jury deliberations than do female jurors (see Marder, 1987; Hastie, Penrod, and Pennington, 1983). Male jurors typically offer forty percent more comments during the deliberation than do female jurors (Marder, 1987: 596). This occurs because, as discussed in the beginning of this chapter, the established "power relation" of male dominance and female submission arises during any communication involving both men and women, whether the communication be verbal or nonverbal:

> When men and women enter the jury room, they do not leave behind the lessons that society teaches about appropriate behavior for men's and women's interaction. (Marder, 1987: 597).

Juror gender also plays a role in the selection of a foreperson, or spokesperson, for the jury (Hastie, Penrod, and Pennington, 1983: 1848). Nancy Marder (1987) points out:

> In the jury deliberations, gender is important from the moment jurors enter the jury room and decide where to sit. One important finding that emerges from empirical studies is that the jury usually selects the foreperson from one of the two people seated at either end of the table. Men are more likely than women to assume the end positions. Not surprisingly, men are also more likely than women to be selected as the foreperson, though their selection is not due solely to their seating choice. (595)

Even when women sit in the end positions at the table, jurors of both gender are less likely to recognize them as potential forepersons because of stereotypes of women as followers, not leaders (Porter and Geis, 1981).

As in other legal settings, the diminution or absence of female communication has a negative impact upon the jury process. Marder explains:

> Women generally need to speak more and men generally need to listen more if the jury is to engage in effective group deliberations that will allow for the articulation of a range of community values and the rendering of accurate verdicts. . . .
>
> Participation during deliberations is critical because the jury performs its task through the verbal communication of ideas. Those jurors who speak the most are viewed as the most persuasive by their peers. The sheer quantity of their comments gives weight to their content. The ideas of male jurors, then, receive more attention than those of their female counterparts. (593, 596–97).

Studies have shown that perceptions and recollections of evidence at trial differ depending on the juror's gender (Williams, 1982; Yarmey, 1979; Powers, Andriks, and Loftus, 1979). Without full participation by jurors of both gender, the jury itself can not take into account these different perspectives when ascertaining facts and then applying the law to those facts.

Courts and judges can encourage more participation on the part of female jurors through the use of a juror handbook, an introductory videotape, and questions during the jury selection process (called "voir dire") that stress the importance of participation on the part of all jurors. Jurors should be educated from the beginning of their service about the effects of gender dynamics on their deliberations. Both male and female jurors must be made aware that the female jurors must speak, and the male jurors must listen, so that both genders are participating equally in the deliberations process.

GENDER PERCEPTIONS AND DIFFERENCES IN OTHER AREAS OF THE PRACTICE OF LAW

Litigation is not the only area of the profession in which issues of gender communication arise. In representing clients in any legal matter, lawyers must communicate with others, whether they be lawyers representing opposing parties, adjudicators, governmental or administrative personnel, or persons not directly involved in the legal matter. Gender perceptions and differences in the way men and women communicate are factors which may influence or have an impact upon the way in which a particular lawyer handles a legal matter and the ultimate resolution of that matter.

For example, gender differences in communication modes play a role in how the negotiations are conducted. Lawyers are regularly called upon to negotiate matters. Business lawyers, for instance, may negotiate complex merger deals, litigation attorneys may negotiate settlements of lawsuits, and labor lawyers may negotiate collective bargaining agreements. In handling these negotiations, research has shown, men and women have different styles of negotiating agreements and approach the process differently (Henning, 1984; Jacker, 1983). Studies have found that women are more trusting and cooperative than men during the initial stages of negotiation, that women tend to take personally certain negotiation tactics, and that, in negotiations between men and women, if a man acts in an aggressive and uncooperative way, a woman tends to react more forcefully than would another man, thereby possibly reducing her effectiveness as a negotiator (Henning, 1984).

Gender differences in communication also appear in the way in which men and women conduct and obtain information from interviews of clients, witnesses, and other persons. It was observed earlier in this chapter that the "female" style of communicating—with more hesitancy and open-ended questions—elicits more information from an interviewee than does the "male" communication mode, because the interviewee is not made to feel as if he or she were in conflict with the interviewer. As Ann Gellis (1991) suggests:

the theory [is] that women will bring another approach to lawyering, one which emphasizes conciliation and mediation of disputes. (964)

Lawyers who study these gender differences and learn techniques and styles of communication from members of the other gender can improve their own skills and more effectively represent their clients. As Henning (1984) points out:

Women, I believe, can teach their male peers how to be better interviewers and counselors, how to listen better, how to elicit all the information that client should reveal, how to develop a more empathetic relationship with their clients. They can also teach male lawyers alot about efficiency and management. Similarly, men can teach women about the "game" of negotiating: how to keep personality out of it, how to distinguish reservation price from principle, how to focus on common goals rather than differences. (15)

Thus, gender differences in legal communication can change from negative to positive perceptions. Instead of clinging to the belief that successful women attorneys must act and communicate like men or that women cannot learn to be effective negotiators because of their personalities, lawyers of both genders should employ both male and female methods of communication, depending on the legal task which they must handle.

Finally, since a lawyer's job is, in essence, to represent his or her client, communication and interaction with that client is paramount. As in the other areas discussed above, gender differences and perceptions also arise in the communications between lawyers and clients. While there has been little study of this area,

> it is empirically proven that the way we perceive other people affects the way we feel about them, talk about them, treat them, represent them, and make decisions about their lives. (Cahn and Schneider, 1987: 388).

Accordingly, if a client prefers a lawyer with whom he or she feels most comfortable (as opposed to selecting a lawyer on skill and reputation), that client might select a male lawyer if the perception is that women lawyers are not as aggressive, bright, well-connected with the court personnel, or other such stereotypes. Lawyers of both genders should be sensitive to the gender perceptions and stereotypes their clients might hold, while continuing to work toward eliminating negative stereotypes and replacing them with a non-gender-based appreciation for legal ability and effective representation.

Gender differences in communication exist in legal settings. The terminology that lawyers use is both gender-based and gender-biased. The training that law schools and law firms provide attorneys creates and perpetuates the notion that only a "male" style of communication is acceptable, and that, if women wish to succeed as lawyers, they must act and communicate as if they were men. Because gender perceptions and differences in communication appear in all areas of the practice of law, all attorneys, of whatever gender, should learn to employ communication techniques that have been identified as male or female, both to eradicate gender bias in the profession and to represent clients more effectively, no matter what the legal setting.

REFERENCES

Adams, E. A. 1988. Study: Female students, lawyers still must battle bias in profession. *National Law Journal*, 23 May: 4.

Bender, L. 1989. Sex discrimination or gender inequality. *Fordham Law Review* 57: 941.

Blodgett, N. 1986. I don't think that ladies should be lawyers. *American Bar Association Journal* 72: 48.

Cahn, N., and N. Schneider. 1987. The next best thing: Transferred clients in a legal clinic. *Catholic University Law Review* 36: 367.

Calhoun, S., J. Selby, and H. Warring. 1976. Social perception of the victim's causal role in rape: An exploratory examination of four factors. *Human Relations* 29: 517.

Dawson, J., W. Harvey, and S. Henderson. 1982. *Cases and Comment on Contracts.* 4th ed., Foundation.

Efran, E. 1974. The effect of physical appearance on the judgment of guilt, interpersonal attraction, and severity of recommended punishment in a simulated jury task. *Journal of Research Personality* 8:45.

Final Report of the Michigan Supreme Court Task Force on Gender Issues in the Courts. 1989, December.

Finley, L. M. 1989. Breaking women's silence in law: The dilemma of the gendered nature of legal reasoning. *Notre Dame Law Review* 64: 886.

_____. 1987. Choice & freedom: Elusive issues in the search for gender justice. *Yale Law Journal* 96: 914.

_____. 1986. Transcending equality theory: A way out of the maternity and the workplace debate. *Columbia Law Review* 86: 1118.

Frug, M. J. 1985. A symposium of critical legal study: Re-reading contracts: A feminist analysis of a contracts casebook. *American University Law Review* 34: 1065.

Gellis, A. J. 1991. Great Expectations: Women in the legal profession, a commentary on state studies. *Indiana Law Journal* 66: 941.

Gilligan, C. 1982. *In A Different Voice: Psychological Theory and Women's Development.*

Ginsburg, R. B. 1986. Some thoughts on the 1980's debate over special versus equal treatment for women. *Law & Inequality* 4: 143.

Greeno, C. G., and E. E. Maccoby. 1986. How different is the "different voice"? *Signs: Journal of Women in Culture and Society* 11: 310.

Hastie, R., S. D. Penrod, and N. Pennington. 1983. What goes on in a jury deliberation. *American Bar Association Journal* 69: 1848.

Henning, J. 1984. New approach needed in training of women; there's a difference, studies say. *The National Law Journal* 1 October: 15.

Jack. R., and D. C. Jack. 1989. Women lawyers: Archetype and alternatives. *Fordham Law Review* 57: 933.

Jacker, N. S. 1983. Learning to negotiate: Techniques, psychology. *National Law Journal* 21 March: 15.

Jacobson, G. 1981. Effects of victim's and defendant's physical attractiveness on subjects' judgment in a rape case. *Sex Roles* 7: 247.

Kaye, J. S. 1988. Women lawyers in big firms: A study in progress toward gender equality. *Fordham Law Review* 57: 111.

Karst, K. 1984. Woman's constitution. *Duke Law Journal* 447.

Littleton, C. A. 1987. Reconstructing sexual equality. *California Law Review* 75: 1279.

MacCrate, R. 1989. What women are teaching a male-dominated profession. *Fordham Law Review* 57: 989.

MacKinnon, C. 1982. Feminism, Marxism, method and the state: An agenda for theory. *Signs: Journal of Women in Culture and Society* 7: 515.

————. 1983. Feminism, Marxism, method and the state: Toward feminist jurisprudence. *Signs: Journal of Women in Culture and Society* 8: 635.

Marder, N. 1987. Gender dynamics and jury deliberations. *Yale Law Journal* 96: 593.

Martin, E. 1990. Men and women on the bench: Vive la difference? *Judicature* 73: 204.

Morris, J. E. 1991. Graham & James program beats back discrimination. *Judicature* 73: 204.

Moss, D. C. 1988. Would this happen to a man? *American Bar Association Journal* 74: 49.

Porter, A., and K. Geis. 1981. Women and nonverbal leadership cues: When seeing is not believing. Mayo, C. and Henley, N., eds. *Gender and Nonverbal Behavior.*

Powers, C., D. Andriks, and E. Loftus. 1979. Eyewitness accounts of females and males. *Journal of Applied Psychology* 64: 339.

Rumsey, G., and H. Rumsey. 1977 . A case of rape: Sentencing judgments of males and females. *Psychological Report* 41: 459.

Taber, J., M. T. Grant, M. T. Huser, R. B. Norman, J. R. Sutton, C. C. Wong, L. E. Parker, and C. Picard. 1988. Project: Gender, legal education, and the legal profession: An empirical study of Stanford law students and graduates. *Stanford Law Review* 40: 1209.

Tobias, C. 1990. Commentary: The gender gap on the federal bench. *Hofstra Law Review* 19: 171.

Wald, P. 1983. Women in the law: Stage two. *University of Missouri at Kansas City Law Review* 52: 45.

Weiss, C., and L. Melling. 1988. The legal education of twenty women. *Stanford Law Review* 40: 1299.

White, J. 1967. Women in the law. *Michigan Law Review* 65: 1051.

Williams, P. 1984–85. Equality's riddle: Pregnancy and equal treatment/special treatment debate. *New York University Review of Law and Social Change* 13: 325.

————. 1982. The equality crisis: Some reflections on culture, courts and feminism. *Women's Rights Law Reporter* 7:175.

Yarmey, A. 1979. *The Psychology of Eyewitness Testimony.*

CHAPTER 12

COMMUNICATION IN HEALTH CARE SETTINGS

AUTHOR   Elaine Bass Jenks, West Chester University

POINTS TO BE ADDRESSED
- Role expectations of female and male patients
- How the patient's gender affects communication with doctors: Psychosomatic diagnoses
- Role expectations of female and male doctors
- How the doctor's gender affects communication with patients: Insufficient evidence
- Role expectations of female and male nurses
- How the nurse's gender affects communication with doctors and patients: An indirect "game"

Interpersonal interactions in health care settings are, quite literally, critical events. Somewhere amidst the difficult and complicated process of accurately conveying information, interpreting meanings, and creating understanding among doctors, patients, and nurses lies the crucial concern of a patient's well-being and possibly even his or her life. Unlike any other setting, the medical context is one where an individual's health depends directly on the communicative interactions that occur.

The available research concerning any form of communication in health care settings is enormous and unwieldly, examining topics as varied as drug advertisement messages (G. Stimson, 1975) and the rhetoric of medical artwork (R. Swiderski, 1976). This chapter will concentrate on gender issues related to interpersonal interactions in health care settings. The focus will be on the communicative implications of the most prevalent gender patterns in interpersonal relationships between doctors, patients, and nurses.

Overall, communication practices in medical contexts have been found to be unsatisfactory. For example, patients are accused of not understanding doctors while doctors are accused of not speaking in understandable language (R. Shuy, 1983). Patients are blamed for noncompliance with doctors' orders and doctors are blamed for not making their directions clear (S. Lane, 1983). Patients are criticized for not participating in decisions concerning their health and doctors are criticized for not allowing patients to participate in these decisions (S. Fisher, 1983).

Introducing gender as an issue in medical interactions invites the inclusion of nurses for consideration as well as doctors and patients. Nurses are vital participants in health care settings, yet they are all but ignored in most health communication studies. Communication does not occur in isolation and all identities require an "other" (R. Laing, 1969: 82). Accordingly, in this chapter, I consider the interactants in health care settings in relational groupings. In exploring the communicative relationship between doctors and patients, I focus first on the gender of the patient and then on the gender of the doctor. Next I examine the role of the nurse in the doctor-patient relationship. Each of these sections outlines research findings regarding gender patterns in the relationships and then discusses communicative issues raised by the gender patterns.

The momentum to study gender patterns in medical contexts emerged from the women's movement of the 1960s and 1970s, when female patients began speaking out about controlling their bodies, especially concerning the issues of childbirth and contraceptives (G. Corea, 1977). At the same time, more females were attending medical school (J. Gray, 1982) and female nurses were beginning to examine their role in the health care process (C. Vance, et al., 1985). Thus, literature on gender issues in the medical context is relatively new and, to date, most researchers have focused on the woman's place in the health care setting. With the exception of a few reports on male nurses (G. Brookfield, et al., 1982, G. Kreps, 1987; B. Snavely and G. Fairhurst, 1984), the role of men in the medical context has not been specifically studied. Consequently, while the following discussion notes various issues concerning males, this chapter centers primarily on female patients, female doctors, and female nurses.

HOW THE PATIENT'S GENDER
AFFECTS COMMUNICATION WITH DOCTORS

According to the *1990 Statistical Abstract of the United States*, approximately one-third more female patients visit doctors than male patients every year, with women making three visits to doctors for every two visits males make. Beyond the United States, there are also more female than male patients in Canada (M. Stewart, 1983), Scandinavia (K. Malterud, 1987b), and Australia (F. Hausfeld, 1976). While it is clear that there are more female patients and that females make more visits to doctors, it is not immediately apparent why this situation exists.

GENDER PATTERNS

There are four possible reasons why more women visit doctors and do so more frequently than men. The first reason is that, owing to their reproductive roles, women visit doctors as *well* patients more than men (Hausfeld, 1976; J. Wallen, et al., 1979). Specifically, doctors see women throughout pregnancy as well as to dispense and monitor birth control methods, even though females are usually not ill when carrying children or using contraceptives.

A second reason for women's more frequent visits is that they often manage the health care of others in their families and see doctors as "non-patient clients" (Hausfeld, 1976: 540). Here, females take the responsibility for the health of their children, husbands, and parents (C. Weisman, 1987). While the first reason offered can be attributed to biological distinctions in the reproductive capabilities of the sexes, this second reason moves into social distinctions between the genders. Society traditionally puts pressure on males to be financially responsible for their children, their wives, and sometimes their parents, but it is women who are expected to be the caretakers of their families and, by extension, to feel guilt for a relative's illness. Hausfeld (1976) mentions not only the familiar point that mothers often blame themselves for their children's illnesses (B. Korsch, et al., 1968), but also the irony that women are often blamed for their husbands' obesity and heart problems because they cook for their families (even though they cook for their families because food preparation is part of the traditional female role in society).

The female role, itself, is a third reason that more women visit doctors more often than men. Specifically, the role of the patient is more traditionally associated with female attributes than with male characteristics (M. Gray and S. Meginnis, 1978). As Corea (1977) writes, "From childhood, a female is encouraged to admit her pain, to freely ask for help and to expect and accept weakness in herself" (81). Patients are expected to be obedient (P. Entralgo, 1979) and to cooperate with doctors (T. Parsons, 1951). Overall, it is more appropriate for women to express suffering and accept assistance than it is for men (C. Nathanson, 1975). However, by expressing pain and asking for help, women leave themselves open to "learned helplessness," which is the repeated inability to exert influence over one's own situation (Malterud, 1987b). Learned helplessness leads to a condition where one chooses to play the role of the incapable and allows the stronger partner, in this case, the doctor, to take control of the situation.

This focus on the patient role mirroring the female role in society is prevalent in the literature (S. Borges, 1986; B. Bernstein and K. Kane, 1981; Gray and Meginnis, 1978; Hausfeld, 1976; Malterud, 1987b; Nathanson, 1975). The situation is magnified when the patient is an older female. Older female patients may be willing to "play the stereotypical role of an old woman" and list her complaints in detail to the doctor (M. Root, 1987: 155). This emphasis on the female being willing, and in fact encouraged by society, to speak of her symptoms indicates that it is considered appropriate for females of all ages to seek help for illness and to passively accept the doctor's assistance.

This linking of the female role to the patient role emphasizes, by conspicuous omission, that the patient role is not a role expected of men. Thus, it is less appropriate for males to complain of symptoms and receive help than it is for females. While this may allow males to escape the condition of learned helplessness, it may also push males into the potentially dangerous position of not asking for help when it is needed.

The fourth reason for more numerous female medical visits seems on the surface to be a physiological reason, but actually involves a social explanation. That is, more women visit doctors simply because females *are* ill more often than males. However, the reason for this apparent physical distinction is partially social; females become sick because of the stress from fulfilling their female roles in society (Nathanson, 1975). For example, a female might be expected to take care of her family even while she works outside the home. Or a female might be expected to care for her children while also caring for her aging parents. These forms of stress can cause physical illnesses which lead women to visit doctors.

This last reason brings up the most frequently reported issue concerning the female patient. It is well-documented that doctors routinely diagnose females as having more psychosomatic illnesses than males (Bernstein and Kane, 1981; Hausfeld, 1976; Malterud, 1987a, 1987b; Nathanson 1975; Wallen, et al., 1979; Weisman, 1987). Repeatedly, studies have shown that women are prescribed more tranquilizers than men because females are more often identified as having illnesses that begin in their minds, not in their bodies. This tendency is compounded by the assumption that the stress caused by the female role does not actually produce physical illness. The obvious danger of this position is noted by Corea (1977) who writes, "Everyone has heard stories of women who complained of blinding headaches, were dismissed with tranquilizer prescriptions and had strokes two days later. No one knows how often such incidents occur" (79).

The stress created by the male role in society may also cause physical illness in men who feel pressure to succeed in their careers and provide for their families. However, society seems to take ill males more seriously than unwell females, particularly because the male role is not linked to the patient role. It might be assumed that if a male complains, he really is sick. Evidence that society focuses on the physiological, not psychological, reasons for male illness is demonstrated by the appropriation of public health money. For example, the 1988 study which advocated patients taking an aspirin a day to thwart heart attacks was conducted entirely on males even though men and women die from heart disease at almost equivalent rates (K. Ames, 1990).

To review, more women visit doctors more often than men because: 1) females make more well-patient visits; 2) females make more non-patient visits with family members; 3) the female role in society has similar characteristics to the patient or sick role in our culture and women are expected to play these roles; and 4) women actually are more physically ill owing to the stress of maintaining the female role in society.

COMMUNICATIVE ISSUES

Four communicative issues emerge from the fact that more women visit doctors more frequently than men. The first three relate to the point that females are diagnosed more often than males with psychosomatic illnesses.

First, there is simply no language for "ill-defined" conditions in the medical context (Malterud, 1987a: 206). "Disease" is the term often used to describe physical abnormalities while "illness" is used to refer to the patient's feelings of unwellness and the effects of these feelings. As Malterud (1987a) points out, "Illness that does not result from disease is not as respectable in our society as illness that does" (206). Thus, if there is no clear name of a disease available for an illness, the patient is often diagnosed as suffering from either a psychosomatic disease or from a non-disease. Patients are clearly being told that their illnesses are in their heads or that their illnesses do not really exist at all. And these patients are usually women.

Second, the fact that the patient speaking is a female may also influence how the speaker is heard by the doctor. Bernstein and Kane (1981) found that both male and female patients who mentioned personal problems were judged more quickly to have psychosomatic conditions by doctors than patients who mentioned only medical symptoms. However, this study also found that both expressive and non-expressive females were diagnosed as having psychosomatic conditions "as though women were *a priori* more emotional than men" (606). Thus, a male had to behave in a "female" manner—that is, more emotionally—to be labelled with a non-disease illness, while all females, both emotional and stoic, were more likely to be labelled with psychosomatic conditions.

Third, *how* females are allowed to be heard can also influence whether or not a women is diagnosed with a psychosomatic illness. M. Paget (1983) explored how questions are used by doctors both to request responses to topics and to follow patient replies, which, in turn, leads to meaning construction. Specifically, a doctor reconstructed a patient's fear of recurring cancer into a simple case of nerves. The case was followed over time and the patient was later diagnosed by another doctor, not with nerves, but with cancer of the spine. The control of the conversation through the use of questions by the first doctor led to the construction of the meaning of her illness, which was then acted upon, or in this case, not acted upon, by the doctor. Doctors' control of medical conversations has been reported in studies of both male and female patients (M. Coulthard and M. Ashby, 1975; S. Fisher, 1983; R. Shuy, 1983; C. West, 1983) and this situation may be a function of the asymmetrical relationship between doctors and patients rather than an issue unique to female patients.

The final communicative area concerning female patients focuses on information flow or the explanations women receive from their doctors. Considering the three preceding issues, it might be assumed that females would not receive very much information from their doctors. This assumption is based on the points that women may have symptoms for which there are no scientific names, that women might be perceived as highly emotional, and that women do not control their conversations with doctors.

However, it has been found that female patients regularly receive more information or more explanations than male patients (T. Adamson, J. Tschann, D. Gullion, and A. Oppenberg, et al., 1989; J. Hall, D. Roter, and N. Katz, 1988; Wallen, H. Waitzkin, and J. Stoeckle, et al., 1979). It has also been found that female patients receive more time with doctors than male patients

(Waitzkin, 1984; Wallen, Waitzkin, and Stoeckle, 1979). The reason for these trends seems to be that females routinely ask more questions of their doctors than males (Hall, Roter, and Katz, 1988; Waitzkin, 1984; Wallen, Waitzkin, and Stoeckle, 1979). Thus, female patients receive more explanations from doctors because they request these explanations. Women may ask more questions because they visit doctors more often and have more practice making queries, and because they feel responsible for understanding the health care concerns of their family members (Wallen, Waitzkin, and Stoeckle, 1979).

Interestingly, it was found by Wallen et al. (1979) that females often receive explanations from doctors that are less technical than the questions asked. Doctors were more likely to match the level of technicality used by male patients, but to "undershoot" the level employed by female patients (142). Thus, women may use more questions and receive more explanations simply because they are not being given sufficient information and must request further explanations from their doctors.

To this point, we have seen that the gender-linked patterns of communication during medical appointments are not without consequences. While little research has focused directly on male patients, female patients are more often diagnosed with psychosomatic illnesses and are more frequently prescribed tranquilizers than men. The question that arises now concerns the individual who makes these diagnoses and who writes these prescriptions. Are doctors who treat female patients differently than male patients more likely to be male or female?

HOW THE DOCTOR'S GENDER
AFFECTS COMMUNICATION WITH PATIENTS

Although there are more female patients than male patients, there are far fewer female doctors than male doctors. As noted above, according to the *1990 Statistical Abstract of the United States*, for every six patients, four are female. However, for every six doctors, only one is a woman.

GENDER PATTERNS

Women who help cure others have had enormous difficulty being accepted in societies controlled by males for centuries (Corea, 1977; D. Scully, 1980). It is estimated that nine million individuals were killed for being witches from the late 15th century to the early 18th century. Most individuals accused of being witches were women and many were midwives who helped women deliver their babies (Corea, 1977).

While we do not execute female healers any longer, we also do not make it easy for females to become doctors. Women still have difficulty getting into medical school, entering certain specialties, receiving admission to internship and residency programs, and obtaining faculty positions in medical schools (Corea, 1977). Women doctors gravitate toward the areas most accepting of females—pediatrics, psychiatry, and public health (Gray, 1982). These specialities have lower mean incomes than surgery where women are "underrepresented" (J. Bobula, 1980: 827), but female doctors have noted that surgery is an area they feel is "closed to them" (M. Heins, et al., 1979: 1136).

These difficulties are compounded by the fact that females are socialized by society to play female roles and that medical schools socialize individuals differently. Women are socialized to be "caring, soft, gentle, emotional, involved and nurturing" (Gray, 1982: 167). While these qualities may seem ideal for a doctor, it has been noted that medical school takes an approach that is analytical and rational, focusing on curing, not caring (Gray, 1982; Malterud, 1987a).

The assumption here is that the doctor role is a male role, and therefore, male doctors do not experience the same role conflict when becoming physicians that their female colleagues find. However, doctors of both genders have other tensions to balance. For example, doctors are expected to always be precisely correct in their diagnostic and treatment decisions while also accurately judging how individual patients would like to be communicated with during medical appointments (E. Jenks, 1989). This pressure to be somewhat of a deity where medicine is concerned and simultaneously human when communication is involved is a tension shared by both male and female doctors.

Additionally, female doctors experience the pressure that most females in predominantly male fields share; that is, females may be superb professionals, but they often are not seen as complete women until they marry and have children (Corea, 1977; Gray, 1982). Thus, female doctors may excel professionally, but because they have "broken sex-role stereotypes to some extent by becoming physicians" (Weisman and M. Teitelbaum, 1985: 1120), they must also prove their femininity to society by becoming wives and mothers. But by being wives and mothers, female doctors leave themselves open to the criticism of not being dedicated to their field (Corea, 1977). While it is not easy for anyone, male or female, to be a physician, the doctor role and the female role clearly contain contradictory requirements that are difficult to reconcile (Gray, 1982; Weisman and Teitelbaum, 1985).

COMMUNICATIVE ISSUES

If females are socialized differently than males and if women have a more difficult time becoming doctors, it might be assumed that female doctors treat their patients in a different manner, in a more caring way, than male doctors. It has been demonstrated repeatedly that, in general, females and males display differences in the use of verbal communication (A. Haas, 1979; C. Kramer, 1977; D. Maltz and R. Borker, 1982; B. Thorne and N. Henley, 1975) and nonverbal communication (Henley, 1977). It would follow that the same differences would be found between male and female doctors.

This assumption might be stated by the hypothesis, if the doctor is female, then she will communicate in a more nurturing, relational, "female" way. However, the answer to this hypothesis is a resounding, "maybe." A few researchers state there are some differences (M. Heins, et al., 1979; K. Langwell, 1982;

A. Mendez, et al., 1986), but other researchers have found no differences in the communicative behaviors of male and female doctors (C. Murphy-Cullen and L. Larsen, 1984; Weisman and Teitelbaum, 1985; Weisman, et al., 1988; J. Young, 1975). Moreover, others searched for differences in the patient's expectations of male and female doctors instead of the doctor's communicative choices (L. Comstack, et al., 1982; Paluszny and Poznanski, 1971; Weisman and Teitelbaum, 1985). Each of these areas will be discussed in turn.

Most of the researchers finding differences between male and female doctors have not focused directly on communicative behaviors. For example, in a study on incomes of male and female doctors, it was found that female doctors see fewer patients per hour than male doctors (Langwell, 1982). This number could indicate that female doctors spent more time communicating with patients because they were more concerned with the doctor-patient relationship and possibly more nurturing. Admittedly, since interpersonal communication was not the focus of this study, disparity in appointment lengths does not necessarily indicate more caring communication, though the perception of having enough time with a doctor is important to patients (Jenks, 1989).

Likewise, doctors' attitudes were examined by M. Heins (1979) and the study found that female doctors are significantly more egalitarian and more sensitive than male doctors. These findings suggest that female doctors may treat patients with more equality and would be more caring, but again, this study looked at attitudes, not communicative behaviors resulting from these attitudes.

Verbal and nonverbal communicative behaviors of male and female doctors were directly examined by A. Mendez, J. Shymansky, and M. Wolraich (1986). However, the results do not loudly proclaim female doctors to be more caring, or even very different, communicators than male doctors. Even so, this study did find that female doctors asked more questions designed to elicit the patient's feelings and made more attempts to restate the patient's feelings in a non-judgmental manner. Therefore, female doctors "were more prompt in dealing with the affective dimension of the interaction" (Mendez, et al., 1986: 441). However, no differences were found in twelve other verbal categories, such as statements designed to elicit a patient's knowledge and comments aimed at explaining medical jargon. Nor were differences found in any nonverbal aspects of communication even though both vocalics and hand gestures were examined.

Thus, the literature that has identified communicative differences between male and female doctors describe either small differences or distinctions in areas surrounding communication such as attitude and length of appointments. But no pronounced differences in interpersonal communicative behaviors are evident.

Additionally, no differences in male and female communication were found by researchers who studied malpractice claims among obstetrician-gynecologists (Weisman, et al., 1988), patient satisfaction with family practice residents (Murphy-Cullen and Larsen, 1984), and symptom disclosure concerning private and non-private parts of the body (Young, 1979). All of these studies worked from the assumption mentioned earlier—that female doctors should communicate in a more caring, nurturing manner. Yet the studies found that the doctor's gender did not affect whether or not a doctor was sued (Weisman, et al, 1988), whether or not a patient was satisfied (or dissatisfied) with a doctor (Murphy-Cullen and Larsen, 1984), or whether or not a patient would be willing to disclose symptoms to a doctor (Young, 1979).

Researchers who have found no differences in the communicative behaviors of male and female doctors caution that perhaps none have been found because the percentage of female doctors is low, even though it is the highest it has ever been. Thus, perhaps differences are not observed because there are just beginning to be enough female doctors to study (Weisman and Teitelbaum, 1985). Additionally, when female doctors are studied, they are usually younger than their male counterparts and distinctions that may be explained by age variations might be mistakenly attributed to gender differences.

Patient expectations of male and female doctors have been the focus of other researchers. Here, instead of studying how doctors communicate with patients, the emphasis was on how patients' expectations affect their interpersonal interactions with doctors. One of the first areas studied was patient acceptance of female doctors, and it was found that experience with female doctors increases patients' satisfaction with female doctors. Basically, this means that patients like the idea of female doctors more after they have been treated by a woman (Weisman and Teitelbaum, 1985).

Another area studied is the preferences of female patients. One study found that female patients were more satisfied with female doctors than male patients and more satisfied than all patients were with male doctors (Comstack, et al., 1982). Others have found that female patients prefer female doctors in situations where female doctors are perceived as more "credible" such as obstetrics-gynecology and psychotherapy (Weisman and Teitelbaum, 1985: 1123).

Focusing on psychotherapy, researchers have examined the reactions of patients to the pregnancy of the therapist. It was found that patients reacted differently, and some showed temporary setbacks, but no permanent harm was witnessed during this period (M. Paluszny and E. Poznanski, 1971). From the female doctor's perspective, Scully (1980) noted that some female residents reported feeling more patient toward women in labor after experiencing childbirth themselves.

The studies of patient expectations, preferences, and reactions to the gender of the doctor are incomplete owing to the scarcity of female doctors. There are some researchers advocating same-sex dyads—with male patients visiting male doctors and female patients seeing female doctors—as the preferred relational pairing in health care settings, or one that is deserving of further study (A. Kaplan, 1985; Weisman and Teitelbaum, 1985; Young, 1979). However, it should be noted that even if this were shown to be the ideal pairing, with so many female patients and so few female doctors, it may never be a genuine possibility.

Overall, it is unclear why few distinctions have been found between male and female doctors' communicative behaviors. It may be because there have not been enough studies conducted owing to the small amount of female doctors. Or it may be that female doctors have been socialized in medical school in the same manner as male doctors and, thus, have taken on male communicative behaviors in their professional interactions. Female patients *are* treated differently by doctors, but it is not clear if they are treated differently by male doctors alone or by all doctors. The discussion now moves to the place of the nurse in the doctor-patient relationship.

HOW THE NURSE'S GENDER AFFECTS
COMMUNICATION WITH DOCTORS AND PATIENTS

Although males have begun to enter the field of nursing, the overwhelming majority (97%) of nurses are still female (J. Lewis, et al., 1990). The beginning of the female dominance of nursing dates back to Florence Nightengale (B. Bullough, 1975; M. Manthey, 1989). While Nightengale did much to facilitate the training of nurses, she also did much to establish nurses as inferior to doctors (Bullough, 1975).

Prior to Nightengale, nurses often worked independently from doctors, such as the male nurses in Ancient Rome who cared for wounded soldiers on the battlefields (Bullough, 1975) and the female midwives who delivered babies for hundreds of years (Corea, 1977). To allow her nurses to practice with suspicious, non-welcoming doctors during the Crimean War in the 1850s, Nightengale told her nurses not to give care until "ordered" to do so by a doctor (Bullough, 1975). She saw nurses as "not in control but under control" (Corea, 1977: 58). Nightengale's philosophy of nursing spread from her own nursing school in England to nursing schools in other countries that employed her model (Bullough, 1975).

Hospitals, and the nurses required to staff them, have been affected by military systems, because nurses were needed during wars, and by religious systems, because hospitals were often run by religious orders between wars. Both of these systems are authoritarian organizations where traditionally women are not the individuals at the top of the hierarchy (Manthey, 1989). It is of little surprise, then, that the main gender issue in the doctor-nurse-patient relationship is power.

GENDER PATTERNS

There are four gender patterns concerning the concept of power in relation to nurses and other individuals in the health care setting. The first, and most prevalent, issue is the imbalance of power between doctors and nurses in relation to the treatment of patients (M. Allen, et al., 1980; L. Bacon, 1986; H. Griffith, et al., 1991; S. Hutchinson, 1982; B. Kalisch and Kalisch, 1982; E. Katzman and J. Roberts, 1988; C. Kennedy and B. Garvin, 1981; B. Ott, et al., 1989; M. Tellis-Nayak and V. Tellis-Nayak, 1984).

The reasons doctors wield more power than nurses are not only historical, but also social. The two professions differ in societal status, with doctors being in the more valued profession. Moreover, doctors and nurses often come from divergent backgrounds, with nurses having middle and lower class upbringings and doctors coming from the upper class (Hutchinson, 1982; B. Kalisch and P. Kalisch, 1982). Additionally, because doctors are usually men and nurses are usually women, their obligations beyond the workplace to their families often differ considerably (Hutchinson, 1982). The most important distinction, however, is that doctors and nurses are educated differently, with doctor training focusing on curing while nurse training focuses on caring (Hutchinson, 1982; Kalisch and Kalisch, 1982; Tellis-Nayak and Tellis-Nayak, 1984). Moreover, the doctor-nurse relationship is discussed in detail throughout a nurse's education, but rarely, or not at all, during a doctor's time in medical school (Bacon, 1986).

These social distinctions in status, background, responsibility, and education have led the nurse to be seen as a helper or "handmaiden" to the doctor rather than a medical professional in her own right (Allen, et al., 1980; Katzman and Roberts, 1988; Muff, 1982a). The role of the nurse has changed somewhat since Florence Nightengale, particularly in the amount and types of medical responsibilities nurses now carry out. However, the socialization of nurses has not changed along with these increasing responsibilities (Allen, et al., 1980). In fact, nurses' responsibilities have now increased to the point where doctors sometimes bill patients for services nurses provide (Griffith, et al., 1991; Ott, et al., 1989).

The second power issue concerning nurses relates to a nurse-nurse relationship. Specifically, some nurses are managers in charge of other nurses. There are status distinctions between registered nurses with bachelor's degrees and licensed practical nurses with less education, as well as between nurses and various hospital aides. These groups "do not support each other in struggling for decent pay, training programs and decision-making power" (Corea, 1977: 71). Rather they often strive to assert or hold their respective status by maintaining solidarity with individuals in the same position and challenging the legitimacy of others' roles.

Moreover, nurse managers have the added pressure of being female bosses to their employees. Some authors advise female managers to behave more androgynously to be successful (C. Camden and Kennedy, 1986; A. Sargent, 1979) while another warns that it is up to female nurse managers to keep the "humanism" in health care (S. Fuller, 1979: 770). Nurses in management roles have the difficulty of being females in supervisory positions. And supervisory positions elsewhere in society are traditionally held by males.

The third power issue also concerns a nurse-nurse relationship, but this time the groups are male and female nurses. While only three percent of nurses are male (Lewis, et al., 1990), gender distinctions exist in the profession. Just as the female role and the doctor role have conflicting tensions, so do the male role and the nurse role. Specifically, male nurses are often assumed by society to be effeminate and/or homosexual (G. Brookfield, et al., 1982). But within the medical profession, there is evidence that male nurses are valued more highly than female nurses. Studies of tokenism have not shown that male nurses are treated negatively in either nursing school or in practice (Kreps, 1987; B. Snavely and G. Fairhurst, 1984). In fact, being male may actually enhance men's status as nurses because males traditionally hold higher status in society (Snavely and Fairhurst, 1984). The most obvious evidence of this is that male nurses are paid better than their female colleagues. According to the *Handbook of Labor Statistics* (1989), between 1984 and 1988, male registered nurses averaged $2,200 a year more in earnings than female registered nurses. These role and salary differences led one male nurse to label his "minority status" as "pleasurable" (Brookfield, et al., 1982: 276).

The fourth power issue concerning nurses exists in the relationship between lay females and nurses. This may seem odd initially because most nurses are female, but the issue here is how nursing is valued by non-nurse females in society. The women's movement has had a "profound influence" on nursing by encouraging action toward the empowerment of nurses (C. Vance, et al., 1985: 33). However, the relationship between women's rights and nursing is not smooth mainly because of the assumption that women should have wanted to become doctors, not nurses, once equal opportunities became available. And nurses today, both male and female, are often asked why they did not attend medical school (S. Gordon, 1991; J. Muff, 1982b). Nurses, however, want the work they do to be valued by society even if it is considered "women's" work (Muff, 1982b; Vance, et al., 1985). The image of the nurse has not been helped by the mass media who portray nurses not only as doctors' helpers, but also as sex objects, such as "Hot Lips" Hoolihan in the film and television series *M*A*S*H*, or as mean, battle-axes like Nurse Rachet in the book and film *One Flew Over the Cuckoo's Nest* (Muff, 1982a).

In summary, there are four issues of power and gender in nursing relationships. These issues are: 1) the asymmetrical balance of power between doctors and nurses with doctors holding virtually all control over decisions concerning patients; 2) the difficulties nurse managers face both wielding power and being female; 3) the power imbalance between male and female nurses, particularly over the issue of comparable worth; and 4) the problems nurses face in trying to become more powerful in a society that devalues their profession.

COMMUNICATIVE ISSUES

The primary communicative issues that stem from these gender issues concern how nurses and doctors speak to each other. In 1967, Stein wrote an influential essay titled "The Doctor-Nurse Game." The "game" is actually a series of indirect communication behaviors that allow the nurse to make recommendations about a patient to a doctor without appearing to be making a recommendation. Additionally, the game allows the doctor to request advice without appearing to be asking for advice. The doctor must not seem to be accepting advice from a non-doctor while the nurse must not appear to be giving medical recommendations. Actually, nurses may not legally offer medical opinions even when called as expert witnesses in lawsuits (Creighton, 1988).

Nurses learn this "game" in their training. They are told not to insult doctors by giving them advice. But paradoxically, nurses are taught that they are valuable assets to doctors, particularly because nurses spend their entire shifts with patients that doctors may see for only minutes. Thus, a nurse may have information about a patient that is unknown to a doctor. Stein (1967) notes that this game reinforces sex-role stereotypes society holds for males and females.

A nurse can choose to make recommendations or not, but the same is not true for orders from doctors. Nurses must communicatively manage the situation that arises when they disagree with a doctor's order. Bullough (1975) notes that nurses tend to use indirect strategies, or a form of "feminine gamesmanship," to respond to doctors (230). However, M. Cunningham and J. Wilcox (1984) found that nurses initially use indirect strategies if they disagree with an order, but use more direct and forceful communicative behaviors if their initial comments are disregarded. Additionally, a nurse's chosen response is mediated by how serious the consequences of the order will be for the patient as well as how angry the doctor might become (Cunningham and Wilcox, 1984).

This communication issue of "inappropriate orders" (Cunningham and Wilcox, 1984: 764) given to nurses by doctors moves beyond concerns of collegiality into the legal realm. Nurses can be named in lawsuits: 1) if they follow an order they believe is inappropriate and some harm comes to the patient; 2) if they refuse to follow a doctor's order they believe is inappropriate and the patient is harmed by their refusal (M. Manthey, 1982; J. Rabinow, 1989); and 3) if they incorrectly follow a doctor's order causing harm to the patient (H. Creighton, 1989). Thus, more and more nurses are purchasing separate liability insurance to protect themselves from situations their hospitals' policies may not cover in the event of a malpractice suit (S. Feutz, 1991; Rabinow, 1989). This legal point is actually a communicative issue because a lawsuit would focus on what doctors and nurses say to each other concerning a specific order.

Beyond the question of how nurses give advice to doctors and follow orders from doctors, the asymmetry of the doctor-nurse relationship is communicatively demonstrated in other ways. Doctors routinely call nurses by their first names, but nurses often call doctors by their titles and surnames, particularly in front of patients (Katzman and Roberts, 1988; Tellis-Nayak and Tellis-Nayak, 1984). The imbalance is demonstrated nonverbally as well in the dress of doctors and nurses because nurses usually wear uniforms, but doctors often wear only lab coats over their street clothes. The use of space also reflects the doctor's superior position: doctors have private offices and separate lounges in hospitals, and their space is usually protected by secretaries and nurses; nurses have no private space and often no separate lounge area. Also, the time of doctors is valued more highly than nurses because they are salaried or work on a fee-for-service basis while nurses are hospital employees, paid by the hour and working in shifts (Tellis-Nayak and Tellis-Nayak, 1984).

Nurses' communication relationships with patients have been examined in light of the nonverbal issue of touch. Lane (1989) studied female nurses beliefs that male patients would be less receptive to touch than female patients, however, the opposite results were found. Male patients found touch more positive than female patients, perhaps because males are not routinely touched in society and enjoyed the experience more. Likewise, perhaps societal views of appropriateness of touch led female nurses to feel more comfortable touching same-sex rather than opposite sex patients (Lane, 1989). Overall, minimal research has addressed gender as a factor in patients' perceptions of nurses (A. Molzahn and H. Northcott, 1989).

The communication issues surrounding the asymmetry of the doctor-nurse relationship are more consequential than simply a power struggle between two professions because doctors and nurses are in the business of helping patients. While the issue of nurses questioning doctors' orders may be potentially healthy for patients, the considerable conflict that exists between predominantly male doctors and mainly female nurses is troublesome to patients of all genders.

CONCLUSION

The health care setting mirrors society in that those holding the power are usually male while those without power are predominantly female. The medical context also reflects the recent changes in society as individuals have begun to cross traditional sex-role barriers in their career choices. Much more research needs to be done, but the preliminary findings seem to indicate that females take on the behaviors of those in power when moving into the traditionally male area of the medical profession while males bring their power with them into the mainly female area of nursing.

The only role in the medical context that traditionally is a male role is that of the doctor, and doctors usually communicatively control their relationships with patients and nurses. Male patients are less prevalent than female patients because men do not bear children and do not routinely take responsibility for the health of others. Also, males are not expected by society to display illness or to seek assistance. Male nurses are unusual, perhaps because society labels men in traditionally female roles as effeminate, even though within the medical profession, male nurses are valued highly.

Female patients are diagnosed with psychosomatic illnesses and prescribed tranquilizers more often than males. They also have the responsibility for caring not only for their own, but also for their families' health. Female doctors have difficulties becoming physicians and then must balance their femininity with a traditionally male role. Female nurses are medical professionals with little autonomy in relation to doctors, patients, and even other nurses.

C. Gilligan's (1982) discussion of the "ethic of care" (30) points out the unique relational attributes of females in society. And S. Gordon (1991) believes females should value this special characteristic and bring their caring, relational attitude with them into the health care setting. Instead of embracing the traditional "marketplace values that have always denigrated care," women should change the contexts they enter (Gordon, 1991: 46).

These gender patterns and communicative issues stir up many questions to which few definitive answers are available. Would everyone—doctors, nurses, and patients—be better off with more "femaleness" in the health care setting? Or does this view simply put more pressure on females to excel in dual roles, that of a medical participant and that of a woman? Is it fair to ask women to bring the caring along with the expertise to the medical context without asking men to bear some of the responsibility? Perhaps if all individuals in the health care setting practice and value caring, as much as they traditionally practice and value curing, patients, doctors, and nurses of both genders would find improved interpersonal interactions.

ACKNOWLEDGMENT

The author would like to thank William K. Rawlins for reading and commenting on this chapter. This chapter was aided by a grant from Indiana University Southeast.

REFERENCES

Adamson, T. E., J. M. Tschann, D. S. Gullion, and A. A. Oppenberg. 1989. Physician communication skills and malpractice claims: A complex relationship. *Western Journal of Medicine* 150: 356–360.

Allen, M. L., D. Jackson, and S. Younger. 1980. Closing the communication gap between physicians and nurses in the intensive care unit setting. *Heart and Lung* 9: 836–840.

Ames, K. 1990. Our bodies, their selves: A bias against women in health research. *Newsweek*, 17 Dec.: 60.

Bacon, L. L. 1986. The nurse-physician relationship: Conflict to collaboration. *Nebraska Nurse* 19: 6–17.

Bernstein, B., and R. Kane. 1981. Physicians' attitudes toward female patients. *Medical Care* 19: 600–608.

Bobula, J. D. 1980. Work patterns, practice characteristics, and incomes of male and female physicians. *Journal of Medical Education* 55: 826–833.

Borges, S. 1986. A feminist critique of scientific ideology: An analysis of two doctor-patient encounters. In S. Fisher and A. D. Todd., eds., *Discourse and Institutional Authority: Medicine, Education, and Law*, Norwood, NJ: Ablex, 26–48.

Brookfield, G., A. Douglas, R. S. Shapiro, and S. J. Cias. 1982. Some thoughts on being a male in nursing. In J. Muff, ed., *Socialization, Sexism, and Stereotyping: Women's Issues in Nursing*, St. Louis: The C. V. Mosby Company, 273–277.

Bullough, B. 1975. Barriers to the nurse practitioner movement: Problems of women in a woman's field. *International Journal of Health Services* 5: 225–233.

Camden, C. T., and C. W. Kennedy. 1986. Manager communicative style and nurse morale. *Human Communication Research* 12: 551–563.

Comstock, L. M., E. M. Hooper, J. M. Goodwin, and J. S. Goodwin. 1982. Physician behaviors that correlate with patient satisfaction. *Journal of Medical Education* 57: 105–112.

Corea, G. 1977. *The Hidden Malpractice: How American Medicine Treats Women as Patients and Professionals*. New York: William Morrow and Company, Inc.

Coulthard, M., and M. Ashby. 1975. Talking with the doctor. *Journal of Communication* 25: 140–147.

Creighton, H. 1988. The nurse as an expert witness. *Nursing Management* 19: 22–23.

————. 1989. Nurse's failure to follow physician's orders. *Nursing Management* 20: 18–22.

Cunningham, M. A., J. R. Wilcox. 1984. When an M.D. gives an R.N. a harmful order: Modifying a bind. In R. N. Bostrom, ed., *Communication Yearbook 8*. Beverly Hills, CA: Sage, 764–778.

Entralgo, P. L. 1979. What does the word *good* mean in *good patient*? In E. J. Cassell and M. Siegler, eds., *Changing Values in Medicine*, New York: University Publications of America, Inc., 127–143.

Feutz, S. A. 1991. Do you need professional liability insurance? *Nursing* 21: 56–57.

Fisher, S. 1983. Doctor talk/patient talk: How treatment decisions are negotiated in doctor-patient communication. In S. Fisher and A. D. Todd, eds., *The Social Organization of Doctor-Patient Communication*, Washington, D.C.: The Center for Applied Linguistics, 135–157.

Fuller, S. 1979. Humanistic leadership in a pragmatic age. *Nursing Outlook* 27: 770–773.

Gilligan, C. 1982. *In a Different Voice: Psychological Theory and Women's Development*. Cambridge, MA: Harvard University Press.

Gordon, S. 1991. Fearing of caring: The feminist paradox. *American Journal of Nursing* 91: 45–48.

Gray, J. 1982. The effect of the doctor's sex on the doctor-patient relationship. *Journal of the Royal College of General Practitioners* 32: 167–169.

Gray, M. J., and S. Meginnis. 1978. Role of the gynecologist and the emerging woman. *Clinical Obstetrics and Gynecology* 21: 173–181.

Griffith, H. M., N. Thomas, and L. Griffith. 1991. MDs bill for these routine nursing tasks. *American Journal of Nursing* 91: 22–27.

Haas, A. 1979. Male and female spoken language differences: Stereotypes and evidence. *Psychological Bulletin* 86: 616–626.

Hall, J. A., D. L. Roter, and N. R. Katz. 1988. Meta-analysis of correlates of provider behavior in medical encounters. *Medical Care* 26: 657–675.

Hausfeld, F. 1976. Women and the doctor-patient relationship. *Australian Family Physician* 5: 534–543.

Heins, M., J. Hendricks, L. Martindale, S. Smock, M. Stein, and J. Jacobs. 1979. Attitudes of women and men physicians. *American Journal of Public Health* 69: 1132–1139.

Henley, N. M. 1977. *Body Politics: Power, Sex, and Nonverbal Communication*. Englewood Cliffs, NJ: Prentice-Hall.

Hutchinson, S. A. 1982. Four perspectives on physicians, nurses, power and games. *Florida Nurse* 30: 9–12.

Jenks, E. B. 1989. An interpersonal perception analysis of doctor-patient communication. Unpublished doctoral dissertation, Department of Speech Communication, Pennsylvania State University.

Kalisch, B. J., and P. A. Kalisch. 1982. An analysis of the source of physician-nurse conflict. In J. Muff, ed., *Socialization, Sexism, and Stereotyping: Women's Issues in Nursing*, St. Louis: The C.V. Mosby Company, 221–233.

Kaplan, A. G. 1985. Female or male therapists for women patients: New formulations. *Psychiatry* 48: 111–121.

Katzman, E. M., and J. I. Roberts. 1988. Nurse-physician conflicts as barriers to the enactment of nursing roles. *Western Journal of Nursing Research* 10: 576–590.

Kennedy, C. W., and B. J. Garvin. 1981. The effect of status and gender on interpersonal relationships in nursing. *Nursing Forum* 20: 274–287.

Korsch, B. M., E. K. Gozzi, and V. Francis. 1968. Gaps in doctor-patient communication: Doctor–patient interaction and patient satisfaction. *Pediatrics* 42: 855–871.

Kramer, C. 1977. Perceptions of female and male speech. *Language and Speech* 20: 151–161.

Kreps, G. L. 1987. Organizational sexism in health care. In L. P. Stewart and S. Ting-Toomey, eds., *Communication, Gender, and Sex Roles in Diverse Interaction Contexts*. Norwood, NJ: Ablex.

Laing, R. D. 1969. *Self and Others*. New York: Penguin Books.

Lane, P. L. 1989. Nurse-client perceptions: The double standard of touch. *Issues in Mental Health Nursing* 10: 1–13.

Lane, S. D. 1983. Compliance, satisfaction, and physician–patient communication. In R. N. Bostrom, ed., *Communication Yearbook 7*, Beverly Hills, CA: Sage Publications, 772–799.

Langwell, K. M. 1982. Factors affecting the incomes of men and women physicians: Further explorations. *Journal of Human Resources* 17: 261–275.

Lewis, J. D., M. Snodgrass, and F. H. Larkin. 1990. Men in nursing: Some troubling data. *American Journal of Nursing* 90: 30.

Malterud, K. 1987a. Illness and disease in female patients I. *Scandinavian Journal of Primary Health Care* 5: 205–209.

_____. 1987b. Illness and disease in female patients II. *Scandinavian Journal of Primary Health Care* 5: 211–216.

Maltz, D. N., and R. A. Borker. 1982. A cultural approach to male-female miscommunication. In J. J. Gumperz, ed., *Language and Social Identity*, Cambridge: Cambridge University Press, 196–216.

Manthey, M. 1989. Just what are doctors' orders anyway? *Nursing Management* 20: 26–28.

Mendez, A., J. A. Shymansky, and M. Wolraich. 1986. Verbal and non-verbal behaviour of doctors while conveying distressing information. *Medical Education* 20: 437–443.

Molzahn, A. E., and H. C. Northcott. 1989. The social bases of discrepancies in health/illness perceptions. *Journal of Advanced Nursing* 14: 132–140.

Muff, J. 1982a. Handmaiden, battle-ax, whore: An explanation into the fantasies, myths, and stereotypes about nurses. In J. Muff, ed., *Socialization, Sexism, and Stereotyping: Women's Issues in Nursing*, St. Louis: The C. V. Mosby Company, 113–156.

_____. 1982b. Why doesn't a smart girl like you go to medical school? The women's movement takes a slap at nursing. In J. Muff, ed., *Socialization, Sexism, and Stereotyping: Women's Issues in Nursing*, St. Louis: The C. V. Mosby Company, 178–185.

Murphy-Cullen, C. L., and L. C. Larsen. 1984. Interaction between the socio-demographic variables of physicians and their patients: Its impact upon patient satisfaction. *Social Science and Medicine* 19: 163–166.

Nathanson: C. A. 1975. Illness and the feminine role: A theoretical review. *Social Science and Medicine* 9: 57–62.

Ott, B. B., H. Griffith, and J. Towers. 1989. Who gets the money? *American Journal of Nursing* 89: 186–188.

Paget, M. A. 1983. On the work of talk: Studies in misunderstandings. In S. Fisher & A. D. Todd, eds., *The Social Organization of Doctor-Patient Communication*, Washington, D.C.: The Center for Applied Linguistics, 55–74.

Paluszny, M., and E. Poznanski. 1971. Reactions of patients during pregnancy of the psychotherapist. *Child Psychiatry and Human Development* 1: 266–274.

Parsons, T. 1951. *The Social System*. Glencoe, IL: Free Press.

Rabinow, J. 1989. You stand in the eyes of the law. *Nursing* 19: 34–42.

Root, M. J. 1987. Communication barriers between older women and physicians. *Public Health Reports Supplement*: 152–155.

Sargent, A. G. 1979. The androgynous manager. *Supervisor Nurse* 10:23–30.

Scully, D. 1980. *Men who Control Women's Health: The Miseducation of Obstetrician-Gynecologists*. Boston: Houghton Mifflin.

Shuy, R. W. 1983. Three types of interference to an effective exchange of information in the medical interview. In S. Fisher and A. D. Todd, eds., *The Social Organization of Doctor-Patient Communication*, Washington, D.C.: The Center for Applied Linguistics, 189–202.

Snavely, B. K., and G. T. Fairhurst. 1984. The male nursing student as a token. *Research in Nursing and Health* 7: 287–294.

Stein, L. I. 1967. The doctor-nurse game. *Archives of General Psychiatry* 16: 699–703.

Stewart, M. 1983. Patient characteristics which are related to the doctor-patient interaction. *Family Practice* 1: 30–36.

Stimson, G. V. 1975. The message of psychotropic drug ads. *Journal of Communication* 25: 153–160.

Swiderski, R. M. 1976. The idiom of diagnosis. *Communication Quarterly* 24: 3–11.

Tellis-Nayak, M., and V. Tellis-Nayak. 1984. Games that professionals play: The social psychology of physician-nurse interaction. *Social Science and Medicine* 18: 1063–1069.

Thorne, B., and N. Henley. 1975. Difference and dominance: An overview of language, gender, and society. In B. Thorne and N. Henley, eds., *Language and Sex: Difference and Dominance*, Rowley, MA: Newbury House Publishers, Inc., 5–42.

U. S. Bureau of the Census (1990). *Statistical Abstract of the United States: 1990.* 110th ed. Washington, D.C.: U.S. Government Printing Office.

U. S. Department of Labor (1990). *Handbook of Labor Statistics.* Washington, D.C.: U.S. Government Printing Office.

Vance, C., S. W. Talbott, A. B. McBride, and D. J. Mason. 1985. Coming of age: The women's movement and nursing. In D. J. Mason and S. W. Talbott, eds., *Political Action Handbook for Nurses: Changing the Workplace, Government, Organizations, and Community*, Menlo Park, CA: Addison-Wesley Publishing Company, 23–37.

Wallen, J., H. Waitzkin, and J. D. Stoeckle. 1979. Physician stereotypes about female health and illness: A study of patient's sex and the informative process during medical interviews. *Women & Health* 4: 135–146.

Waitzkin, H. 1984. Doctor-patient communication: Clinical implications of social scientific research. *Journal of the American Medical Association*, 252: 2441–2446.

Weisman, C. S. 1987. Communication between women and their health care providers: Research findings and unanswered questions. *Public Health Reports Supplement*: 147–151.

Weisman, C. S., and M. A. Teitelbaum. 1985. Physician gender and the physician patient relationship: Recent evidence and relevant questions. *Social Science and Medicine* 11: 1119–1127.

Weisman, C. S., M. A. Teitelbaum, and L. L. Morlock. 1988. Malpractice claims experience associated with fertility-control services among young obstetrician-gynecologists. *Medical Care* 26: 198–306.

West, C. 1983. "Ask me no questions . . ." An analysis of queries and replies in physician-patient dialogues. In S. Fisher and A. D. Todd, eds., *The Social Organization of Doctor-Patient Communication*, Washington, D.C.: The Center for Applied Linguistics, 75–106.

Young, J. W. 1979. Symptom disclosure to male and female physicians: Effects of sex, physical attractiveness, and symptom type. *Journal of Behavioral Medicine* 2: 159–169.

CHAPTER 13

GENDER AND COMMUNICATION IN THE HOSPITALITY INDUSTRY

AUTHOR   Judi Brownell, Cornell University

POINTS TO BE ADDRESSED

- The symbolic/cultural approach to understanding organizational communication
- The impact of culture on gender and communication
- Cultural aspects unique of the hospitality industry
- Gender issues in hospitality organizations
- Communication behaviors and organizational culture: Changing the way men and women interact at work.
- Implications of the symbolic/cultural approach to improving the way men and women communicate

Service industries are one of the fastest-growing segments of the U.S. economy. Well over 70 percent of the working population is engaged in some form of service activity, and this number is steadily increasing. There are over eight million people in today's hospitality workforce alone; by the 21st century, that figure will have increased significantly.

If you think about it, you can probably name several friends or relatives who have worked in service organizations. Perhaps you've even waited tables or delivered pizzas. If not, you've still played a part as a consumer; you've stayed at a hotel, visited a health care professional, or flown in a plane. It's likely, then, that you know something about service organizations already.

This chapter explores gender and communication in one segment of the service industry—hospitality organizations. The hospitality industry includes such businesses as hotels, restaurants, airlines, clubs, resorts, and casinos. We will be observing communication between men and women in these organizations from a particular viewpoint called the symbolic/cultural perspective.

First, the basic assumptions of the symbolic/cultural approach are defined because they reveal important characteristics of hospitality organizations and provide a framework for better understanding how gender affects behavior in the workplace. The unique aspects of the hospitality industry are emphasized and their influence on gender and communication is discussed. Two significant issues related to gender are then explored—sexual harassment and women in management.

Finally, specific communication behaviors and strategies for addressing common problems of communication between men and women are presented. The skills of listening, communicating verbally, and communicating nonverbally are discussed because they can modify an organization's culture toward more effective male/female communication. In closing, we take a look at the implications our discussion has for gender and communication in the hospitality industry.

APPROACHES TO STUDYING ORGANIZATIONS

Over the years, scholars and researchers have viewed organizational communication and behavior from a number of different perspectives (L. Bolman and T. Deal, 1983; Frank and Brownell, 1989). Each perspective provides a slightly different lens, enabling us to focus on specific aspects of communication and behavior. Our job here is to identify the lens best suited to examining communication between men and women at work.

Early classical theorists such as Max Weber (1947) applied mechanistic, highly rational models that emphasized formalized rules, specialization of roles, and organizational structure. If things didn't go well in their organizations, classical theorists might recommend creating another department or restructuring lines of authority.

The human relations theorists, pioneered by researchers like Barnard (1938) and E. Mayo (1933), were interested in human resources issues and in the individual worker. D. McGregor's (1960) Theory X and Theory Y clearly distinguished classical theories from the newer human relations approaches that took the needs of the individual and the influence of personal and social factors into account. Human relations theorists were concerned with employee satisfaction, morale, and quality of worklife issues. If an organizational communication problem arose, their approach might be to survey workers, to implement training programs, or to create additional opportunities for employees to participate in decision-making processes.

Still other researchers were interested in the sets of properties and patterns that make organization possible. Some of the first applications of systems theory to organizational behavior were described by D. Katz and R. Kahn (1966) and J. Miller (1972). These researchers viewed organizations as integrated systems and emphasized the functional relationships among all parts. Any time a problem was identified, its solution would ultimately affect all aspects of the organization.

Each framework highlights certain aspects of human behavior in organizations, and allows us to see with varying degrees of clarity a particular aspect of organizational life. When our subject is gender and communication, we discover that focusing our lens on yet another approach, the symbolic/cultural perspective, provides the clearest and most revealing view. An understanding of the symbolic/cultural framework is essential to our subsequent discussions of gender and communication.

THE SYMBOLIC/CULTURAL APPROACH

From a symbolic/cultural perspective, communication makes organization possible. Think for a moment about the implications of this statement. The symbolic/cultural approach to studying organizations focuses on the ways in which individuals "make sense" of their experiences and "negotiate meanings" in the process of their daily interactions. It is through communication—symbolic interaction—that organizational meanings are created, maintained, and shared, and organizational values transmitted. Human communication is seen as sense-making activity; it generates a core of basic assumptions that, in turn, influence members' subsequent perceptions and behaviors.

Through the actions of organizational leaders and the daily activities of members, each organization develops a unique culture that influences behavior as it is itself created through employees' interactions. As M. Louis (1980) explains, culture is the "process of learning the expectations of others and how to act in terms of context-specific assumptions." A portion of those assumptions, as we will see, pertains to gender and communication.

The concept of symbols and symbolic action is also basic to understanding how an organization develops a particular social reality for its members and affirms basic cultural values. You can determine what a symbol means to an organizational member by observing his or her behavior in response to a particular word or gesture. In one instance, a "great waitress" might mean that a woman has provided efficient, courteous service. In another, the implication might be that she has performed related activities as well—brought your little sister crackers or put extra ice in your water. The meaning of a symbol is strongly influenced, then, by the organizational context in which it is used. As Kreps (1990) explains, culture influences

> . . . the attitudes and values of members; the specialized jargons and languages they use; the social and professional rituals they engage in; the company history that is passed on; the company philosophies that are held; legends, stories, and jokes that are told; informal norms and logic used to guide actions; the visions that organizational members have of the organization's future; and the identification of organizational friends and foes. (126–127)

How does all of this relate to gender and communication? In the next section you will discover that notions of what it "means" to be male or female are socially constructed.

Gender and Symbolic Action

Communication creates gender (J. Pearson, 1985) just as it creates other organizational realities. It is through interactions with others that we learn what it "means," within a particular framework, to be male or female. You may have Asian friends, for instance, who grew up in an environment where appropriate behavior for women was strikingly different from what you experienced in the United States. Consequently, you and your friend may have disagreements about how women should respond in various situations. The symbolic/cultural perspective helps us view more critically our basic assumptions about gender and, further, recognize how these assumptions are created and perpetuated within organizational environments.

Think, for a moment, about your past experiences as a man or woman in organizations. Although women are generally accepted in "soft" professions like marketing and personnel, many employers still have reservations about hiring women in construction, finance, or other areas traditionally associated with male-linked characteristics such as mathematical ability and physical strength. In spite of many recent changes, it is still unusual to find male secretaries or female groundskeepers.

In addition, gender itself may be a significant variable in influencing individual perceptions. E. Hackett and his colleagues (1991) discovered that women's expectations about new technology, for instance, were significantly more pessimistic than mens'. Women did not anticipate as much job improvement and, in fact, expected some aspects of their work to get even worse. His conclusion was that differences in perceptions could be attributed to gender; men and women simply perceived and interpreted the same experience in different ways.

Another study (B. Nelsen, 1990) examined upper-level hospitality managers' perceptions regarding whether there are gender-based differences that affect women's career progress. The findings are revealing.

MEN AGREED AND WOMEN DISAGREED THAT:

- female managers are more visible and this increased exposure has a positive effect
- that women network in similar ways to men
- that upward mobility is equal for men and women

MEN DISAGREED AND WOMEN AGREED THAT:

- women are perceived as not being tough enough
- women have a better record of staying with a company
- women and men use mentors with equal success
- women rely less on organizational power politics

As S. Kenton (1989) summarizes, if the above findings reflect organizational realities, then it may be that females must indeed be superior to men in order to achieve equal results. J. Peters (1988) agrees, noting that credibility still doesn't appear to come easily for women in the workplace.

What is responsible for these perceptual differences? One explanation might be that from their earliest years, men and women have different social experiences that subsequently influence the way they see and interpret the world (L. Arliss, 1991). As children, boys and girls are reinforced and recognized for different sorts of behavior. While girls who are pretty and clean may receive attention, boys are more often rewarded for their athletic ability and other physical accomplishments. Each gender is provided different types of stimuli and sent different messages about what is valued or appropriate.

In addition to the influence of their parents or significant adults, the media, children's literature, and early peer groups also contribute to the impressions that children form about what it means to belong to a particular gender group. These attitudes continue into adulthood. Recent literature (J. Gregg and P. Johnson, 1990) suggests that even when women and men have similar educational backgrounds and produce similar products, they have "different work-related experiences" (12).

Informal networks, the social contacts that often help to define the organization's norms and expectations, are often different for men than they are for women (Peters, 1988). Women often have more difficulty gaining access to career-relevant information because the "old boy network" operates on golf courses and at happy hours as well as in the organization's hallways and cafeterias.

Many employees treat colleagues of both genders in a manner consistent with their gender role expectations regardless of the person's organizational role (B. Gutek, A. Cohen, and A. Konrad, 1990). If men have been raised to believe that women need to be protected, or that they should take care of social events, or that they are easily upset, these assumptions will affect how women are treated at work. Later, you will see some vivid examples of this problem as two fictional characters, Sylvia and Beth, attempt to communicate with their male colleagues.

As L. Smeltzer and J. Werbel (1986) suggest, although there are few documented differences between male and female communication behaviors, "stereotypical assumptions, perceptions, and expectations concerning the . . . behavior of the sexes persist" (42). The stereotype of women as gentle, clean, and nurturing may be in sharp contrast to their role requirements on the job. Yet, the way she is treated cannot help but influence a woman's subsequent behavior as she receives cues regarding what it means to be a woman in that particular workplace.

Because attributing certain characteristics to one gender or another is likely to produce behavior that is "based on stereotypes rather than on individual talents and abilities" (Catalyst, 1987: 42), it is clearly in the best interest of the organization to develop a culture in which expectations are not gender-linked and self-fulfilling prophecies do not have opportunities to grow (Abbey, 1982). As Liza Dolittle noted in the well-known story of her transformation from uneducated urchin to a well-mannered woman, "I'll always be a flower girl to Professor Higgins, because he treats me like a flower girl and always will." Those who treat her like a lady, however, empower her to behave in a more appropriate and productive manner.

Although Pearson (1985) warns that perceptions of behavior are often confused with actual behavior, the truth is that our perceptions are our reality. What we believe is what is true: our beliefs influence our subsequent attitudes and behavior.

You can see how the symbolic/cultural approach draws attention to some important aspects of gender and communication. We have examined how employees are affected by the values and culture of their organization and how expectations of gender behavior influence our perceptions. Now, let's focus on the specific ways in which the hospitality environment shapes employees' gender-related behavior.

The Service Industry: A Special Culture

A growing body of literature suggests that service industries are unique in several important ways. The nature of service, as discussed earlier, requires that organizational members deal not only with internal communication but with the expectations and definitions of their publics as well. In the hospitality industry, quality service is often defined by whether or not the provider meets the customer's expectations. Because a portion of the service occurs during a transaction between two individuals, the meanings negotiated during this encounter become particularly significant.

Internal communication in hospitality industries is affected not only by verbal behavior, but by nonverbal communication as well. The next section reviews some of the characteristics that distinguish hospitality organizations and make them challenging environments for gender communication.

SYMBOLS AND ENVIRONMENTAL CHARACTERISTICS OF SERVICE CULTURES

Kathleen Talbert, director of the French Culinary Institute, tells of her problems placing women graduates (Peters, 1988). Many chefs, she reports, are reluctant to hire females:

> . . . They say, You are going to ruin the spirit of my kitchen if you send me a woman because then the other chefs aren't going to pay attention to their work, they are going to be chasing after her. (118)

Toni Knorr, corporate director of food and beverage at Hyatt Hotels in Chicago, explains how she has to take the dynamics of a particular environment into account when placing women graduates; some cultures, she believes, are so strong and male-dominated that women find it almost impossible to be successful (Peters, 1988). Clearly, aspects of the foodservice environment make it particularly difficult for women to succeed.

Pearson (1989) suggests that three elements determine an organization's work environment: (1) performance standards, (2) business concepts that define how the company operates, and (3) the values that define what it's like to work in the particular organization. Although performance standards and business concepts may vary from one property or firm to the next, the service industry in general has strong values that guide member behaviors within the service culture (Wood, 1990).

The symbols and the environment inherent in hospitality organizations (both verbal and nonverbal) are strong forces in shaping the way in which men and women communicate. Hospitality implies meeting needs, having a good time, doing whatever it takes to satisfy. Images of the industry include wine glasses and moonlit patios, whirlpools, and breakfast trays. Symbols of romance, of feeling good, of pampering, predominate.

The work environment itself also influences behavior. Many employees work in close proximity to one another. Their shifts are long and irregular, often including evening and nighttime hours. The duties of hospitality workers are likely to take them into settings traditionally associated with sexual behavior—bedrooms, bars, and lounges. In other instances, employees work poolside in a casual, informal atmosphere.

In addition, hospitality employees are often hired, in part, because of outgoing personalities and physical attractiveness. Airline stewards and stewardesses, club managers, front desk personnel—all project their organization's image to the public and, in that regard, are likely to be personable and attractive. In many instances their dress accentuates gender differences and sexuality. The combination of work environment and personal characteristics makes hospitality employees' work experience quite unlike any other.

Note, too, that different cultures mix sex and business in different ways (R. Axtell, 1990). The changing composition of the hospitality workforce brings together men and women with very different experiences and assumptions because of their cultural backgrounds. Awkward situations are likely to develop when initial expectations are highly discrepant. From the symbolic/cultural approach, this means that organizations need strong cultures with clear norms and expectations to socialize new employees and communicate what it means to work for that particular company.

Although all organizations confront internal problems associated with gender and communication, the nature of service industries poses additional challenges. Not only do employees communicate regularly with co-workers, but their customers and guests represent yet another potentially problematic dimension.

Service and Symbolic Action

In addition to providing a framework for viewing organizational members' interactions as well as the physical and symbolic aspects of the workplace, the symbolic/cultural approach also provides insight into the nature of service encounters. There are few more elusive concepts in today's business world than that of effective service. Difficult to measure or describe, "good service" is largely in the eyes of the customer. It has, most specialists agree, little to do with what the provider believes it is and a lot to do with the customers' perceptions and expectations (Davidow and Uttal, 1989). In fact, good service is frequently defined not by any standard of quality, but rather by behavior that exceeds the customer's expectations. You can see the usefulness of the symbolic/cultural approach in understanding how the meaning of service is negotiated. Because of its subjective nature, the most meaningful approaches to studying service organizations are those that emphasize the dynamic aspects of the service encounter.

In hospitality organizations, service can be viewed as emerging from the coordinated efforts of service employee and customer; it is the social interaction itself that defines what service *means* to the guest (Mills and Morris, 1986). At the moment of service, the organization's representative and the specific customer interact to produce the "product" (Worsfold, 1989).

In one sense, then, the customer becomes a "partial employee" (Barrington and Olsen, 1987), affecting the time of demand, the exact nature of the service, and the quality of the service provided. Clearly, such high-contact systems have a high degree of uncertainty within their daily operations, and room for interpretations regarding appropriate gender behavior. Just as with internal communication, customers have sets of expectations regarding how they will be treated. These expectations involve patterns of rights, privileges, and obligations between the guest and the service provider. Some of these expectations, to be sure, have to do with gender-related behaviors.

Basic assumptions about the importance of "satisfied customers" often force employees to conform to expectations that may not be in keeping with their understanding of what their job entails. If, for instance, a customer's "meaning" of barmaid includes services that the employee does not feel obligated to provide, problems are likely to result.

A customer ordering a drink, then, will define his or her experience not only by the quality of the beverage, but also by the extent to which the employee meets his or her expectations regarding service behavior. Expectations for women, who have traditionally been perceived as service providers (mother, helper) or sexual objects may go beyond the organization's definition of what constitutes appropriate action. The patron who has been drinking and invites the waitress to sit on his lap, or the hotel guest who suggests that the maid give him a backrub, demonstrate this discrepancy. As Chase (1978) explains, interactions with the customer make the worker "part of the product" (139). In some cases, this notion can be taken to the extreme.

There is also a degree of discretion on the part of the service provider. As Mills and Morris point out, some customers are extended far more and varied service than others. Often, service employees have been coached in advance and are prepared to extend more complete or quality service to selected guests. It's not uncommon for the front desk manager to insist that when Mr. Warren arrives, he should be "given priority treatment." Even in these cases, however, problems arise when employees are asked for specific services on the basis of their gender in addition to—or instead of—their organizational role.

Employees must also manage what Albrecht and Zemke (1985) have called "moments of truth." Moments of truth are the specific employee decisions or behaviors that have an impact on the customer and his or her impressions of the particular organization. These moments of truth contribute to customer's definitions of what service means in a particular organization. The way in which employees respond to inappropriate gender-related behaviors, as we will see in a later section, is critical to the success of any given encounter.

Gender Issues

In addition to the moment-by-moment decisions that are made as men and women communicate at work, gender poses several more encompassing concerns as well. Among these are issues of sexual harassment and the difficulties women have had securing and maintaining managerial positions. Because of the pervasiveness of these problems, the next section is devoted to a review of these two issues as they pertain to hospitality organizations.

HARASSMENT

As we have seen, the nature of the hospitality workplace, with its higher male-female contact and its sex-associated symbols, provides an environment where the potential for sexual harassment is particularly high.

Recent statistics on sexual harassment indicate that over half of all employees have been exposed to some form of sexual overture from a co-worker of the other sex. Few women, however, take formal action in such situations. Although an estimated 10 percent of women have quit a job because of sexual harassment (Gutek, Cohen, and Konrad, 1990), many researchers believe that a large percentage of harassment situations go unreported. These findings are striking; yet, R. Nozar (1990) proposes that sexual harassment in the hospitality industry may exist at twice the rate it does in other types of organizations.

Harassment in the service industry takes place between managers and subordinates and between service personnel and customers or guests; however, the majority of violations occur among colleagues. In her study of harassment in the hospitality industry, Eller (1989) found that over 40 percent of the women she surveyed said they contended with insulting sexual comments; 28 percent reported experiencing insulting looks and gestures and sexual touching.

As Eller (1989) emphasizes, in an industry already faced with "rampant turnover, high labor costs, and a diminishing supply of works" (84), sexual harassment is a serious problem. On a national level, sexual harassment cost U.S. taxpayers approximately 267 million dollars between 1985 and 1987.

There are a number of reasons why hospitality workers are particularly susceptible to sexual harassment. Most of these have already been discussed as aspects of the service culture. Clearly, there is frequent physical contact among co-workers. Unusual hours, with peak and slack periods, create an environment where harassing behavior is likely to occur. Because sociability and attractiveness are valued and emphasized, attention is drawn to employees' gender identities. In some situations, skimpy uniforms or other aspects of employees' required dress contributes to the problem still further.

One study that is particularly relevant to gender communication in the hospitality industry was conducted by Gutek, Cohen, and Konrad (1990). A review of their work raises some interesting and relevant issues.

Are you familiar with the phrase, "sexualization of the workplace"? It's the concept Gutek, Cohen, and Konrad (1990) propose for examining gender and communication in organizations. The authors suggest that a simple measure—the amount of contact between individuals—can partially explain gender behavior in organizational settings. A "sexualized" work environment, or one in which there is a great deal of physical contact, is more likely to encourage people of both genders to make sexual overtures. The degree to which a work environment is sexualized also reflects the acceptability of social-sexual behavior (570).

Gutek and her colleagues believe that understanding the sexualization of a workplace is important because of its "pivotal mediating role" (572) in facilitating both sexual harassing and nonharassing behavior. Managers, they believe, can work to desexualize the contact between men and women at work by establishing appropriate standards of language, conduct, and dress. These responses will be discussed in a later section of this chapter when we examine culture change. For now, let's continue by focusing on the second significant issue pertaining to gender and communication—women in management.

WOMEN IN MANAGEMENT

A group of female executives sits around a table. The main topic of conversation is the growing number of women who are leaving excellent corporate careers because they believe gender discrimination will prevent them from obtaining senior positions (Rogers, 1986).

Women account for nearly one half the graduates of foodservice management programs. Although the majority of service employees are women, fewer than a third of management positions are filled by women (Gregg and Johnson, 1990). A 1988 study conducted by Lodging determined that fewer than eight percent of the service companies sampled had a woman president (B. Nelsen, 1990). This statistic is comparable or slightly higher than those provided for U.S. corporations generally. Bernstein (1990) reported that only 3 of the 500 chief executives of the highest volume U.S. companies and only three percent of senior executives nationwide are women.

There seems to be little question that although women may manage "differently," they are as effective as their male counterparts in accomplishing personal and organizational goals (J. Baird and P. Bradley, 1979; C. Baytosh and B. Kleiner, 1989). In fact, some researchers believe (Bass, 1991) that women may be better suited than men to serve as transformational leaders in the twenty-first century. Leadership in the decades ahead is likely to be characterized by a variety of social and technical skills, some traditionally male-linked and some female-linked. In a 1987 report, Catalyst, a New York-based research and advisory organization, proposes that:

> In an increasingly service-driven economy, characterized by a diverse labor force and changes in the nature of work itself, there has been a re-evaluation of the stereotypical "female" managerial characteristics and of their viability in management. (40)

Although increasing numbers of women are moving into managerial positions, men have not "demonstrated a corresponding interest in the lower-paid, female-dominated" (G. Powell, 1989: 47) roles like waitperson or housekeeper. In addition, it appears that once women assume managerial roles, there is often a glass ceiling that prevents further upward mobility. Part of the problem may be due to a culture that perpetuates stereotypes and assumptions about women's role and abilities as a manager.

Mary, for instance, has been an assistant manager at a 300-room full ser-vice hotel for two years. Dick, her boss, has surrounded himself with an all-male clique that purposely excludes women. The members of the clique advance, often leap-frogging over women like Mary who have impressive qualifications but who may not participate in the same social activities (DeLuca, 1988: 10).

Men have traditionally used informal networks to help move ahead profes-sionally. As more women reach middle management positions, they have found such contacts unavailable to them (S. DeWine and D. Casbolt, 1983). As one author observes, the service industry's challenge is to "open its doors for female executives all the way to the board room—which is still very much an all-male arena" (Marshall, 1989: 19).

Bernstein (1990) agrees, noting a study where at least four out of five of 1,000 corporate chief executives conceded that "stereotyping and preconcep-tions by men were blocking women from reaching top management" (51). As Leonard Roberts, chairman and chief executive officer of Shoney's, Inc., said to his chain's top management: "Wake up and smell the coffee. She isn't mak-ing it anymore" (29).

Another problem women face as a result of their poor representation in upper-level management is the lack of appropriate role models. Laura Hay-den, personnel director of Pizza Hut, noted in an interview that role models for women simply aren't there at the corporate level—at least not in the hospi-tality industry, at least not yet (Peters, 1988). Although women have the option of turning to men as their models and mentors, as Peters (1988) explains, "subtle social and sexual pressures can make women feel uncomfort-able in these relationships" (128).

Although women in organizations face numerous challenges, the symbolic/cultural approach provides a means of identifying and addressing some of the most pressing issues. The next section of this chapter provides some sugges-tions for how individuals can influence organizational cultures so that the environments in which they work promote healthy communication between men and women. First, you'll be introduced to Sylvia and Beth, managers at The Fortune. Then, you'll discover how listening, verbal communication, and nonverbal behavior can be used to modify organizational culture.

GENDER AND COMMUNICATION: MODIFYING CULTURE

GENDER AND COMMUNICATION AT THE FORTUNE

The Fortune Hotel, one of several well-established, smaller but exclusive hotels in Chicago, has a long tradition of quality and service. Fortune's culture is strong, and over 40 percent of its salaried employees have been with the organization for more than 10 years. Ned Brown, general manager, has made several significant changes within the past five years. One of the most striking was to hire two women managers, Sylvia Thorz and Beth Westbrook. Although rumor has it that Ned was under a lot of pressure from his peers in other properties to demonstrate his commitment to equal opportunity, his staff never knew for sure. In any event, the long-standing tradition of an all-male management team had been permanently disrupted.

Clearly, both women were well-qualified for their positions. Sylvia, Food and Beverage Manager, received her Bachelor of Science degree in Hotel Administration from the University of Nevada, Las Vegas. Prior to joining The Fortune she had been the Assistant Banquet Sales Manager at the Beverly Wilshire Hotel in Dallas. Soft spoken and somewhat shy, Sylvia nevertheless had proven to be a very capable and employee-centered manager. Her staff loved her because she was so committed to their welfare.

Beth was hired five years ago as Assistant Manager of Marketing for Fortune, having earned an MBA from Dartmouth and having spent two years at Lever Brothers, Inc., in their Marketing Department. After years of hard work, she was passed over for a promotion to Director of Public Relations when Sid Adams retired after 38 years at Fortune. Although Beth filed no formal grievance, she did speak out and questioned Ned's decision in hiring an old college buddy of his to replace Sid. She criticized The Fortune's corporate philosophy and questioned whether there were any opportunities for women to be successful within such a male-dominated culture. Soon she had a reputation as a troublemaker and "bitch." Her behavior seemed to strengthen the opinion most of her colleagues shared; women make excellent housekeepers and waitresses, but keep them out of management!

One of the strongest aspects of Fortune's culture was its regular meetings, held every Tuesday morning. As the eleven-member management team convened, the sound of jokes and good-natured bantering could be heard down the hall. "Hey, Steve," Jeff Car, the Front Desk manager, said as he grabbed the arm of The Fortune's new director of finance. "Listen to this." As Jeff turned around he saw Sylvia taking a seat across the room. "Well, maybe I'd better wait on that one. We don't want to offend any of our colleagues—right Sylvia?" The two men laughed as they went back to the table. Sylvia caught Beth's eye and she shook her head. She could tell it was going to be one of those days, and began fidgeting with her bracelet.

"You have met the better-looking members of our team, haven't you?" Jeff said as he motioned to the women at the table. "Yes," Steve nodded. "I've had the pleasure." "Well, we'll fill you in on what really goes on around here when we hit the 19th hole next Saturday! These girls may look . . ." Jeff was stopped abruptly by the loud thump of Ned's hand hitting the table as he brought the group to order.

The meeting was a long one, as usual, drawn out by discussions that wandered from the main issue and by the fact that Ned, although a solid businessperson, was not a particularly good discussion leader. After over an hour of reports and various debates, Ned pushed back his chair. "All right gentlemen," Ned began. "I know this has been long, but I think we've about come to the end." He looked down for a moment at his agenda. "Hold it," he said with emphasis, "I almost forgot. We've got one last item on the agenda. It's a problem that Sylvia is having with several of her employees. Sylvia, why don't you explain your problem to the rest of us?"

Sylvia could feel herself becoming angry, not only at the way Ned was presenting her situation to the rest of the management team, but also because both times in the past when she had proposed a discussion topic, it had been put at the very end of Ned's agenda. In spite of her anger, she took a deep breath, smiled, and began.

"You all know Karen Duncan, one of our most loyal employees. She came in to talk with me last week about a concern she has with the way our guests have been treating the barmaids. Ever since the staff began wearing, ah, those new uniforms, verbal abuse—which they always had to put up with to some extent—has drastically increased. They're just, ah, I don't think they're appropriate. Last week a guest, um, actually pulled Mary Sanders onto his lap and wouldn't let her up. I guess she was really frightened and refused to work the late night shift again.

"Anyway, the employees, well, the employees attribute some of the problem to their new uniforms. They think the short, low-cut uniforms invite suggestive comments and more aggressive behavior. And, well," Sylvia looked down at the table but continued, "Karen even suggested that, um, a couple of the F & B assistant managers were giving the women a hard time. So," she rushed on, "I've been asked to discuss this with you and, um, see if we can't propose some action plan."

"I'll give them a little action," Tony, the F & B manager, quipped. Several of his buddies chuckled. "I wish I had problems like that," Jeff commented. "All those cute girls down at the bar won't have anything to do with me—heaven knows I've tried!"

"Okay, okay, guys," Ned said as he raised his hand to quiet the group. "Sylvia needs help, and the least we can do is make some suggestions."

"If you want my opinion," Tony said as he leaned back in his chair, "it's the way the girls act toward the guests, not the uniforms. If they want to be treated like professionals, they need to act like professionals. I've seen them strutting around down there in the bar myself. What do they expect? They're dealing with men who are away from home, who have been working hard all day. Those barmaids are just what the doctor ordered.

"In fact," Tony continued, leaning forward in his chair, "Remember Marge? Well, she was one of our best barmaids. Used to sit on the table and laugh at all the bad jokes. When her customers were ready to leave, she'd give them this pink note that said, 'Hurry back now.' She knew how to increase business."

Beth had been silent, listening to the conversation. She could see that Sylvia was about to cry—or leave the room—and wondered what she could say that would help. She raised her hand. Ned seemed to look past her as he took suggestions from two more managers. Finally Beth had had enough. "Ned," she said with irritation, "I know you don't care what I think, but I've been trying to present my opinion and I wondered if you could be quiet and listen."

"Right on, Beth," Mark said with a grin. "Go for it."

"I think you men are animals with no sensitivity whatsoever. What is the matter with you? Sylvia has brought up a very legitimate problem and you guys just think it's funny. What does it take to get your serious attention?"

"More coffee!" Tony said as he stood up. "And more time. I think we've had enough for one meeting. Tell you what, Sylvia. I'll sleep on it—" there were a few isolated chuckles from the group—"and let you know what I think next week."

Others quickly agreed that the meeting had gone on too long already, and Ned offered no resistance. "Fine," Ned said in closing. "See you next Tuesday."

Sylvia and Beth walked out of the room together. Although they had seemed eager to adjourn, most of the others stood around and shared reactions to the recent Lakers-Knicks game. Although Sylvia and Beth had both been with The Fortune almost five years, they still felt as if they were the "new kids on the block" when it came to the tight old boy network that had been in existence when they arrived. Golf on Saturdays, bowling Thursday nights, racquetball on noon hours—there was a whole world from which they were excluded.

Upset by the events of the meeting and annoyed to discover that no one was really in any hurry to get back to work, Sylvia and Beth headed for Beth's office so they could talk in private.

COMMUNICATION BEHAVIOR AND
ORGANIZATIONAL CULTURE

Sylvia and Beth were frustrated in their efforts to communicate with their male colleagues. The Fortune's culture is strong; an old-boy network has been well-established, and the women's efforts to gain credibility will obviously be hard won. The male managers seem friendly, but discounted Sylvia's problems or made them low priorities. Both she and Beth felt frustrated and resented the attitudes they perceived were keeping them from participating fully in their professional activities. Do you think this situation still exists in many organizations? Unfortunately, it does. Do you think there's hope?

The answer to the second question may depend on how you view the situation. Some consultants or theorists would suggest redesigning the organization's structure. Others would recommend that Ned make a strong policy regarding gender issues. Others may advocate changes in the formal communication systems. Once again, we will take a symbolic/cultural perspective and argue that, indeed, Sylvia and Beth can modify The Fortune's culture through their own communication behaviors. By gradually leading their colleagues to new interpretations of how "women managers" at The Fortune behave, they can facilitate a change toward more constructive patterns of interaction between men and women.

We know that organizational culture can be modified or changed. Recall that culture is learned or negotiated through communicative events. As a new manager, Steve gained a number of insights from the meeting. One of the strongest may have pertained to what it means to be a woman manager—or employee—at The Fortune. In order to change culture, Sylvia and Beth must begin to change the way in which other employees think about women managers and, subsequently, the way they act toward women managers.

The most productive way to begin redefining what it means to be a woman manager is through their own communication behaviors. In essence, Sylvia and Beth need to create new definitions of what gender means in the context of The Fortune. They must change organizational members' assumptions so that their vision of a fair, equitable workplace is realized.

Although changing culture isn't easy, there are actions that Sylvia and Beth can take to make a difference in their organization's culture. The next section examines three aspects of communication: listening, verbal communication, and nonverbal behavior. Each is discussed as it could be used to modify aspects of The Fortune's culture.

LISTENING

Individuals who influence their organizations do a great deal of listening. As you discovered earlier, it is through effective listening that new and long-time employees learn the values, assumptions, priorities, and expectations of other organizational members. Only when members align their actions and activities can an organization move forward to accomplish its larger goals.

Active listening, therefore, is important to accurately understand culture. We have discussed how definitions of gender—what it "means" to be male or female"—are embedded in a culture. It is essential, therefore, that employees first listen in order to determine exactly what definitions currently exist. As we discussed earlier, men and women may hold different views regarding appropriate gender-related behavior. It is possible that men and women may view the same action, but interpret it differently. Therefore, both men and women in organizations must listen carefully to each other so that differences in perceptions are recognized and addressed.

If Sylvia and Beth listen carefully, they will quickly realize that the men exclude them from conversations and that the nature of these conversations makes it almost impossible for the women to participate. Nonverbal communication, too, is important to observe; nonverbal cues suggest an "in" group—winks, laughing, holding on to an arm, nudging, and other signs of comradery.

The women also notice that Ned put Sylvia's request at the end of his agenda. When he finally raises the issue, his language suggests that "Sylvia has a problem" and that she "needs help" from the others. Sylvia has the impression, from the conversation, that no one takes the problem seriously; in fact, some of the others do not even define the situation she describes as a problem at all.

These women must first make sure that they understand organizational members' perspectives—in this case, the attitudes and assumptions they want to change. Then, they can move on to choosing appropriate verbal and nonverbal communication strategies.

VERBAL BEHAVIOR

Sylvia and Beth can begin right away to model the verbal behavior and style they believe will best communicate a professional image to their peers. If they want organizational members to think of women as competent and credible, then they need to examine their own behaviors. What verbal behaviors did each woman demonstrate at the management meeting? Do you think that Sylvia and Beth demonstrated effective communication skills?

Unfortunately, neither Sylvia nor Beth made a good impression on the group. First, Sylvia was so passive that her agenda item almost didn't get discussed. When she was asked to describe the situation, her speech was full of nonfluencies and hesitations that reduced the impact of her ideas. In addition, when the group began to get rowdy, she did nothing and let Ned step in to maintain control of the group. Similarly, when Tony suggested the problem was with the barmaids not the guests, she said nothing. It is not surprising that when male managers observe this kind of behavior from one of a very few women managers, they form assumptions that inevitably undermine the women's ability to be effective in the workplace.

Yet Beth's behavior was no more productive. Although she spoke out, her hostility and anger were inappropriate. By opening with "I know you don't care what I think," she set the stage for an adversarial relationship. Then, rather than assertively stating her position, she resorted to name calling, referring to her colleagues as "animals with no sensitivity."

Professional women on the job learn to assert themselves in ways that reduce defensive communication. They are concerned with the quality of their relationships and work to develop teammanship as well as credibility. They seek opportunities, such as the one Sylvia had, to demonstrate their ability to analyze situations and problem solve. As Sylvia and Beth change the way they communicate, they will begin to change the impressions their colleagues have of them. Slowly, their peers will begin to make more positive associations regarding what it means to be a woman manager at The Fortune.

Culture is also transmitted through stories like the one Tony told about Marge. If you think about this story in light of the symbolic/cultural perspective, you'll see that it perpetuates a particular framework and communicates to others expectations regarding how a "good" barmaid at The Fortune behaves.

If Sylvia and Beth want to change The Fortune's culture, one way to go about it is to begin telling different stories, stories that illustrate how effective barmaids handle difficult situations. Clearly, the story Sylvia and Beth would tell may not resemble the one Tony passed along.

In addition to modifying their verbal behavior, Sylvia and Beth can also use nonverbal communication to establish their credibility and change the mens' perceptions about their female colleagues.

NONVERBAL COMMUNICATION

Organizational members send messages through their appearance, their office furnishings, their gestures and posture, their facial expressions, eye contact, touching, and possessions. No wonder the expression "You cannot not communicate" is repeated so frequently.

Often, individuals' nonverbal communication is unintentional and unplanned. Sylvia, for instance, probably didn't realize that by fidgeting with her bracelet she was sending messages about her anxiety and insecurity. It's likely she didn't give much thought to the seat she took at the table, or her eye contact as her glance moved quickly around the room.

Over a decade ago, Dowling (1981) was among those who noted that women in organizations tend to simply do a good job day after day, assuming that their work will be recognized and rewarded. Many of those in higher level management positions got there because they were at the right place at the right time—their career movement was more coincidence than the realization of personal goals. Unlike those who wait patiently for something to happen, individuals who want to improve communication between men and women must take deliberate actions.

Sylvia might also examine her office after the meeting. Has she hung her degrees on the wall? Does the office communicate orderliness and efficiency? Or are there obvious signs of confusion and a mixture of personal and professional items? If she wants to communicate an image of seriousness and competence, Sylvia needs to take that extra pair of stockings and curling iron out of her top drawer and put them in the very back of her filing cabinet. The picture of her frolicking at the beach with her family might be replaced with a studio portrait. Attention to detail is key in managing the impression you make.

REVISITING THE FORTUNE

At the moment, being a woman in management at The Fortune means that male managers probably don't listen to you. It means that you are excluded from important conversations, and that no one really values your ideas. It may also mean that you get the least desirable office, the weekend shifts, and the late lunch breaks. Although Steve came from a work environment where he was supervised by a woman, he is quickly learning that at The Fortune, women managers aren't taken seriously. Although he empathizes with Sylvia and Beth, he doesn't feel in a position to speak out. After a few months, he may not even notice that they are discounted by their colleagues because he will have become accustomed to "the way things are" at The Fortune.

Culture cannot be changed overnight. By modifying their communication behavior, however, Sylvia and Beth can move a long way toward gaining equal status in the workplace. First, they must listen carefully to fully understand just how other organizational members interpret their role. Then, by telling different stories and responding in a more appropriate way to the incidents that arise, they can begin to alter the way they are perceived by their peers. Although their male counterparts may now assume that they are somehow less capable, the women are in a position to redefine currently held meanings and modify the beliefs organizational members hold. By intentionally using nonverbal communication to communicate their professionalism and competence, Sylvia and Beth can begin to change organizational members' understanding of what it means to be a woman manager at The Fortune.

You should now be able to use the symbolic/cultural approach to analyze the way men and women communication in organizations. The symbolic/cultural approach focuses on the meanings of gender that are created through symbolic action, and how these meanings subsequently affect organizational members' behavior. This perspective is particularly appropriate because it suggests that an individual's choice of communication strategy can, over time, have a direct impact on an organization's culture.

Communication between the genders in the hospitality industry is particularly challenging because of several unique aspects of the industry. Irregular hours, close proximity among employees, and guests' expectations all affect gender and communication. Symbols associated with hospitality organizations—bedrooms, bars, and parties—contribute to the difficulties women may have in maintaining a work environment where their professional contributions are recognized and rewarded.

Women are entering the hospitality workforce at an unprecedented rate; greater numbers are also moving into management positions. To be successful in traditionally male-dominated environments, both men and women must learn and practice appropriate communication behaviors. The need for effective listening will increase as men and women negotiate their respective roles and expectations in each organizational context. Those who are able to "listen to their organization's culture" will be in the best position to take appropriate actions and make appropriate decisions.

If an ideal culture is one in which men and women are treated with equity and fairness, then organizational members can best promote this kind of environment by deliberately managing some of the most apparent culture indicators. They can begin to tell stories to new employees that reinforce desirable behaviors and attitudes. They can choose symbols—both verbal and nonverbal—that represent their vision of what the organization should be like. Through their artifacts, actions, and words, men and women in the 1990s can create a workplace characterized by mutual respect and understanding.

REFERENCES

Abbey, A. 1982. Sex differences in attribution for friendly behavior: Do males misperceive females' friendliness? *Journal of Personality and Social Psychology* 42: 830–838.

Albrecht, K., and R. Zemke. 1985. *Service America—Doing Business in the New Economy.* Homewood, IL: Dow-Jones Irwin.

Aldrich, H. E. 1989. Networking among women entrepreneurs. In O. Hagan, C. Rivchun, and D. Sexton, eds., *Women-Owned Businesses.* New York: Praeger: 103–132.

Arliss, L. 1991. *Gender Communication.* Englewood Cliffs, NJ: Prentice-Hall.

Axtell, R. E. 1990. Culture shock: The "S" word. *Meetings and Conventions*, 25(3): 132.

Baird, J. E., and P. H. Bradley. 1979. Styles of management and communication. A comparative study of men and women. *Communication Monographs* 46: 101–111.

Barrington, M. N., and M. Olsen. 1987. Concept of service in the hospitality industry. *International Journal of Hospitality Management*, (3)6: 131–138.

Barryman, C. L. 1980. Attitudes toward male and female sex-appropriate and sex-inappropriate language. *Communication, Language, and Sex.* C. L. Barryman and V. A. Eman, eds., Rowley, MA: Newberry House.

Barryman-Fink, C. L. 1983. Changing sex-role stereotypes. *Personnel Journal*, 62(6): 502–504.

Bass, B. M., B. J. Avolio, and L. Goodheim. 1987. Biography and the assessment of transformational leadership at the world class level. *Journal of Management*, 13: 7–20.

Baytosh, C. M., and B. H. Kleiner. 1989. Effective business communication for women. *Equal Opportunities International*, 8(4): 16–19.

Bernstein, C. 1990. Unified effort vital to women's advancement; Stereotypes remain barrier to the executive suite. *Nations Restaurant News*, 24: 29.

Bielby, W., and J. N. Baron. 1984. A women's place is with other women: Sex segregation within organizations. In B. F. Reskin, ed., *Sex Segregation in the Workplace.* Washington, D.C.: National Academy Press, 27–55.

Blair, J. 1989. CHRAQ news and reviews: "I" for improvement. *Cornell Hotel and Restaurant Administration Quarterly*, 30(2): 110.

Bolman, L. G., and T. E. Deal. 1984. *Modern Approaches to Understanding and Managing Organizations.* San Francisco: Jossey-Bass.

Borisoff, D., and L. Merrill. 1985. *The Power to Communicate: Gender Differences as Barriers.* Prospect Heights, IL: Waveland Press.

Brophy, B., and L. Lennon. 1987. Why women execs stop before the top. *U.S. News and World Report*, 5 Jan.: 72.

Campbell, K. E. 1988. Gender differences in job-related networks. *Work and Occupations*, 15(2): 179–200.

Catalyst. 1987. A matter of personal ability, not gender. *Management Solutions*, 32(11): 39–45.

Chase, R. B. 1978. Where does the customer fit in a service operation? *Harvard Business Review.* 43, 137–142.

Collin, J. 1989. Can men and women learn to communicate? *Successful Meetings*: 38(3), 36A–36D.

Conte, M. 1987. Sexual harassment: Ignorance is no defense. *Food Management*, 22(2): 100–104; 192–196.

Crossen, C. 1990. Pssst! The new way to network is . . . softly. *Working Woman*, 15(9): 154–156.

Cullins, E. G. C., and T. B. Blodgett. 1981. Sexual harassment: Some see it . . . some won't. *Harvard Business Review*, 59(2): 76–95.

DeLuca, M. 1988. Female lodging executives dealing with glass ceiling. *Hotel & Motel Management*, 203(15): 10.

DeWine, S., and D. Casbolt. 1983. Networking: External communication systems for female organizational members. *The Journal of Business Communication*, 20(2): 57–67.

diTomaso, N. 1989. Sexuality in the workplace: Discrimination and harassment. In J. Hearn, G. Burrell, D. Sheppard, and P. Tancred-Sheriff, eds., *Sexuality in the Organization*. London: Sage Publications, 71–90.

Dowling, C. 1981. *The Cinderella Complex*. New York: Summit Books, Inc.

Driskill, L. P., and J. R. Goldstein. 1986. Uncertainty: Theory and practice in organizational communication. *Journal of Business Communication*, 23(3): 41–56.

Duerst-Lahti, G. 1990. But women play the game too: Communication, control, and influence in administrative decision making. *Administration and Society*, 22(2): 182–205.

Eakins, B. W., and R. G. Eakins. 1978. *Sex Differences and Human Communication*. Boston: Houghton/Mifflin Company.

Eller, M. E. 1989. Sexual harassment: Prevention, not protection. *Cornell Hotel and Restaurant Administration Quarterly*, 30(4): 84–89.

Epstein, C. F., and B. Bass. 1991. Ways men and women lead. *Harvard Business Review*: 150–160.

Ezell, H., C. Odewahn, and J. D. Sherman. 1981. The effects of having been supervised by a woman on perceptions of female managerial competence. *Personal Psychology*, 34(2): 291–299.

Feathes, N., and J. Simon. 1975. Reactions to male and female success and failure in sex-linked occupations: Impressions of personality, causal attribution and perceived likelihood of different consequences. *Journal of Personality and Social Psychology*: 20–31.

Fernsten, J. A., L. L. Loury, L. K. Enghagen, and D. Hott. 1988. Female managers: Perspectives on sexual harassment and career development. *Hospitality Education and Research Journal*, 12(2): 185–196.

Fish, S. 1990. Interpretive research: A new way of viewing organizational communication. *Public Administration Quarterly*, 14(1): 67–74.

Foss, K. A., and S. K. Foss. 1983. The status of research on women and communication. *Communication Quarterly*, 31: 195–203.

Fraker, S. 1984. Why women aren't getting to the top. *Fortune,* 101(8): 40–45.

Frank, A., and J. Brownell. 1989. *Organizational Communication and Behavior: Communicating for Improved Performance (2+2 = 5).* New York: Holt, Rinehart, & Winston.

Freedman, S. M., and J. S. Phillips. 1988. The changing nature of research on women at work. *Journal of Management,* 14(2): 231–251.

Gattiker, U. E., and L. Larwood. 1990. Predictors for career achievement in the corporate hierarchy. *Human Relations,* 43(8): 703–726.

Grauerholz, E., and R. T. Serpe. 1985. Initiation and response: The dynamics of sexual interaction. *Sex Roles,* 12: 1041–1059.

Gregg, J. B., and P. M. Johnson. 1990. Perceptions of discrimination among women as managers in hospitality organizations. *FIU Hospitality Review,* 8(1): 10–22.

Gutek, B. A. 1985. *Sex and the Workplace: The Impact of Sexual Behavior and Harassment on Women, Men, and Organizations.* San Francisco: Jossey-Bass.

Gutek, B. A., A. G. Cohen, and A. M. Konrad. 1990. Predicting social-sexual behavior at work: A contact hypothesis. *Academy of Management Journal,* 33(3): 560–577.

Hackett, E., P. H. Mirvis, and A. L. Sales. 1991. Women's and men's expectations about the effects of new technology at work. *Group and Organization Studies,* 16(1): 60–85.

Hagen, R., and A. Kahn. 1975. Discrimination against competent women. *Journal of Applied Social Psychology,* 5: 362–376.

Hall, J. 1984. *Nonverbal Sex Differences: Communication Accuracy and Expressive Style.* Baltimore, MD: Johns Hopkins University Press.

Hirokawa, R. Y., R. A. Kodama, and N. L. Harper. 1990. Impact of managerial power on persuasive strategy selection by female and male managers. *Management Communication Quarterly,* 4(1): 30–50.

Jansen, S. C. 1989. Gender and the information society: A socially structured silence. *Journal of Communication,* 39(3): 196–215.

Kalleberg, A. L., and K. T. Leicht. 1991. Gender and organizational performance: Determinants of small business survival and success. *Academy of Management Journal,* 34(1): 136–161.

Katz, D., and R. Kahn. 1966. *The Social Psychology of Organizations.* New York: Wiley.

Kenton, S. B. 1989. Speaker credibility in persuasive business communication: A model which explains gender. *The Journal of Business Communication,* 26(2): 143–156.

Konrad, A. M., and B. A. Gutek. 1986. Impact of work experience on attitudes toward sexual harassment. *Administrative Science Quarterly,* 31: 422–438.

Krippendorff, K. 1980. *Content Analysis: An Introduction to its Methodology*. Beverly Hills, CA: Sage.

Laudadis, D. M. 1988. Sexual and gender harassment: Assessing the current climate. *Hospitality Education and Research Journal*, 12(2): 411–415.

Loden, M. 1985. *Feminine Leadership, or How to Succeed in Business Without Being One of the Boys*. New York: Times Books.

Louis, M. R. 1980. Surprise and sense-making: What newcomers experience when entering unfamiliar organizational settings. *Administrative Science Quarterly*, 23: 225–251.

Loy, P. H., and L. P. Stewart. 1984. The extent and effects of sexual harassment of working women. *Sociological Focus*, 17: 31–43.

Maltz, D., and R. Borker. 1982. A cultural approach to male-female miscommunications. In J. J. Gumperz, ed., *Language and Social Identity*, 56–82. London: Cambridge University Press.

Mann, B. C. 1989. Management theory: Networking in the 1990s. *Club Management*, 68(10): 22–24.

Marshall, A. 1989. Women: The best solution to industry's talent shortage. *Hotel and Motel Management*, 204(16): 18–19, 48.

_____. 1987. Employee dress codes can give hoteliers headaches. *Hotel and Motel Management*, 202(2): 18–19.

Mayo, E. 1933. *The Human problems of industrial civilization*. New York: Macmillan.

McCall, M. W., Jr., and M. M. Lombardo. 1983. What makes a top executive? *Psychology Today*, 17(1): 26–31.

McGregor, D. 1960. *The human side of enterprise*. New York: McGraw-Hill.

Miller, J. C. 1972. Living systems: The organization. *Behavioral Science*, 17: 1–182.

_____. 1980. Individual and occupational determinants of job satisfaction: A focus on gender differences. *Sociology of Work and Occupations*, 7: 337–366.

Mills, P. K., and J. H. Morris. 1986. Clients as 'partial' employees of service organizations: Role development in client participation. *Academy of Management Review*, 11: 726–735.

Nelsen, B. J. 1990. Perceptions of sexism in F & B oriented corporations. *Lodging*, 15(5): 51–52.

Nozar, R. 1990. Winking at sexual harassment demeans lodging. *Hotel and Motel Management*, 205(7): 6–7.

O'Donnell, H. 1985. Leadership effectiveness: Do sex and communication style make a difference? *English Journal*, 74(3): 65–67.

Papa, A. 1985. Protecting your staff from sexual harassment. *NRA News*, 19: 18–19.

Pearson, J. C. 1985. *Gender and Communication.* Dubuque, IA: William C. Brown.

_____. 1986. Gender and communication: Sex is more than a three-letter word. Chapter 3, 154–162.

Peters, J. 1988. Bridging the gender gap: RB Women's council challenges the status quo. *Restaurant Business,* 87(13): 115–131.

Peterson, N. 1984. How do women manage? *The Executive Female,* 7: 45–48.

Pincus, J. D. 1987. How CEOs view their communication roles. *Communication World,* 4(12): 18–22.

Plummer, D. 1987. New rulings on sexual harassment: Policies and procedures to guide professional conduct. *Executive Housekeeping Today,* 8(3): 8–9.

Powell, G. N. 1988. *Women and men in management.* Newbury Park, CA: Sage Publications.

_____. 1989. Male/female work roles: What kind of future? *Personnel,* 66(7): 47–50.

Rawls, D. J., and J. R. Rawls. 1968. Personality characteristics of successful and less successful executives. *Psychological Reports,* 23: 1032–1034.

_____. 1974. Toward earlier identification and development of managerial success. *Psychological Reports,* 35: 819–822.

Remland, M. S., and T. S. Jones. 1985. Sex differences, communication consistency, and judgments of sexual harassment in a performance appraisal interview. *Southern Speech Communication Journal,* 50(2): 156–176.

Rogers, J. 1986. Gender dynamics and the business meeting. *Successful Meetings,* 35(11): 39–45.

Rosener, J. 1990. Ways women lead. *Harvard Business Review,* 68(6): 119–125.

Smeltzer, L. R., and J. D. Werbel. 1986. Gender differences in managerial communication: Fact or folk-linguistics? *Journal of Business Communication,* 23(2): 41–50.

Snaver, P. and C. Hendrick. 1987. *Sex and Gender.* Beverly Hills, CA: Sage.

Steckler, N. A., and H. Rosenthal. 1985. Sex differences in nonverbal and verbal communication with bosses, peers, and subordinates. *Journal of Applied Psychology,* 70: 157–163.

Sterkel, K. S. 1988. The relationship between gender and writing style in business communications. *The Journal of Business Communication,* 25(4): 17–38.

Stockard, J., and M. M. Johnson. 1980. *Sex Roles: Sex Inequality and Sex Role Development.* Englewood Cliffs, NJ: Prentice-Hall.

Stringer, D. M., H. Remick, J. Salisbury, and A. B. Ginorio. 1990. The power and reasons behind sexual harassment: An employer's guide. *Public Personnel Management,* 19(i): 43–53.

Tannen, D. 1990. *You Just Don't Understand: Women and Men in Conversation.* New York: William Morrow.

Watson, C. 1988. When a woman is the boss: Dilemmas in taking charge. *Group & Organization Studies,* 13(2): 163–181.

Weber, M. 1947. *The Theory of Social and Economic Organization,* trans. A. Henderson and T. Parsons, trans. New York: Free Press.

Welch, M. S. 1980. *Networking: The Great New Way for Women to Get Ahead.* New York: Harcourt Brace Jovanovich.

Wheeless, V., and C. Berryman–Fink. (1985). Perceptions of women managers and their communication competencies. *Communication Quarterly,* 33(2): 137–147.

Wholey, D. R., and J. W. Brittain. 1986. Organizational ecology: Findings and implications. *Academy of Management Review,* 11: 513–533.

Wiley, M. G., and A. Eskilson. 1985. Speech style, gender stereotypes, and corporate success: What if women talk more like men? *Sex Roles,* 12: 993–1007.

Williams, J. E., and D. L. Best. 1982. *Measuring Sex Stereotypes: A Thirty Nation Study.* Beverly Hills, CA: Sage.

Women and the Politics of Empowerment. 1988. Bookman, A., and S. Morgan, eds. Philadelphia: Temple University Press.

Women in the industry. *Lodging,* 14(3): 44–46.

Worsfold, P. 1989. A personality profile of the hotel manager. *International Journal of Hospitality Management,* (1)8: 51–62.

WOMEN IN BROADCASTING

AUTHOR   Marcia Rock, New York University

POINTS TO BE ADDRESSED
- Paternalism in the broadcast industry
- Obstacles to gender equality in the industry
- Challenges to male dominance
- Women in broadcast news and broadcast entertainment
- Portrayals of women on television

INITIAL OBSTACLES

The story of women in broadcasting is the story of latent gender prejudice by a male-dominated industry slowly changed by the women in the
industry fighting for their rights. Those women were supported by the
Women's Movement, the adoption of the word "sex" in the Civil Rights Act,
and government pressure to enforce Equal Employment Opportunity policies.
It is also the story of the women in the industry becoming aware of the image
of women on television and trying to make that image better reflect reality.
This chapter will focus on the women who were pioneers in the broadcast
news industry, the challenges they faced, and their methods for change; it will
also survey the success of women in the entertainment side of broadcasting
and, finally, it will review the depiction of women on television through the
types of roles, professions, and economic brackets given them.

Women first entered broadcast journalism during World War II when
Edward R. Murrow needed radio reporters overseas. The women were hired
on an ad hoc basis. Only a few were allowed to narrate their own stories
because the male management in New York thought women's voices lacked
authority. Few women were offered jobs after the War when the men came
home. One exception was Pauline Frederick.

After Frederick graduated from college in the 1930s, she worked for the
Washington Star interviewing the wives of diplomats. A woman at NBC
thought these columns would make good radio features and hired Frederick on
a freelance basis. It was the practice of the news media then to have the few
women journalists cover "women's" topics like women celebrities, fashion, and
food. After the war, Frederick worked for ABC doing stories on the shortage of
nylon stockings and how to get a husband, even though she had not managed to

do that for herself. Her break came when none of the men wanted to cover the United Nations and she did. ABC would only use her voice, though, if she got an exclusive. Otherwise a man would record the audio track.

When television came along and convention coverage was extremely competitive, ABC hired her to interview the candidate's wives. At that time, how one should look on television was of major import to Frederick:

> One of her concerns was wondering how one was supposed to look on television. The only information she could get out of the network was not to wear black, white, or red. As for makeup, no one had any information at all. So she scurried over to Elizabeth Arden's to ask if they could help. They knew nothing about television either, but outfitted her with a kit of makeup suitable for still photography which they hoped would work. When she got to Philadelphia and the two conventions, she found that not only did she have to do her own makeup and interview the likes of Helen Gahagan Douglas and Mrs. Harold Stassen, but she found she was expected to do their makeup too, and she did. (M. Sanders and M. Rock, 1988: 10)

The women who worked behind the scenes during the war and then continued afterwards to build their careers fared a bit better. They did not have to fight the prejudice against the female voice, and because female expectations of success were limited, the women were grateful for being hired at any level. One would think that today the public accepts women's voices and that the old prejudice has been laid to rest. In 1986 the Screen Actor's Guild commissioned a study to rebuke that prejudice still held by advertising agencies who prefer men to women in voice-overs (the off-camera voice in commercials). The study, conducted by McCollum/Spielman, found that "it makes absolutely no difference whether a male or female voice is used as a commercial voice-over." In fact, the data indicated that "women are more effective presenters" (McCollum/Spielman, 1986). This study was conducted by recording two commercials with both female and male voice-overs. The test audience, composed of males and females, was then asked to select a brand for inclusion in a prize market basket. Eleven percent responded to the male voice and 12 percent responded to the female voice for the Listerine product. Forty-two percent responded to the male voice and 46 percent responded to the female voice in the Nestle Morsels commercial. This study also found that the respondents were not very much aware of whether the voice was male or female. The study implies that the voice could readily be female rather than the customary male voice.

Female reporters' voices are now accepted and female anchors' voices are accepted on local television news. It is still being debated whether a woman's voice could hold the nation's attention in the anchor position on the main network news broadcasts.

PATERNALISM

Another attitude that women broadcast journalists faced—and still face to a degree—is paternalism. Male supervisors, with the self image of father/protector, often feel uncomfortable sending women into dangerous situations or being in dangerous situations with a woman. Correspondent Betsy Aaron believes this is true because there is still a lingering fear on the part of management that the death of a female correspondent would be more embarrassing to the network than the loss of a man (Aaron, 1986). One way women have worked around this problem is to do feature stories in war zones and dangerous areas. This was acceptable because women didn't have to be on the front lines.

In the early 1980s, Aaron went overseas to do a story on the plight of Amerasian children. While she was praised for her work, she says it never seemed to earn her the right to go back without having to fight for the opportunity. Despite Aaron's track record of dangerous overseas assignments, Ted Koppel asked if she had her husband's permission to go to Lebanon.

In 1977, when Aaron was a CBS news correspondent out of Atlanta, she was seriously injured during a Klan rally in Americus, Georgia, when a sports car plowed into the crowd. Her knee was badly damaged and surgery was required, followed by years of physical therapy. Despite residual leg problems, she did not hesitate to take an assignment in Afghanistan. Several men had turned down the assignment, feeling, Aaron says, that it would not do anything for their careers. Therefore the assignment was available to a woman, with the added pressure of succeeding or being regarded as a sissy, unwilling to take the risks of a real correspondent. Aaron and her crew had to walk most of the 150 miles they finally covered, in order to report on the rebels' resistance to the Soviets.

Another problem that women correspondents and producers have in competing with men on international assignments is sustaining a meaningful personal life. Male correspondents, then and now, often have their families with them on a foreign assignment. Their presence provides a refuge and helps make a stressful life bearable. When women began to cover foreign news, few could find that kind of comfort. The women who become foreign correspondents are almost always single (Sanders and Rock, 1988).

Aaron was a widow during her thirties, and although she is now happily married, she says her generation got a heavy dose of the message that women's lives were only validated if they became wives and mothers. Aaron wanted to be a reporter as well, but still feels somehow incomplete because she did not fulfill those expectations of motherhood. Aaron feels that women often have to compromise if they want to have it all.

FAMILY AND CAREER

Many women prefer local news specifically because it does not require much travel. The hours may be long but it is possible to see your family every day. Network correspondents have to make some difficult choices. Lesley Stahl joined CBS News in 1972 as a Washington-based reporter. She is married and had a daughter while in her late thirties. Caring for her daughter affected her career choices. In 1986 she wouldn't consider a *60 Minutes* assignment, "because I have a child and it would be a sacrifice . . ." (Stahl, 1986). The *60 Minutes* correspondents are on the road about 70 percent of the time. By 1991, Stahl obviously felt ready for the assignment when she replaced another woman, Meredith Viera. Viera was taken off the show because she was pregnant with her second child and wanted another year of part-time work.

Viera had just completed two seasons of part-time work to care for her first child. Don Hewitt, the executive producer of *60 Minutes* felt that was enough. He had agreed to the part-time arrangement for her first child but he needed a full-time correspondent to replace the retiring Harry Reasoner and could not extend that arrangement for another year (S. Daley, 1991). Some feminists argued that CBS should consider time-sharing and hire several women for that position, but Hewitt maintains that "the program is built around the idea that viewers would become familiar with five top-flight journalists seen almost every week" (Daley, 1991).

Viera was not fired but was not immediately reassigned either. At age 37, she feels trapped by her predicament: "If I don't have children now, I'm not sure I can do it later. . . . But if I had kids earlier, I'm not sure I could have established myself" (Daley, 1991). Viera's concerns are understandable. According to the *New York Times* only 35 to 40 percent of successful women over forty have children as compared to 93 percent of their male colleagues (Basler, 1986).

White House correspondent Andrea Mitchell is divorced and has no children. She's not sure the ambitious women of her generation made all the right choices and thinks perhaps they were too available to their jobs. "I guess the bottom line is still that if it's a choice between an important personal commitment and being at a presidential news conference, I'm going to still choose the presidential news conference," she says (Mitchell, 1986). But she thinks ambitious women are not treated the same way as ambitious men.

> Sometimes I think women get criticized in subtle and not so subtle ways for being aggressive or ambitious. We're called pushy, bitchy, if we pursue a line of questioning at the White House aggressively. I get dumped on by the press secretary, but if Bill Plante [CBS News] or Sam Donaldson [ABC News] do it, it's OK. It's really a matter of male expectations that we behave in a certain way. (Mitchell, 1986)

The greatest complaint by young women correspondents and producers is their feeling of being out of control. After facing intense competition to get their jobs and after working hard to get promoted, they find themselves having to make difficult choices between their careers and their families.

Local Chicago reporter Renee Ferguson encountered more problems on a personal than on a company level when she was pregnant and a correspondent for CBS. She did not feel she was as strong a presence in an interview: "When I go on a story I approach people with a certain strength, power that's important to me. I felt more vulnerable while pregnant, less powerful. It changed the way I'd walk into the room." She overcame that and worked as long as she could but took an early maternity leave though because, "People started to cover for me. I felt I was imposing so I left." Ferguson sees a change in attitude toward day-care and maternity leave when more women are in management and can make decisions on company policy and flexible time arrangements (Ferguson, 1986).

Having women in supervisory positions does not necessarily ensure better treatment. Former ABC producer Betsy Rich decided to leave the news business because of her treatment by another woman. She'd been on the road for over a week and was told that she'd have to go to Washington, D.C., to edit the story. Her senior producer was enraged that Rich refused to go because she wanted to see her child (Rich, 1986, 1988).

Sometimes Rich feels the women's movement put too much pressure on young women to prove that they could have it all. "It sounds strange, but I feel I was sold a bill of goods to come to expect I could have everything." Faith Daniels, *Today Show* news anchor and anchor for the daytime program, *A Closer Look*, has two children and her husband is a local news executive producer. When Daniels looks around the newsroom she feels she deserves the same as the men. "Certainly you don't think Peter Jennings is less professional because he has two children, and Dan Rather has a family." Daniels is optimistic. "Women have come a long way in a short period of time. We still have a long way to go, but yes we can do it. It's a very demanding job but you can have a life on the side. For me, my family comes before work, although it is nice to have both" (Daniels, 1986, 1987).

FIGHTING FOR RIGHTS

In the 1970s, the few women in broadcasting faced similar problems to those of women in publishing: pay equity, promotion, and a clear policy on maternity leave. Women at *Newsweek* filed a complaint with the state attorney general's office in 1970, newswomen negotiated changes in their Newspaper Guild contracts in 1972, and the National Organization of Women (NOW) filed a petition with the Federal Communications Commission (FCC) asking that broadcast licensees be required to file affirmative action reports regarding the employment of women in 1970.

In 1969 the FCC agreed to add the word "sex" to various antidiscrimination rulings they already had, and in May 1971 a new requirement was added to the license renewal process: television stations were to file affirmative action plans for women with their application (Sanders and Rock, 1988). Stations had to go beyond merely not discriminating on the basis of race, creed, or sex; they had to take steps to hire women and minorities to remedy the effect of past practices. NOW's strategy for change was to challenge the broadcast licenses of some of the network's owned and operated stations in major markets and thus get the publicity about these issues. NOW claimed that the stations did not act in the "public interest," and thus violated the station's mandate by the Federal Communications Commission when awarded a television license. Attorney Nancy Stanley outlined the following violations in 1971: under the standards of equal employment opportunity, women on the staffs of the stations were underrepresented, underemployed, and underpaid; the stations' ascertainment process (evaluating the community's programming needs) was incomplete because they did not include women as a significant community group; and the stations violated the Fairness Doctrine, a provision that stated a licensee has an affirmative duty to present contrasting views of an issue in its overall programming, because the role of women in society is a bona fide controversial issue of public importance and licensees were not portraying contrasting views of that role in their overall programming (Stanley, 1971).

NOW challenged stations WRC in Washington, D.C., and WABC in New York City, two network flagship stations whose prominence would draw a lot of media attention. Litigation began in 1972. NOW claimed that WRC had very few women employed in management, technical positions, and sales, and had discriminatory policies on wages and maternity leave. It charged that WABC consistently failed to report serious women's issues and, after studying ABC programs for two years, complained that women were portrayed in disparaging roles.

Neither license renewal challenge was successful but the four years of litigation brought publicity to NOW's grievances. Change came indirectly as a result of these legal actions. Stations around the country started hiring women and became aware of their female employees' problems. "Consciousness-raising," a new phrase in the language, was forced on the television brass. They began to look around, not only at how their own companies were run, but also at the articulate, able women lawyers facing them across the table. Interestingly, station legal departments became receptive to women and that was one area where changes took place rather rapidly (Sanders and Rock, 1988).

At the network level, change came more slowly. Women did not have the legal avenue of license renewal challenges because networks are not licensed by the government as are individual television stations. But the networks were covered by a Labor Department ruling that required that such companies draw up affirmative action programs to remedy the underutilization of women. Organizing the women at networks was not easy because the companies were large and encompassed women on all different levels, from secretaries to correspondents. ABC women were organized indirectly through the license challenge of the local ABC station in New York City. NOW charged that Channel 7 had not hired or promoted enough women. The station replied it couldn't find qualified people. Lawyers for the women's group turned to several network women for consultation.

During all this, a female executive at ABC stated that no woman had ever complained about any problems at the network. The ABC women suddenly realized that they needed to speak up, but first they had to get together and find out what was wrong. That's when the women realized that they had no avenue of communication and no place to meet. The first solution was to put notices in the place they all frequented, the lavatory. Eventually the newly formed Women's Action Committee (WAC) got permission to post notices and use board rooms for meetings. Their grievances were generic: no job posting; women in line for promotions, frustration because outside men, often younger and with less experience, were brought in for them to train for jobs the women should have had; an unresponsive personnel department; the deep disappointment with being stuck in dead-end jobs; and salary discrepancies.

It was common for men to be hired from the outside for the same level job as a woman, but at higher pay. The myth went that a woman didn't "need" the money. Perhaps her husband had a good job, or maybe she was single and didn't need that much. The WAC felt salaries should reflect individual worth, not someone's uninformed speculation on another's needs. When men negotiate salary, no chart is made of their family obligations. How many single women support elderly parents, assist younger siblings in college, or are saving for their old age—or just plain deserve to be paid well? (Sanders and Rock, 1988).

The ABC group had a few triumphs. They got job postings even though many jobs were filled before posting. ABC hired a manager to recruit minorities and women. An informal employee grievance committee procedure was established wherein a woman (or a man for that matter) with a complaint against a boss did not have to face him alone, but could call on a WAC member to accompany her to a meeting with her superior.

The most difficult attitudinal problems to solve were deep-seated cronyism. Women were not members of the "old boys club," were not on the lunch and golf circuit with them, had not come through the same employment route, and were, therefore, not considered for some of the top jobs. After a protracted series of discussions, management agreed that some kind of sensitivity training was needed.

There were several specific accomplishments by the WAC. In 1972, when it was organized, two women held the title of vice president and only half a dozen women, exclusive of performers, earned more than $20,000 a year. The female portion of the broadcasting division totaled just under 30 percent. By mid-1975, the proportion of women was up to 32 percent and approximately fifty women on the talent payroll earned more than $20,000 a year. There were still only two vice presidents, but there was a female corporate officer and a woman put on the board of directors. Those gains were not astounding by any means, but were at least in the right direction (Sanders and Rock, 1988).

At CBS, the most militant step taken was over the issue of clothes. In 1970, when pantsuits were the latest vogue, a memo was issued by a middle manager in news to the effect that "it is not company policy nor the discretion of the immediate supervisor for female employees to wear slacks during the course of their normal working day. . . ." The women acted swiftly, and the next morning almost all of them appeared in pants. The event merited coverage in the *New York Times*. The rule was rescinded.

Following the pants revolt in 1970, no organized activity by the women of CBS occurred until 1973. Oddly enough, the women got together as a result of a "policy statement on women" distributed company-wide from the network president. The memo declared that every employee at CBS should receive equal opportunity, that there was a policy of equal pay, and that five part-time women's counselors would be appointed to handle women's "aspirations and gripes." The memo was intended to head off law suits like the one at NBC. Although change came slowly, the numbers improved. In the news division in 1972, only 22 women were in producers' jobs, but by January 1979, there were 40 more. Where there had been three female technicians, the number rose to 15.

While the managements of ABC and CBS were by and large conciliatory in the 1970s, NBC was so hostile that legal intervention became necessary. The women at NBC had not initially wanted a lawsuit. One of their grievances was that secretaries were graded according to the standing of the men they worked for. A secretary to a vice president was paid more than a secretary to a lower-level person. No matter how well they did their jobs, they were treated as appendages. Their initial appeals to personnel to change this practice were ignored. Money was not the main issue; the women wanted fairness.

At their second meeting with management, the women's grievances went beyond employment; they charged that women's concerns were ignored on the air as well. The men made a counterpresentation charging that they dealt with women's issues on soap operas: adultery, abortion, rape, homosexuality, and incest. These were certainly sensational subjects and surefire ratings grabbers, but they were not what the women had in mind. The management's definition of "women's issues" underscored for the NBC women's group just how far apart they were from management in the comprehension of the issues (Sanders and Rock, 1988).

Soon after that, with the help of the New York City Human Rights Commission, the 16 NBC women decided to sue. A crucial development helped to conclude the litigation. The case was joined by the Equal Employment Opportunity Commission, which filed its own charges. NBC first tried to settle out of court for $500,000 but the women turned them down. Money, they repeated, was not the whole problem. The settlement finally included a payment of $2 million, but much more was involved.

The bulk of the agreement involved a broad range of affirmative action designed to bring more women into previously male-dominated management and technical positions, to improve the salaries and job assignments in the primarily female clerical positions, and to provide a more open, documented personnel system. Twenty thousand dollars a year was set aside for monitoring compliance efforts, to end in 1981.

The work of these women's groups was not always lasting. By 1983 the ABC women organized again, unaware of the group that had preceded them by ten years. The discontent began in the news division where there were nearly one hundred correspondents and only fifteen of them were women. When they complained to the Washington bureau chief, he basically told them they were lucky to have jobs. By 1985 they appealed to the news division president. Of the 1,100 employees in the news organization at the time, 500 were women. The women's research revealed large wage discrepancies. They said women producers were paid on the average of 30 percent less than men.

Management expressed disbelief and wanted to know where those numbers had come from. The women pointed out they were reporters and had found a way. The other major issue brought up was sexual harassment. Both were red flags to the network because they spelled possible litigation. The women also wanted a Woman's Advisory Board to serve as a watchdog group, and a full-time recruiter to hire qualified women as well as minorities. They wanted job postings and a system of employee evaluations. Instead of bad-mouthing people behind their backs, the women wanted evaluations on a regular basis. Lastly, the women asked for a pay equity study.

The company responded positively to several of those demands. In January 1986, a female news recruiter was hired. Job posting did begin, but top jobs, like senior producer, were not listed. A company salary study revealed discrepancies, but ABC explained that was caused by different hiring patterns. Women tended to rise within the company, restricted by the company policy of a 10 percent limit on raises. Men often came in from high-paying outside jobs. However, the company study resulted in substantial raises for more than 40 producers, 15 of them men. Although this second group was successful in effecting change, by 1988, the women's group was having difficulty arranging any meetings at all with management.

In 1990 women network correspondents suffered a decline in airtime on the three major networks. In 1989, they reported 16 percent of the news stories and in 1990 the figure dropped to 15 percent. Out of a total of 457 stories monitored by the Women, Men and Network News study, men covered 390 and women covered 67. ABC had the worst record, with only 13 reports by women. CBS had a better record with women reporting 30 stories. PBS's MacNeil-Lehrer had the best record, with 40% of the stories reported by women. This report did note a 2% increase in the number of women newsmakers shown on network news (Women's Media Project and NOW Legal Defense and Education Fund, 1990).

ON-CAMERA PRESSURES

Anchors in local news were experiencing other kinds of pressures that began interfering with their work. Christine Craft was hired as a local news anchor at a Metromedia-owned station, KMBC-TV, in Kansas City in 1981. She brought a discrimination suit against them in 1983. Her complaint was indicative of the problems on-camera women were having in an industry where news is seen as entertainment.

KMBC had hired a research consulting firm, Media Associates (now known as Audience Research and Development), to find them a female anchor who could bring "warmth" and comfort to the news. Media Associates went all over the country taping local talent off the air. They liked Craft because she looked "laid back with California energy." In 1980 KMBC-TV in Kansas City, the 27th-sized market, offered her the anchor job at a salary of $35,000.

Craft was wary of consultants and disliked makeup artists. In her negotiations with Ridge Shannon, news director for KMBC, she stressed the fact that she wanted to be hired for her journalistic abilities and not because her appearance would fit into some consultant's categorization. Although her boss assured her otherwise, when the ratings did not go up management sent in a consultant to "help" her. They "helped" her with her makeup and developed a clothes calendar for her to improve her image. Nine months after she began she was called into news director Shannon's office and told that he was taking her off the anchor position and assigning her as a reporter. Craft's description of his reasons for demoting her was that she was "too old, too unattractive and not deferential enough to men." Shannon later denied making this statement (Craft, 1986: 68).

Craft wanted to be evaluated on her journalistic abilities; she resented the emphasis on the look of her hair and clothes, and on her audience ratings, so she decided to take her case to court, claiming three things: "sexual discrimination in an advisory capacity," the violation of the Equal Pay Act (her male co-anchor was making $52,000), and fraud, because KMBC said they hired her for her journalistic abilities but she was fired for her appearance. A major focus in the trial was on the validity of the kind of research conducted by Media Associates through the use of surveys and focus groups. (Focus groups are small groups of people who experience something together and then are questioned by a trained leader about their immediate reactions.)

In the focus group organized to study Craft's presentational style, the leader began the discussion by asking the group whether the anchorwoman was a "mutt"; he is also reported to have said: "Let's spend thirty seconds destroying Christine Craft, and "if we all chip in we can buy her a ticket back to California" (Craft, 1986). The leader claimed that those remarks were meant to loosen up the group so they wouldn't be afraid to criticize her. The participants in the focus group had not been tested for sexual preference, that is, for whether they liked a man or a woman anchor better. It did try to find out what *kind* of woman they wanted to see, whether they preferred a woman with youth, beauty, and a nonaggressive style. Later, the lawyers defending Craft claimed that the method of testing violated Title VII of the Civil Rights Act of 1964 because of the sexual stereotypes encouraged in the testing setup. They said the focus group leader encouraged a negative reaction to Craft's dress and makeup. Most physical appearance requirements are illegal under Title VII. There can be a dress code but not a grooming standard applied more strictly to women than to men (Gielow, 1985: 444). The focus group seemed to demand more from her in terms of appearance than they did from her male co-anchor. Based on these evaluations, the news director is reported to have said that "the audience perceived [Craft's] dress, appearance, makeup, and presentation as stumbling blocks" (Craft, 1986: 127). Craft claimed that this kind of reason for demotion was sexual discrimination against women in the category of appearance and demeanor.

The first jury found in favor of Craft on the sex-discrimination and fraud charges and recommended an award of $500,000 in damages. But Judge

Stevens threw out the jury's award and ruled that KMBC-TV had not been guilty of sex discrimination in insisting that Craft improve her appearance; it demanded the same of men. Stevens said the only discrimination to be found in the case was the ironic one that, "but for the fact that she is female, [Craft] would not have been hired as a co-anchor in December 1980, regardless of her other abilities" (*Broadcasting Magazine,* 7 November 1983). Judge Stevens did order a new trial on the fraud charge (that Craft was hired under false pretenses).

The second jury also found in favor of Craft and advised the judge to award her $325,000. Metromedia appealed the case yet again and took it to the Eighth Circuit Court of Appeals, where three male judges, Reagan appointees with histories of anti-civil rights rulings, ruled against Craft, stating that they "didn't feel there was enough evidence for a 'reasonable' jury to conclude there had been fraud" (Craft, 1986: 194). Craft decided to go the next step and take her case to the United States Supreme Court. On 3 March 1986 the Supreme Court refused to review the Appeals Court decision because of insufficient evidence on sex discrimination (Sanders and Rock, 1988).

The Craft case highlights many of the issues affecting the status of women in television news. It is undeniable that television is an entertainment medium and that one's appearance does affect one's reception by an audience. Most women on television do care whether they look attractive. But that should not be the only criterion by which a female newscaster is judged. Sadly, the lesson from the Craft case may ultimately be about language. Reuben Frank commented when he was president of NBC News in 1983, "What will happen is legal departments will instruct news executives on what to say" (*New York Times,* 1983: 17). Others were more optimistic. CBS News correspondent Lesley Stahl "hopes . . . that a person's ability to write and get a story and convey the story to the public will be considered first" (*New York Times,* 1983: 17).

WOMEN IN MANAGEMENT

Because there are a limited number of power positions in any system, including broadcasting, questions of promotion are inherently questions of politics. Promotions often come from within and occur among friends. Women are not usually part of the in-group. Those few women who do advance are often not particularly anxious to help or identify with other women. If women are going to change corporate structures, they will only do so when their numbers increase to a critical mass—then, if so inclined, they can act without fear of being overruled or mustered out.

One obstacle for women is called the "comfort factor." Professor Richard L. Zweigenhaft, of Guilford College in Greensboro, North Carolina, is credited with coming up with the phrase in the course of a study commissioned by the Institute of Human Relations of the American Jewish Committee. In his 1984 report called "Who Gets To The Top?," he examined executive-suite discrimination in the 1980s through a study of the Fortune 500 companies. He interviewed graduates of the Harvard Business School as far back as the 1960s, and included women, blacks, and Jewish men.

One Harvard woman MBA from the class of 1975, told him that management now knows the right things to say. She said the problem surfaces when one wants to advance beyond the assistant vice president level. She said,

> Way up at the top, a lot of business gets conducted in non-structured ways, over a golf game, or even in the men's room after a meeting. It's not really the old boy's network, but a lot like that, and women just aren't in it. It's hard for them to get into it because people at that level still are born and raised with the belief that women belong at home. They might make an exception, but they don't do it in general. They don't have the same comfort with women. (Zweigenhaft, 1984: 62)

A 1980 graduate told Zweigenhaft, "They're so used to dealing with women in a teasing sense, or in a non-business sense. Socially, it's still difficult to be a woman in management. Men still perceive you either as their daughter or their mistress. They find it difficult to relate to you as a co-worker" (Zweigenhaft, 1984: 62).

60 Minutes senior producer Phil Scheffler feels the exclusion of women from top management has to do with the kinds of friendships men tend to form with each other. He says men are not intimate or very personal, even with someone they consider a best friend. They talk about externals. They view women, probably correctly, as more comfortable with intimacy, more personal, demanding more of people. He felt that men, by and large, like keeping work relationships on an impersonal level in terms of emotional content. Admitting women into their midst would therefore threaten the kind of casual, comfortable relationships the men have with each other. Possibly it does not occur to them that women can be impersonal and cool on the job and will not necessarily transfer their out-of-office conduct to the workplace (Sanders and Rock, 1988).

When Marlene Sanders was vice president and Director of Documentaries at ABC, she noticed that her relationships with former colleagues and with other vice presidents, usually men, changed. She also noticed the informal friendships that her five male colleagues established among themselves were somewhat different from her own relationships with them. They would usually go out to lunch together but rarely invited her unless she initiated the invitation. The men were not conscious of the exclusion and thought it was merely because her office was in a different building; but Sanders thinks it was that they were just more comfortable with each other.

Many of the younger women in middle management today believe men in management are beginning to change their attitudes toward women. NBC senior producer Cheryl Gould is optimistic about the men coming up through the ranks who are in their thirties and don't think it's a big deal if a woman is the boss. Older men often feel awkward. Gould has to make choices when dealing with them: "one correspondent was always condescending to me, always calling me 'dear' and saying that I reminded him of his daughter. I made a conscious decision not to object. My approach was to ignore it"

(Gould, 1987). But she doesn't hesitate to be critical when appropriate, regardless of age or sex.

Mary Alice Williams is optimistic about women working equally with men. When she was anchor and vice president of Cable News Network in New York she felt not only people but the organization was starting fresh:

> CNN started with a clean slate. We began in 1980 with the values of 1980. It's not fair to generalize, but men over forty have to be educated. Men under thirty-five are used to us. They've had women bosses, their favorite professor in college was a woman, or something. So they have some experience with this. The men over forty have not." (Williams, 1986)

WOMEN IN BROADCAST ENTERTAINMENT

Women in the entertainment side of broadcasting face many of the same problems as the women in broadcast news. Hollywood is a one-company town where that company is dominated by men. Women have made inroads, but in specific areas such as situation comedies which have a large female audience.

According to Sally Steenland in "What's Wrong with this Picture: The Status of Women on Screen and Behind the Camera in Entertainment TV," 25 percent of writers are women. The show with the highest percentage of women is *Designing Women* (83%) and the show with the lowest number of women, zero, is *Just the 10 of Us*. The newest network, Fox, has the highest number of female producers (26%) and ABC the lowest (8%). Overall, 15 percent of producers on prime time television are women. Women fare the worst in the area of directing, where only 9 percent are women. The one exception is *A Different World*, which has almost all women directors (Steenland, 1990).

Women in Hollywood suffer from stereotyping. Women writers are deemed only able to write for comedies with female characters; how could a woman write action adventure with chase scenes and shoot-outs? Yet Hollywood has no problem hiring men to write shows about women. Two men and a woman are the writers for the series *Sisters*, a one-hour drama. One woman sitcom writer sensed the gender prejudice on her first day at work: "I went in . . . thinking I was a writer. They saw me as a woman. I never wore a dress after that—I was afraid to do anything that would accentuate my gender" (Steenland, 1990). Eve Brandstein is an exception, but she was hired to bring in a female audience to these predominantly male shows. She is an executive producer and writer for Stephen J. Cannell Productions, a company that produces *Booker, Hunter*, and *Wiseguy*.

Men dominate the executive positions in the major studios and production companies. The executives sell shows to the networks so they are the ones who have to approve an idea. They tend to be uncomfortable with women leads in one-hour dramatic shows, although women make up a large proportion of the television audience. The executives prefer women as comedy queens such as Lucille Ball and Candice Bergen.

It is difficult for women to advance into that executive world. Nearly two-thirds of network entertainment executives are men and nearly 90 percent are under age forty (Steenland, 1990). Brandstein sees the glass ceiling preventing women who are in top production positions from being promoted to executive vice presidents, but she sees young men groomed early on for those positions. "In Hollywood," Brandstein says, "the grooming happens at the poker and tennis games where groups of men hang out." Because careers are built on who you know, on friendships, on who will take your call, women are often left out of the loop (Brandstein, 1991).

The male executives have an added asset—their wives. Brandstein sees these women concentrating on their husband's social obligations; they give parties, organize charity events, and help give their men a high profile in the community. Few women have husbands who are in the position to help their wives in that way.

Women like Brandstein are the least optimistic about the progress of women in Hollywood. Like their counterparts in news, they have seen great advancements in the 70s and retrenchments in the 80s. They see change in Hollywood coming when there is more than one woman executive making programming decisions, when men as well as women redefine the manic, twelve-hour days of Hollywood executives, when decision making becomes more of a group effort and not the sole territory of one man, when community pressure demands more women in leading roles.

THE PORTRAYAL OF WOMEN ON TELEVISION

Male characters outnumber women characters by almost two to one in television dramas (Steenland, 1990). "What's Wrong With This Picture" points out that action dramas are the exclusive world of men and most women characters are clustered in sitcoms. Most characters on television are in their 20s and 30s. At 40, the number of women characters drops sharply. Most television characters are middle class, which is a realistic change from past seasons filled with shows like *Dynasty* and *Dallas*. The most common female job portrayed on television is clerical work, but a greater number of women on TV have professional careers. The number of full-time homemakers has increased in the past few seasons. Although television families are mostly headed by two parents, men are more likely to be portrayed as the single parent, contrary to reality. The report concludes that men have most of the leading roles in TV and women tend to be supporters and sidekicks (Steenland, 1990).

The results of this study reveal some progression and regression for the portrayal of women on television. Women no longer inhabit only a domestic world; they are often depicted as secretaries, which does reflect reality. There are few women bosses. Murphy Brown is a rare television character; she is ambitious, powerful and likeable (Steenland, 1990). Despite characters like Murphy Brown, too many female characters remain extensions of male fantasies. This is especially true in the male-dominated world of action adventure (Steenland, 1990).

Young men are plentiful on television but there are few teenage women. "What's Wrong With This Picture" quotes a producer/writer's explanation, "Teenage boys are inherently more interesting than girls; they go through rites of passage. Basically, only one thing happens as a girl grows up—she tries to be pretty so boys will like her. But boys have sports rituals, sexual development, preparation for careers, the growing responsibility of manhood, the father-son conflict. Girls don't have that much going on" (Steenland, 1990: 31). This female producer articulated the commonly held belief that boys have more interesting lives than girls.

Women in the broadcast entertainment and broadcast news see a narrow road for advancement with many obstacles. Having a full, personal life is difficult, the "old boys' club" is a powerful networking tool that excludes women, and stereotypes about a woman's abilities is a constant barricade to opportunities. One successful producer in Hollywood observed a difference between the way men and women work, and liked it. She observed women as being more collaborative and less competitive and perhaps creating a better work environment (Steenland, 1990). In the two decades since women started entering both fields in substantial numbers, change is evident. A few major studios have child-care centers for their employees; women executives do change the atmosphere in a board room and restrict off-color jokes and comments that some men are uncomfortable with as well; and slowly women are covering wars and writing action adventures.

The broadcast industry has a high profile in the American society and the women on television news and the women characters in television comedies and dramas influence the way Americans see themselves. Neither television news nor entertainment is in a growth period. There is little government or community pressure to change the number of women working in or portrayed on the small screen. Women are making progress but it is slow and the future does not portend a quickening of the pace unless the pressure comes from the next generation of viewers and consumers.

REFERENCES

Aaron, B. 1986. Personal interview: 14 Oct.

Basler, B. 1986. Putting a career on hold. *New York Times Magazine*, 7 Dec.: 159.

Brandenstein, E. 1991. Personal interview: 9 March.

Craft, C. 1986. *Christine Craft: An Anchorwoman's Story*. Santa Barbara, CA: Rhodora/Capra Press.

Daley, S. 1991. Networks, motherhood and careers. *New York Times*, 4 March: C16.

Daniels, F. 1986. Personal interviews: 8 Oct. 1986, Feb. 1987.

Ferguson, R. 1986. Personal interview: 8 Nov.

Gielow, L. S. 1985. Sex discrimination in newscasting. *Michigan Law Review* 84: 443: 444.

Gould, C. 1987. Personal interview: 29 March.

McCollum/Spielman & Company, Inc. 1986. *Topline* Feb.: (4).

Mitchell, A. 1986. Personal interview: 18 Nov.

Rich, B. 1986, 1987. Personal interviews: 30 Sept. 1986, 21 Feb. 1988.

Sanders, M., and M. Rock. 1988. *Waiting for Prime Time: The Women of Television News*. Urbana, IL: University of Illinois Press.

Stahl, L. 1986. Personal interview: 19 Nov.

Stanley, N. 1971. Federal communications law and women's rights: Women in the wasteland fight back. *Hastings Law Journal* 23: 15–53.

Steenland, S. 1990. What's wrong with this picture?: The status of women on screen and behind the camera in entertainment television. National Commission on Working Women of Wider Opportunities for Women and Women in Film: 6.

Williams, M. A. 1986. Personal interview: 4 Dec.

A woman's voice sells as well as a man's on tv, Screen Actor's Guild study shows. 1986. Screen Actor's Guild press release: 16 Sept.

Women's Media Project and NOW Legal Defense and Education Fund. 1990. Women, men and network news.

Zweignehaft, R. L. 1984. Who gets to the top? Institute of Human Relations, American Jewish Committee.